History of Twentieth Century Fashion

1 *Fashion dictated by High Society—1900*

History of
TWENTIETH CENTURY FASHION

Elizabeth Ewing

B. T. BATSFORD LTD London

Acknowledgments

In preparing this history I have been generously helped by many people who have been actively concerned with fashion during the period of great change and expansion with which it deals. To all of them I am deeply grateful. In addition I have been greatly indebted to the staffs of the London Library, the Victoria and Albert Museum Library, the London College of Fashion and Clothing Technology Library, and the Museum of Costume, Bath.

For this, the Third Edition, further invaluable help has been given by many of today's representatives of various areas of fashion, especially by Penelope Byrde, Keeper of Costume at the Museum of Costume, Bath, with regard to illustrations; Piers Milligan, on punk fashion; and finally by Timothy Auger and Richard Reynolds, my editors. To all these my sincere thanks.

Elizabeth Ewing
November 1985

First published 1974
© Elizabeth Ewing 1974, 1986
Third edition 1986

ISBN 07134 4682 X

Typeset by Servis Filmsetting Ltd, Manchester
and printed and bound in Great Britain
by Anchor Brendon Ltd, Tiptree, Essex
for the publishers B.T. Batsford Ltd
4 Fitzhardinge Street, London W1H 0AH

Contents

The Illustrations

Unacknowledged photographs are from publisher's archives.

1 Edwardian sunshine for the few, but change in the air, 1900–1909

I

Within the span of this century fashion has changed in everything but name. What had always been the special preserve of the privileged few has become the happy hunting ground of all. Long-treasured traditions of hand craftsmanship, with their slow, infinitely patient methods of making-up, which put fashion out of reach of most people, have in the main been superseded by large-scale manufacture primed with growing expertise and catering for all sections of the consumer market. Fashion now pours off the production lines of innumerable substantial factories and is being reproduced with the technical know-how of a modern work force that numbers hundreds of thousands in nearly every leading Western country and far beyond. Fashion is a vast industry – in New York, the world's largest city, it is the largest of all. In Paris, for centuries the centre of fashion creation, *haute couture* rubs shoulders with an ever-expanding ready-to-wear trade even within the enclaves once sacred to the jealously guarded elegances of *la mode*. Fashion is no longer dictated by High Society; as often as not it is triggered off and swept into favour by the anonymous but compulsive force of this or that section of the masses. It is news. It moves under a constant floodlight of publicity.

How this has happened and what events and people have been the main contributors to it is a story that has no parallel from the past. It would be against all reason if there were. 'Fashion is the outward and visible sign of a civilisation, it is part of social history', says Amy Latour in *Kings of Fashion*. The civilisation and the social history of the twentieth century have swept right out of the context of previous times. The new look that science, industrial development, technology and social and economic changes have given to nearly every aspect of daily life has rubbed

2   A Mirror to Life in 1903

off on fashion which, as one of the *arts mineurs*, has always held up its own mirror to life, reflecting not only basic attitudes and their changes but also playing on lesser variations with something like the momentary flicker of sunlight on water. It is doing all this today, but, in addition, its structure and even its entity have progressively changed in a way that has no precedent.

Fashion, unless we are going to be very anthropological about it, dates from the time when, about 1300, people in the Western world stopped wearing the various kinds of loose hanging or draped robes which, with little basic change, had served them as clothing all over the world through practically all civilisations, and began to wear fitted clothes. These immediately showed signs of acquiring a history and almost a life of their own. They changed continually, though at varying rates of speed, borne along by an impetus whose source has been the subject of endless enquiry and speculation. The trouble is that no one's findings have ever wholly satisfied anyone else. Fashion was not. Fashion came; could it also go?

To start with, and for a considerable period, fashion applied equally to the clothes of men and women. In medieval, Tudor and Stuart times and even for much of the eighteenth century man was often the proud peacock who outshone the contemporary lady. But in more recent times fashion has come to be generally accepted as applying to women's dress and this is the meaning to be given to it here – although the trend of the recent 'sixties and the present 'seventies threatens to reverse use and wont and dazzle the world again with male and female – and, for good measure – unisex fashions.

One immutable feature of fashion up to this century was that it was dictated from the top. The ruling classes – which meant the Court or some aristocracy of rank or wealth – made fashion. They were its accepted, unquestioned leaders, and from them it spread downwards. The descent was usually fairly slow and it never reached anything like the whole of the community. Fashion was a minority movement. When William Hazlitt said in an essay on the subject: 'Fashion is an odd jumble of contradictions, of sympathies and antipathies. It exists only by its being participated among a number of persons and its essence is destroyed by being communicated to a greater number,' he stated what was true in the early nineteenth century. The very meaning of fashion implies freedom to follow it and for the majority of people such freedom did not exist in Hazlitt's time. If a fashion spread to the masses it would not be at their choice and would therefore not be a 'fashion' any more. A century and a half later

Dr. Willett Cunnington made this point when he said: 'So long as there is not a free choice of style of dress, we cannot correctly speak of a "fashion" at all.' But at this time, 1951, he continued: 'Fashion is established only when adopted by the millions, instead of by the hundreds.' Free choice then existed for all. Sir Cecil Beaton, speaking for the 'seventies, sums it up more succinctly: 'Fashion is a mass phenomenon, but it feeds on the individual.' There must be personal originators and when they are followed you have fashion.

Today, accordingly, fashion is for all. Couturiers, speciality shops, department stores, boutiques, chain stores and multiples all offer fashion. In contrast to the past the biggest and the less expensive outlets are even on occasion the most fashionable. It is difficult to realise that at the start of this century millions of women, including a considerable proportion of middle class ones, had no means by which they could follow fashion without endless trouble and contrivances and waste of time. But the writings of the time show that it was so. The spread of fashion, and its availability, moved pace by pace with the emancipation of women, but both moved slowly and laboriously.

3   La Belle Epoque, 1905

Chic Parisien

4 *'Extravagance was the prevailing mood of Society'. 1900*　　5 *The daunting elaboration of her toilette. 1900*

At the start of the twentieth century there was little surface indication of any change in the traditional pattern of fashion for the few. Never had fashion as an expensive, class-conscious spectacle had such a heyday. In France it was *la Belle Epoque* and the name was a tribute to the fashions which flourished there in an extravagance of silks and satins, ribbons and laces, flowers and feathers and jewels, making Paris more than ever before the Mecca of fashion for all the world. America, closely linked with Europe since colonial days, followed Paris closely, with the more wealthy of the fashion-seekers selecting their wardrobes on personal visits, while many others followed Paris's lead through the acquisition of original models or copies obtained from there by the top flight of 'little' – or not so little – dressmakers in their American home towns.

In Britain the Gay Nineties were being followed by the Establishment-style gaiety and splendour of Edwardian days. The shining, almost theatrical allure which was part of this near-

decade finds no more apt symbol than the fashionable lady.
'Extravagance,' says Alison Adburgham, 'was the prevailing
mood of Society, with mature and triumphant womanhood the
focus of all glory, laud and bonheur.' That it was the calm before
the storm gives the period in retrospect a lingering, nostalgic
quality that is hard to resist. 'Edwardian high society,' J. B.
Priestley comments, 'added a little chapter, and surely . . . the
last, to the myth of the lost Golden Age.' And he is no dreamer.

Fashion was securely controlled by the rich and socially
eminent among the upper classes and by those who had achieved
wealth and the limelight of either fame or notoriety, plus the
copious leisure that being in fashion still demanded. Fashion was
a badge of social status and its devotees regarded it with high
seriousness and full absorption. Fantastic, elaborate, shaped as

6   *Dressed for the country. 1901*

7 *Formality for the country weekend. 1904*

nature never made her, the fashionable Edwardian lady is infinitely beguiling in the aplomb and serenity with which she carries off the daunting elaboration of her toilette. Those immense, yard-wide hats, laden with plumes and feathers or with basket-loads of artificial flowers; those rustling, frothing bell-shaped skirts that swept the ground; that giddy confusion of ribbons, lace, embroidery, frills, jewels and beads at every point all contributed to fashion's mighty overspill. Clothes like these were to disappear about 1908 – for what we call the Edwardian age really started before the end of the nineteenth century and was in eclipse before the end of Edward VII's reign. Nothing like these fashions has been seen since then, nor is it likely to be, but she was blissfully unaware, the Edwardian lady, that hers was a sunset song and that, even in her own time, she was becoming an anachronism.

The fashionable world, to which she belonged, revolved round the Court which, under the new King, had an importance unparalleled since then. It included new elements which contributed to its luxury and elegance. Beautiful and wealthy American women, most of whom had married into the British peerage, were brought into prominence by the King, among them Lady Ribblesdale, Lady Granard, Lady Cunard, Lady Curzon (Mary Leiter), Lady Astor and Consuelo, Duchess of Marlborough (later Madame Jacques Balsan). There were also some notable figures in Court circles who were interlopers from finance and even trade, but they all played the game according to the traditional code. This covered nearly every facet of daily life. It enjoined great formality and immense luxury in women's dress and also demanded close attention to being in the height of fashion and to wearing the correct clothes on all occasions. On the famous week-end country visits, which were a feature of high life, the fashionable lady would change her dress, with all its accessories, five or six times a day. And no outfit should be seen twice during one week-end. Several trunks and immense hat boxes were normal luggage for these visits, with, of course, an attendant lady's maid to manoeuvre the panoply of fashion for its high priestess – or victim.

This was the inescapable ambience of fashion and the blueprint of all who aspired to it in the early years of this century. The clothes for the top ladies of the time came from many dressmakers. Paris was, however, dominant. 'It was the fashion to be dressed by Paris couturiers Worth, Redfern and Callot,' declared American *Vogue*, and London thought likewise. The hypnotic spell Paris cast on the fashion scene was all-embracing.

Paris was a magic word. 'Paris model,' 'copy of a Paris model', these and similar phrases were echoed beguilingly wherever fashion was mentioned. London was, however, beginning to sustain a cluster of outstanding dressmakers who were flourishing in their own right and, though many of them depended upon Paris's lead, some of them were challenging the time-honoured monopoly and were themselves to become international figures. Though many of the most elegant Englishwomen shopped regularly in Paris, there was also developing a patriotic trend to buy British. This was given a lead by Queen Alexandra, both during her reign and previously as Princess of Wales. 'For patriotic reasons she dressed chiefly in London,' says Georgina Battiscombe in her life of the Queen, 'where her favourite dressmaker was Redfern, but occasionally she allowed herself a shopping expedition to Paris. There she would patronise Doucet, then a great name in the world of fashion, also the lesser known Fromont, of the Rue de la Paix.' She had also been known to buy from Worth.

Queen Alexandra was a lifelong maker of fashion – the last Royal lady and indeed the last great lady to achieve this eminence and to give fashion a leadership and quality it has lacked ever since. She was a magnificent figure. In 1909 Lady Oxford described how 'the Queen, dazzlingly beautiful, whether in gold and silver by night, or in violet velvet by day, succeeded in making every other woman look common beside her'. She was 'lovely and gracious, ineffably beautiful', and, again, 'slender, gracious and beautiful'. She was then 64. Where fashion was concerned Queen Alexandra was also, like other great ladies of her time, a leader with a mind of her own. Of her Coronation attire she wrote to Sir Arthur Ellis: 'I know better than all the milliners and antiquaries. I shall wear exactly what I like and so will all my ladies. Basta!'

This royal explosion of defiance was in key with the past, when great ladies would dictate to their chosen dressmakers and on occasion turn their private inspirations and ideas into fashion. But it was also in key with a certain relaxation of rigidity and solemnity which was making itself felt in fashionable life as the twentieth century got under way. 'In this new sunshine did the metamorphosis of taste take place overnight, I wonder?' queries Sonia Keppel in *Edwardian Daughter*. 'Suddenly,' she recalls, 'all Victorian furniture, ottomans, antimacassers &c all disappeared, with Turkey pile, dismal reps. In came chaises-longues, papier maché chairs, lace curtains, midget tables, nebulous colours. . . . Whereas, in Queen Victoria's reign paterfamilias predominated

8 *Queen Alexandra, last Royal fashion leader, in 1905*

9 *A perpetual summer. 1905*

10   The S-shaped corset, introduced in 1900, claimed to follow the natural lines of the figure

and male taste prevailed, now in King Edward's reign, the deification of the feminine was re-established.'

This deification meant that more attention was given to fashion, which also developed a number of new characteristics. Stiff satins, plush, damask, tweed and rigid materials in general went out with other Victoriana, and in came a froth of chiffons and laces, net and ninon, soft faille, tussore, crêpe de Chine, mohair and cashmere. Strong, emphatic or sombre colours were superseded by sweet pea and sugar almond delicacies of tone. Frills, beading, ribbons and trimmings of all sorts ran riot over the fashionable clothes of the time. 'The upper classes of Europe had succeeded in establishing for themselves a perpetual summer, and this fact was reflected in women's dress,' says James Laver of this time. And where the upper classes led others were by now trying hard to follow.

While the elegant, leisured Edwardian woman was setting the fashion scene with these light and airy dresses she was, however, wearing under them a corset that was anything but light and airy and which gave her one of the most extraordinary and constricting shapes that exist in fashion's annals. The famous 'S'-shaped figure of the time was the result of a new corset introduced in 1900. It was invented by a Frenchwoman, Mme. Gaches-Sarraute, who had studied medicine and whose aim was to create a foundation garment which would benefit the health of women by removing the extreme pressure exerted on the waist and diaphragm by the prevalent style of corset. This came high up on the bust and had a curved front busk indented at the tightly laced-up waist. The new design had a straight busk, began lower down on the bosom, which it released, and extended more deeply over the hips. It was named the Health Corset, and it should have lived up to its name, but unfortunately the idea went wrong. The fashionable Edwardian lady did not want to follow nature. The corset was laced up tightly over the large, mature Junoesque curves that were fashion's ideal, for the age of a mature king was also the age – the last – of the mature woman. This corset forced the bosom forward and thrust the hips back, thereby producing what became known as the 'kangaroo stance' as well as the 'S' line. The fashionable shape therefore consisted of a large, overhanging bust, augmented, if nature was sparing,

11   A large, overhanging bust. 1903

12 Hats were perched on top of elaborate hair styles, 1906. These were devised for motoring, travelling, walking and for elegant occasions respectively

13 Spring fashions, 1906, for walking

by a heavily frilled or even boned camisole or bodice, which even, on occasion, included handkerchiefs used as stuffing. The blouse or dress top was pouched lavishly over this. The forward flow of the bosom and the tight waist were counterbalanced by a majestic sweep of curving hips and derrière, outlined by a bell-shaped skirt, a shape new to fashion. The effect was as if the top of the lady was a foot ahead of the rest of her. The skirt fitted closely to the figure to below the hips, then flared to the ground, usually trailing on it and even by day sometimes completed by a train. Various kinds of clips were used to keep it off the ground out of doors.

The general pattern of formal fashion changed very little between 1900 and about 1908. A great many clothes were worn – chemise, corset, corset cover, drawers, a flannel petticoat, one or more cotton petticoats and, to be really elegant, a silk one over all. Large, forward-sweeping hats balanced the rear projection of the figure. Hair was puffed out and built up over pads inserted along the front of the head. These were known as 'rats' and persisted through the first decade of this century and to some degree after that. The back hair was drawn up and supported by combs. Hats were perched on this contraption of hair-styling and secured to it by means of long hat-pins, often with elaborate jewelled or enamelled heads, which speared the hat to the hair. Often they had lethal projecting points which menaced anyone who approached the wearer too closely.

Fashionable hats could be enormously expensive, as much as 50 guineas being not unusual, but the costly ostrich feathers, aigrettes, osprey feathers and other feathered or floral embellishments would be transferred from one hat to another. Hats were always worn, for sport and even by children at play. Other elaborate items contributed to the fashionable *toilette*. Chief of these were ostrich or marabou boas and stoles and, for colder weather, long fur stoles and large pillow-shaped muffs. Parasols were part of the summer ensemble: 'Women of fashion require many parasols during a London season,' says a fashion writer of 1902. Jewellery was worn in great profusion and was a costly item. But a signpost for the future appeared in the *Illustrated London News* when, in a fashion article in 1904, it drew its readers' attention to the Parisian Diamond Company's artificial jewellery, which could be invaluable 'for the succour of those whose worldly wealth will not extend to the limitless thousands that modern fashion desires to spend on pearls and diamonds alone'.

The epitome of elegance at this time and for many years to

come was the tea-gown. It was to become a garment of mystery to future generations, but it symbolised the vanishing world. 'In our own drawing rooms,' rhapsodises Mrs. Eric Pritchard in *The Cult of Chiffon* in 1902, 'when the tea-urn sings at five o'clock, we can don these garments of poetical beauty.' The tea-gown is also 'this garment of mystery which can be a very complete reflection of the wearer'. Going into details, she describes 'the ideal tea-gown of accordion pleated chiffon, lace and hanging stoles of regal furs'. Gwen Raverat, writing of the same time, recalls that her mother 'was in her glory in a tea-gown'. Susan, Lady Tweedsmuir describes her cousin Hilda Lyttleton's appearance 'wearing tea-gowns made by the Italian dress designer Fortuny, whose fanciful but lovely dresses were all the rage in these days. He made for her long straight garments of artfully pleated satin, held at neck, wrists and waist by strings of small iridescent shells.' Lady Diana Cooper remembers that, about the time when she 'came out' in 1911, 'the ladies dressed for tea in trailing chiffon and lace, and changed again for dinner into something less limp'. Top stores also specialised in tea-gowns. Debenham & Freebody said in a 1908 catalogue: 'We have made a special study of Rest, Boudoir and Tea-Gowns, and have now in stock a wonderful variety of these dainty and useful garments. These gowns are our own exclusive design, and are made in our own workrooms from materials that we can thoroughly recommend'. Marshall and Snelgrove in colour catalogues of the same period illustrated some spectacular tea-gowns. There was, for instance, 'Clytie', which was created in ivory satin, veiled with shadow lace, with a narrow insertion of Wedgwood ninon, finished with tiny vieux rose buttons. The coat effect, in a rich quality painted gauze ribbon and ninon to tone. Price 15½ guineas.' 'Delphine' was another prized design, 'in satin with tunic of silk, voile and guipure lace, made to order 15 guineas'. The tea-gown lingered on. In spite of the new outlook and new way of life which resulted from World War I, stores still featured it in 1919 and through the 'twenties, though by then it was being replaced by the afternoon gown and the cocktail dress, symbols of a new and different world.

14 *Tea gown in black satin and chiffon, 1901*

15 *The tea gown lingered on—this 1916 version is in silk crepe and lace, with embroidery*

2

The suggestion that there was hope for those who wanted to be in fashion but could not keep up with it on the scale set by its accepted wealthy leaders was being made increasingly in the 'glossy' magazines of the early nineteen-hundreds. Keeping up with fashion had become a matter of considerable concern to a substantial and growing section of the female members of the rising, prosperous middle classes and also of anxiety and near-despair to the not-so-wealthy elements of this group. Living up to one's 'position' was terribly important. Ways of achieving the fashionable look on a shoe-string budget were a major pre-occupation. The fashionable Edwardian lady was, unknown to herself, the tip of an iceberg of which the huge base was beginning to be visible and significant as the fashion followers increased.

The foundations upon which Edwardian fashion flourished and also one important means by which it was being extended had been laid in the previous half-century in Paris, but paradoxically, by an Englishman, Charles Frederick Worth. He was to Paris fashion what the Emperor Augustus was to Rome. He not only built a brilliant fashion empire of his own but also, although he may not have foreseen all the consequences, he put fashion on a new basis which led in the direction of fashion for all and he opened the way for the immense changes and developments which were to come.

Worth was born at Bourne, in Lincolnshire, in 1825, the son of an unsuccessful lawyer, and after starting work at the age of 12 in a local draper's shop, he went to London as an apprentice at Swan and Edgar's small, elegant shop in Piccadilly, where he served behind the counter, selling shawls and dress materials. In 1845 ambition took him to Paris where, at the fashionable Maison Gagelin, he was soon selling fabrics and also cloaks and mantles – the 'confections' which were among the first steps towards ready-made women's fashions. In 1858 he set up his own dress house. Paris fashion design, then mainly in the hands of undistinguished women dressmakers, had lapsed from the distinction it had achieved earlier in the century, under the régime of Leroy, and had come to consist mainly of ringing the changes on one or two basic styles in innumerable small ways. Worth's genius for original design and his flair for elegance led to spectacular success. He became the favourite dressmaker of the Empress Eugénie, who was the fashion leader of Europe during the Second Empire. Soon nearly every crowned head and other 'royals' from all over Europe, together with women of fashion from a host of other countries, especially and in growing numbers, from America, were making a visit to his handsome and luxurious showrooms a regular routine part of every visit to Paris. Improbably, even Queen Victoria was at times dressed by Worth, though she could well have been unaware of it. Jean

Paul Worth, son of Charles Frederick, and, with his brother Gaston, successor to the business, said: 'We made many a dress to her measurements, and sold it through English dressmakers.' That was a recognised procedure in fashion at the time.

In 1864 Worth was employing over 1000 workers and as he continued to advance it was evident that 'an immense luxury industry had been created for which Worth was largely responsible'. It was, of course, at this time an industry only in size – the sewing machine, which had become a practical reality in 1851, had no significant effect on his craftsman's methods and mass production was as remote as the moon from what he was doing. By virtue of the scale of Worth's activities, however, fashion was being given a new status and dimension and was being extended in a way that was to lead logically to interpretation in commercial rather than individual terms.

The great step by which Worth set on foot the revolution in fashion was his production of models not only for private customers, as in the past, but also for sale to top dressmakers and eventually, as the making of fashion developed, to manufacturers and big stores in France, England and, above all, in America, for copying purposes. Towards the end of his long career this side of his business became the dominating one. By the later years of the nineteenth century he had laid the foundations of the new concept of fashion as big business which was to develop in the twentieth century and had established Paris Couture as its fountainhead.

Worth also introduced mannequins, many of them English, to show his clothes to private clients, shop buyers and dressmaker copyists, instead of using the 'dummies' hitherto customary for this purpose. This was a major step in fashion presentation. There was, however, nothing like the later mannequin parade, and these early model girls are reported as having invariably worn tight-fitting, high-necked, long-sleeved black garments under the fashions they displayed. Much later Balmain, in *My Years and Seasons*, stated that at the beginning of this century mannequins showing evening dresses still wore cover-up garments of this kind. It was not seemly for them to be gowned like the aristocrats of fashion.

All in all, Worth was the first great fashion tycoon. He lived up to his name 'The King of Fashion' and the Second Empire was rightly called the Age of Worth. He lived royally, entertained lavishly, travelled in a private wagon-salon and presented his clothes (the first ever to be produced on a scale that merited the description 'collection') in a drawing-room atmosphere of great elegance. He lived until 1895, active to the last, and left his two sons to carry the name of Worth with undimmed glory well into the twentieth century. The impetus of his achievements in fashion not only contributed to its contemporary brilliance but also, as other new factors began to operate, helped to carry it, during the next century, into the life of every woman, whatever her age, class or way of life. 'The boy from Lincolnshire beat the French in their own acknowledged sphere,' said the *Times* in a

16 Fashions at a Paris Exhibition, 1907

leading article when he died on March 10, 1895. 'He set the taste and ordained the fashion of Paris and from Paris extended his undisputed sway all over the civilised and a good deal of the uncivilised world. He knew how to dress woman as nobody else knew how to dress her.'

By the turn of the century Paris fashion, largely due to Worth, had attained a structure recognisably like that of *haute couture* in more recent years. A considerable number of fashion houses had come into being and were flourishing in a Paris which was drawing more and more visitors from all over Europe, Britain and America. In addition to the wealthy and leisured, the great middle classes were now enjoying the pleasures of 'gay Paree' and among its entertainments were its splendid exhibitions. The great one held in 1900 was a landmark in fashion, because it included a section in which a series of tableaux showed the latest elegancies of fashion. All the leading dressmakers of the day took part – Doucet, Paquin, the Callot Soeurs, Redfern and Worth among them. Mme. Paquin, who was the President of the Fashion Section and who had opened her House in 1891, was the first successful woman in *haute couture*. She numbered Royalty among her customers and by the beginning of this century had set up a branch in London, where Redfern had started his career and where Worth was already established. By 1902 she was advertising her establishment at 39, Dover Street, Mayfair and announcing 'each creation original and produced in Paris and London simultaneously'. Later she also opened branches in Buenos Aires and Madrid. Her contribution to the 1900 Exhibition consisted of a wax figure of her supremely elegant self wearing a beautiful dress. Worth showed a series of fashion tableaux, with figures wearing appropriate *ensembles* for various occasions. This venture was another indication of the growing interest in fashion among the public and so successful was it that police had to be called in to control the crowds.

Another important sign of the widening attention being given to top fashion and a new means of spreading it lay in its close connection with the Stage at the close of the nineteenth and the early part of the present century. The Stage began to take the place of Society as a fashion-setter. 'In the nineteen hundreds,' says Barbara Worsley-Gough in *Fashions in London*, 'the stage reached its fashionable apotheosis. It was the focus of social interest, and its leaders had usurped the leadership of fashion which had been held by the great ladies. Photographs of actresses vied with photographs of the professional beauties in public esteem. Soon they ousted them completely. Fashions in clothes, in hairdressing, even in mannerisms, were set from the stage.' As far more people attended plays than could ever see the Society beauties and study their clothes fashion was widely disseminated. 'The first night of a play had become a fashionable function which both the frivolous and the serious sets attended. Actors and actresses were welcomed, sought after, cultivated, envied. Royalty approved of them. In fact almost everyone in Society did.' To round off the picture, some of the professional beauties, like Lily Langtry and Mrs. Wheeler, became professional actresses.

Leading actresses were dressed with great magnificence by top couturiers, both on and off the stage, and immense public interest was taken in what they wore, especially in the drawing room comedies and romantic plays, which were so popular at this time. But, in addition, historical plays were presented in contemporary fashionable dress, even if the settings were as remote as ancient Rome. So important was stage costume of this kind considered to be that leading newspapers and magazines published detailed reports of the clothes worn on the stage along with their criticisms of the play itself. Eleanora Duse's biographer records that she was dressed by Worth for 30 years, until her death in 1924. Sarah Bernhardt, though she created some of her own spectacular fashions herself, also went to Worth. Réjane was dressed by Doucet.

Among the most elegant and fashionable actresses of the early nineteen-hundreds was the American Maxine Elliott, a leading figure on the stage in the U.S.A., Britain and Europe and a star noted not only for her beauty and glamour but also for her supreme fashion-sense. Some of her sumptuous stage *toilettes* are described in her biography, written by her niece, Diana Forbes-Robertson. In September 1903, starring in a fashionable comedy, 'she would first step upon the stage in a creation of heliotrope chiffon velvet with a chemisette and hanging oversleeves of lace, topped by a large black hat with sweeping ostrich feathers, a black fox stole round her shoulders, and a black fox muff carried lightly upon one forearm. A white satin ball dress draped in classic style with silver trimmings would be the high point in the second act. The clothes were fresh from Paris.'

In her dealings with Paris, however, Maxine displayed an independent attitude. In 1900, when appearing in *When we were Twenty-one,* she told an interviewer that 'French dressmakers were putting sashes on everything, but it spoiled the line, so she removed them. . . . The fact that she was willing to pay the price of a thousand dollars or more for a dress gave her every

17 Actress Eva Moore in an elegant ensemble of 1902

18 Maxine Elliott, most fashionable of
Edwardian actresses

19 Lily Langtry, professional
beauty and fashion leader

right to pick it about as she saw fit.' She also had a plan of
campaign when seeking her own way with great dressmakers;
'You must simply move in on them with your sandwiches in a
bag and sit it out till you get what you want.' She was the most
fashionable of actresses on and off the stage. In July 1905, when
the play *Her Own Way* closed, 'Maxine had six weeks for yachting trips, country visits, and the purchase of a new wardrobe in
Paris'. Then back to New York for her new play *Her Great
Match* in which she was 'exquisite' in a white lace dress and tiny
tiara.

Further evidence of how actresses were recognised as fashion
leaders at this time is recorded by Ruby Miller, one of the
famous Gaiety Girls, in her memoirs, *Champagne for my Supper*.
She retails how 'During Ascot Week, we Gaiety Girls led the
fashions, trailing the lawns wearing gorgeous creations of crêpe
de Chine, chiffon, or lace over petticoats of rustling silk edged
with hundreds of yards of fine Valenciennes lace threaded with
narrow velvet ribbon. Every stitch sewn by hand and no
couturier of repute would have dreamed of copying a model
gown.' With these dresses went 'precious hats trimmed with
plumes and rich satin ribbon from Paris' or, alternatively, small
toques of fresh flowers. 'Our gloves, shoes and stockings,' she

adds, 'always matched' and they carried 'dainty parasols of ruched chiffon, feathers or lace, with the most beautiful handles of carved ivory, mother of pearl or hand-painted porcelain'. They attracted all eyes – and meant much business for the fashionable dressmakers of the day.

3

Splendour and elaboration were the main features of Edwardian fashion, created for and sustained by a special kind of Edwardian lady who was the most spectacular and the most copied by the rest of womankind. But also emerging at this time were other kinds of women due in the long run to oust the Edwardian concept and swing into the future on quite different lines. Their starting point was, appropriately, the New Woman. This phenomenon appeared in the latter part of the nineteenth century, when her 'rights', her education, her social freedom and physical activities all began to be promoted by her own increasing efforts and to be fostered by various happenings, from the achievements of pioneer individuals in breaking down barriers to Acts of Parliament and the invention of the bicycle – the last, with all its implications, being probably the most important of all!

So far as fashion was concerned, the first outward and visible symbol of the New Woman was the tailor-made costume which, to the great credit of Britain's part in female progress as well as to her traditional supremacy in men's tailoring, had become, by the start of the twentieth century, the first British-born fashion to achieve international fame and domination. It had originated some time before that, and was fashionable in Britain in the eighteen-nineties. One view of its origin is that it was first devised by the British tailor Redfern, who also had a Paris house, for yachting wear at Cowes. Made by a man's tailor from materials similar to those used for men and following a similar tradition of craftsmanship, it was the first forward-looking fashion, the first symbol of freedom to come, and in spirit, if not in design, of an equality that was to be loudly claimed in the near future. Its early versions were reminiscent of the riding habit, which was natural, as that outfit was the only one for which women had in the past sought out the tailor.

Charles Poynter, of the London house of Redfern, had set up a Paris branch in 1881 and there were also branches in Edinburgh and New York. He played an important part in taking the tailored suit across the Channel and establishing it in Paris – and

20   The New Woman, in her tailor-made costume, began to rival the more elaborately dressed Edwardian lady. 1900

international – fashion. The claim that it was first introduced to Paris by the English house of Creed was put forward by Charles Creed, of the sixth generation of this family to head the famous British tailoring establishment with the strong Paris link. The first Creed, born in Leicester in 1710, came to London to start a business in tailoring repairs and alterations. His son, Henry, became a tailor in the Strand and his son, also Henry, had a fashionable tailoring business in Conduit Street, where he became the tailor of the Comte d'Orsay, leader of the dandies, and also made 'amazones', or riding habits, for fashion leader

21　The tailor-made and the bicycle were twin symbols of emancipation. 1904

22　Real-life version of the New Woman. My Mother, a career girl, 1902

23 *Smart costumes for practical wear. 1907*   24 *The Sportswoman in her tailor-made costume, 1908*

Empress Eugénie, to whom he was recommended by Queen Victoria. At the Empress's suggestion he opened a second establishment in Paris in 1850 and acquired a distinguished clientèle, rich in crowned heads. He claimed to have made the women's tailor-made a top fashion in Paris at the turn of the present century, when the Duke of Alba, ordering a tweed suit for himself, suggested that Creed should make a costume of the same material for the Duchess. The result proved a sensation and a fashion-maker. The tailored suit is still something few women would be without – and was Creed's creation for the Duchess perhaps the first move towards the 'unisex' that was to make fashion news in the 1960's and the first of many feminine borrowings from men's clothes through the intervening years?

As a result of the Duke's inspiration Henry Creed's clients for tailored costumes soon included the Queen of Italy, the Grand

Duchess Vladimir of Russia, the Infanta of Spain and a galaxy of
famous actresses, including Réjane, Mary Garden and Gaby
Deslys. There was also the famous 'beautiful spy', Mata Hari.
She was executed in a Creed suit, thereby providing the most
macabre piece of fashion publicity in all history.

Although the woman's costume started as a rather severe
fashion, for travelling, walking and for venturesome young
women who were launching out into careers, it became elegantly
elaborate in the hands of the fashionable Edwardian lady. It was
worn for smart daytime events and led to a corresponding
tailored dress which was even worn to weddings. It also led to
the infinite variety of the Edwardian blouse, one of the most
notable and characteristic items introduced into the wardrobe
at this time. Starting in the late nineteenth century as a severe
shirt blouse, based on the man's shirt and complete with stiff
collar and tie, well-suited to the New Woman, the blouse became

*26   The infinite variety of the
Edwardian blouse. 1904*

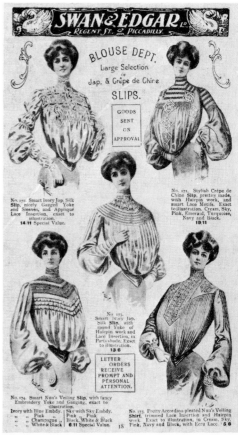

25   Evening blouses. 1907

27 *The Gibson Girl, immortalised by Charles Dana Gibson, the American artist, in tailored blouse and skirt. The wooing of the American heiress by the British nobleman was an important part of the Edwardian social scene. 1903*

a fantasy of lace and embroidery, varying from a costly hand-made creation from a top dressmaker to a home-made effort produced with infinite patient labour. Lady Diana Cooper recalls a German governess of her childhood who spent all her spare time sewing: 'She worked only at a shell pink blouse for herself with lace insertions, all the two years she was with us, and at making pink flannel nightdresses.'

The New Woman in her uniform of tailored skirt and blouse achieved a fame and acclaim without precedent in fashion in the shape of the internationally renowned Gibson Girl, the subject of innumerable pictures and postcards. The creation of the American artist, Charles Dana Gibson, she was inspired by the three famous and beautiful Langhorne sisters, one of whom he married and another of whom became famous in the British political world as Lady Astor, the first woman to take her seat in the House of Commons in 1919. On the American stage the Gibson Girl was portrayed by Camille Clifford, whose name became almost synonymous with the creation. She came to London and first appeared on the stage there at the Shaftesbury Theatre in 1904. The vogue continued until fashion began to change dramatically about 1908, but although Charles Dana Gibson lived until 1944, he never created another fashion figure of such note. Another American fashion symbol, Fluffy Ruffles, a dashing beauty created by artist William Morgan, failed to achieve the international acclaim of the Gibson Girl, but she had considerable fame in serial drawings in the *New York Herald*. The only comparable commercial promotion of fashion on this scale also emanated from America, when the film stars of the great days of Hollywood in the coming 'twenties and 'thirties set fashions that went round the world.

But while the tailor-made pointed the way ahead to a hopeful new world for women, the early years of this century also show a deep, smouldering discontent with existing fashions. Fashion was a status symbol in a very class-conscious society, but keeping up with it remained a besetting financial problem, mainly among the rising groups of the middle classes. The fashions of the time presented them with standards which they found painfully difficult and sometimes impossible to achieve. Fashion was also time-wasting and irrational. The new young women resented its demands, but knew they would lose face if they ignored them. Gwen Raverat, who in *Period Piece* is an invaluable commentator on this aspect of middle-class life in the early 1900's, gives a graphic picture of fashion as she grew up at that time. She describes cycling in 'baggy knickerbockers over frocks, and over our frilly drawers. We thought this horribly improper, but rather grand. . . . I only once saw a woman (not, of course, a *lady*) in real bloomers.' She recalls the boarding school Sunday crocodile for church, with the girls of 1902 in 'their beribboned top-heavy hats, stuck on top of the hair they had spent so long in frizzling and puffing out; and their tightly corseted, bell-shaped figures wobbling down the hill'. Clothes, she declares, brought 'discomfort, restraint and pain' and 'except for the small-waisted, naturally dumb-bell shaped female, the ladies never seemed quite at ease, or even quite as if they were wearing their own clothes. For their dresses were always made too tight, and the bodices wrinkled laterally from the strain; and their stays showed a sharp ledge across the middle of their backs. And, in spite of whalebone, they were apt to bulge below the waist in front, for, poor dears, they were but human after all, and they had to expand somewhere.'

Corsets and hats were forms of torture, and even the tailor-made brought its miseries and was not the embodiment of freedom that it purported to be: 'Skirts were more tiresome than painful, but they could be very tiresome indeed. . . . It was difficult to walk freely in the heavy tweed "walking skirts" which kept on catching between the knees. Round the bottom of these skirts I had, with my own hand, sewn two and a half yards of "brush braid", to collect the worst of the mud, for they inevitably swept the roads, however carefully I might hold them up behind . . . afterwards the encrusted mud had to be brushed off, which might take an hour or more to do. There can be no

28 Camille Clifford. 1906

more futile job, imposed by idiotic convention, than that of perpetual skirt-brushing.' The time wasted in trying to keep up with fashions of such an unaccommodating kind irritated intelligent young women. Susan Tweedsmuir recalls that 'we must have bought literally miles of the kind of beaded trimmings called *passementerie* with which to renovate ageing dresses', and she recalls her cousin Hilda protesting: 'I want to do something better than rush up and down Oxford Street hunting for beastly pieces of tulle.' Rebellion was rife among those 'brought up in the strictest sect of young ladyhood'.

A recurrent figure in the history of the struggle to keep up with fashion, which runs through the records of the early part of this century, is the 'little dressmaker'. Crouched over her sewing, usually working single-handed in her own home or going out by the day for hire, poorly paid and with the manual sewing machine as her only equipment, she existed in such numbers that she played a very considerable part in the making of fashion for the growing number of people who sought it anxiously but could not afford to cross the thresholds of its established sources.

The lack of retail outlets which could meet the increasing needs of the ordinary woman presented a constant problem to which no satisfactory answer could be found at the time. Sometimes the 'little dressmaker' existed in quite exalted circles. Lady Diana Cooper recalls childhood memories of her mother's clothes; 'for big evenings, grand balls or dinners. . . . I remember black tulle over moonlight blue, and flesh-pink satin stuck over with sequins or bunches of rosebuds, always the creation of some little dressmaker, never Paquin or Worth'. Yet the beautiful Duchess of Rutland, a talented painter, was one of the most elegant women of her time. Gwen Raverat recalls how her mother 'used to spend hours superintending a humble daily dressmaker in cutting old clothes to pieces and putting them together again in new permutations and combinations, for that marble-hearted fiend, Economy, who was her evil angel, was always putting in his spoke and preventing her from having things made at a good shop'. For boarding school she remembers that: 'I had a new green tweed coat and skirt badly made by the poor little daily dressmaker, and the skirt had been lined with bright buttercup-yellow cotton, which showed round the edges whenever I moved.' One daily dressmaker, interviewed about 1909, said she was paid 2s. 6d. or 3s. 6d. a day. Another received 2s. a day and in addition was given her food. But such dressmakers were in great demand and had the compensation of

29   The innumerable trimmings and accessories of Edwardian dressing, which irritated the new young woman, continued for many years, even up to 1916

1 U.S.   5 U.S.   3 U.S.   6 U.S.   2 U.S.   4 U.S.

usually being regularly employed by a substantial number of the same families.

Ways of getting round the high cost of fashion were continually being put forward by fashion writers and in nearly every case they advocated the resort to the 'little dressmaker' in some form or other. 'The girl with a limited dress allowance will probably have her lingerie made at some charitable institution or at her own home,' advises one writer of 1902 in dealing with the problem of a trousseau. Again, the woman with a small dress allowance 'cannot go to Paris and buy expensive lingerie, but she can pick up a French model at a sale and have it copied in muslin or nainsook costing from 8d. or 9d. a yard'. The *Illustrated London News* in January 1904 advises that the cost of evening dresses is 'more of a drag on a small dress allowance than any other item. A clever maid, or a girl who has had some dressmaking lessons can often produce at home a sufficiently satisfactory costume for a small dance and the saving is great.'

She must, however, have a paper pattern. This advice is constantly given: 'Buy a really good paper pattern and have it copied by a neat worker.' Summer dresses, for instance, are not prohibitive because 'if you have a good pattern and a clever maid you can have dresses for all sorts of public occasions at not very great cost'. Paper patterns had already been helping women to achieve some degree of fashion at a modest cost for some time. They had been included in the British magazine, *The World of Fashion*, from 1850 and were for bodices, mantles, underwear and various other garments. Rather oddly, several patterns, indicated by different types of outline, were given on a single large sheet of paper, so that the user had to pick out the one she wanted. It must have been enough to try the patience of a saint. A step forward had been taken in 1862 by Ebenezer Butterick, a tailor in Massachusetts, who had the idea of cutting out a pattern for his wife to follow as she busied herself with the family sewing. This led to a great demand for such patterns of all kinds. In 1866 Butterick went to New York, bought a fashion journal there and started selling patterns by mail order – it is believed for the first time anywhere. He set up a branch in Regent Street, London in 1873 and as his business grew his employees numbered 40. Weldons started a similar business in 1879.

During the second half of the nineteenth century women's magazines, which were rapidly increasing in number (48 new titles appeared between 1880 and 1900), ran paper pattern services and also dealt in their correspondence columns with problems of making-up and re-making. From the end of the nineteenth century there was a tremendous expansion in the circulation as well as the number of these publications. Typical was *The Lady*, founded in 1885, which started with a circulation of 1683, rose to 17,687 in 1895 and by 1905 achieved a total of 27,949 copies.

Great attention was given to fashion in women's magazines from the early 1900's, indicating the spread of interest in the subject. *The Queen* had a regular Paris letter and pages of coloured illustrations of Paris models as well as its London fashion feature. Fashions were shown for all kinds of events – 'On the Lawns at Goodwood', 'Toilettes de Casino', 'Fashions behind the Footlights', 'Palais de Glace Costume', 'Charmante Robe de Bal' among them. Often the captions were in French, for Paris had the fashion *cachet*. *The Queen* also offered paper patterns of all kinds, from 'A Dinner Gown' to 'A French Bathing suit'.

The style of writing on fashion in these early years of the twentieth century had a rapturous quality similar to that which is still indulged in at times by writers on wine. Debenham and Freebody, for instance, are described in the *Illustrated London News* as having 'an illuminative way of expressing La Mode here that is immediately inspiring, and have a positive genius for selecting (or is it, perchance, creating?) what we may call the sympathetic little gown'.

From the start of this century social change, improved education and technical progress in printing and production all contributed to the wider dissemination of news about fashion through women's magazines. Such news was increasing too as the fashion trade itself grew. 'The importance of the quality magazines as sources of information on the latest fashion trends grew with the rapid expansion of the fashion trade on both sides of the Channel', says Cynthia White in her study of women's magazines from 1693 to 1968. From the end of the nineteenth century newspaper advertisements also showed fashions obtainable at leading stores and by the early part of this century they were substantial and frequent. Towards the end of the first decade newspapers began to publish illustrated fashion articles, thus bringing fashion to the attention of more and more women.

2 Fashion spreads from the top, and many join in, 1900–1910

Although the forces which were to speed fashion on its course of expansion developed from both the top and bottom, the process by which the traditions of a craft serving a minority were to come to terms with and, to some degree, be absorbed by, big business was a long and involved one. To start with, growth came mainly from the top to meet the aspiring needs of the fashion-seekers, and the years before 1914 saw much happening here. Based on the Paris pattern, already familiar in Britain by virtue of the many private customers and fashionable dressmakers who patronised the fashion houses there, certain fashion houses in London had grown to a considerable size by the early years of this century. They were stimulated by the opening of London houses by Paris couturiers. Among the Londoners were Madame Handley-Seymour (favourite of Royalty), Reville and Rossiter (started in 1906 by two members of the department store, Jays), Russell and Allen, Redfern, Mascotte, Bradleys and Lucile. They were all distinguished and elegant, though not, on the whole, creative designers. Redfern, with houses in London, Edinburgh, Paris and New York, was, however, included by Paul Poiret in *My First Fifty Years* as one of the leading Paris couturiers of the 'nineties, along with Doucet, Paquin, Worth and Maggy Rouff.

The most dramatic personality among the London dressmakers and one who left a series of landmarks in the growth of fashion was Lucile, Lady Duff Gordon. She was not only an outstanding innovator in the general set-up and presentation of fashion, but also the first Englishwoman (or, to be exact, Scots-Canadian with a touch of Irish) to achieve an international reputation as a dressmaker, with a quadruple fashion empire which spread from London to embrace branches in Paris, New

York and Chicago, with collections being shown every season in each city. The irrepressible sister of the equally irrepressible best-selling novelist, Elinor Glyn, she started dressmaking in London in 1890, without capital or staff, to support herself and her young daughter after an early divorce from her first husband. Her only qualifications were some skill in sewing and embroidery, acquired at school, plus the possession of what she called 'chic' – 'nobody had ever heard of the word in England until I brought it in'. From dressing personal friends from a room in her mother's London house, she moved to premises in Old Burlington Street, where the name Maison Lucile was coined (her own Christian name was Lucy), and then to Hanover Square, first to number 17, then to 23, where she was established in 1900, having by then formed a company and married one of the directors, Sir Cosmo Duff Gordon.

In her autobiography, *Discretions and Indiscretions*, published in 1932, when her kind of fashion world had expired and she was writing articles and answering readers' letters for a newspaper, she gives a highly coloured story of her career which is not without affinities to the style of her sister, and in it boldly claims a long series of fashion innovations. Some are important and justified, but others reveal that *folie de grandeur* to which she was prone. Her American assistant, Howard Greer, later to make a name for himself in Hollywood and then as a wholesale manufacturer in America, refers to her 'obsession with greatness' and gives a colourful description of how 'she affected long flowing chiffon veils, white Russian boots and Tosca walking sticks'. She had flaming red hair and had a passion for Pekineses and Chows.

She claims to have been the first to decorate her showroom with drawing room elegance – and that probably was true of London, though Worth had done something of the kind in Paris long before. She was on firm ground in claiming to have introduced the mannequin parade in the style which was to prevail from that time onwards and to be a highly important part of the fashion business at all levels. She describes how the idea grew of 'glorious goddess-like girls' parading in her setting of rich carpets and grey brocade curtains, on a stage with misty olive chiffon curtains as the background and with accompanying music by an orchestra.

The first parade, attended by Princess Alice, Ellen Terry, Lily Langtry, the Duchess of Westminster, Mrs. Asquith and a host of other notabilities, was a triumph, not least for the mannequins. One was 'five feet eleven inches of loveliness (it was the day of tall women and generous curves)'. Another was 'six foot one

30   *'Lucile', Lady Duff-Gordon, in 1922*

inch of perfect symmetry' and a third 'a six foot statuesque beauty. . . . Not one of them weighed much under eleven stone and several of them considerably more.' She gave the girls dramatic names, the most famous being Dolores, and others including Gamila and Hebe.

Another of Lucile's innovations which became general couture practice was that of giving the model clothes names – but what names! 'When Passion's Thrall is o'er', 'Do you Love me?', 'The Sighing Sound of Lips Unsatisfied' replaced the conventional 'pink silk' or 'black velvet'. The show which introduced all this was a tremendous success; 'My star had risen'.

She claims to have revolutionised women's underwear early in her career. 'I was particularly anxious to have a department for beautiful underclothes, as I hated the thought of my creations being worn over the ugly nun's veiling or linen-cum-Swiss embroidery which was all the really virtuous woman of these days permitted herself. . . . So I started making underclothes as delicate as cobwebs and as beautifully tinted as flowers, and half the women in London flocked to see them, though they had not the courage to wear them at first. . . . Slowly they came over to them.' Success again crowned Lucile's efforts. 'I was a pioneer. I loosed upon a startled London, a London of flannel underclothes, woollen stockings and voluminous petticoats, a cascade of chiffons, of draperies as lovely as those of ancient Greece.' It was not quite true – silk underwear had existed in the 1880's and silk stockings were centuries old. But Lucile did usher in glamour in underwear; though taken for granted now it was rare then.

1907 was a splendid year. She had already dressed a number of plays, starting with *The Liars* for Sir Charles Wyndham, but now: 'A new play was launched with a new actress.' This was *The Merry Widow*, with Lily Elsie, and 'the triumph of *The Merry Widow* was also a triumph for me. *The Merry Widow* hat, which I designed for Lily Elsie, brought in a fashion which carried the name of Lucile, its creator, all over Europe and the States.' Lily Elsie and *The Merry Widow* were legendary for years, and Lucile continued to dress her, as well as many other leading actresses and fashion-setters. 'The leading lady's gowns,' says Sir Cecil Beaton of this time, 'were inevitably made by Lucile and were masterpieces of intricate workmanship. . . . Lucile worked with soft materials . . . with bead or sequin embroidery, with cobweb lace insertions, true lovers' knots and garlands of minute roses.' Again, he says: 'In her heyday Lucile's artistry was unique, her influence enormous.'

The Merry Widow hat was more important than it could be

31 Lily Elsie, 1907, in the Merry Widow hat designed by Lucile, which became world-famous in fashion

today, for hats at that time were not only invariably worn by day, but also with evening dress in restaurants and at the theatre. It took Sarah Bernhardt, when she bought her own theatre, to have the courage to ban hats there because they obstructed the view. The smouldering heroine of Elinor Glyn's *Three Weeks*, the sensational best-seller of 1907, wore 'an expensive, distinguished looking hat' on her first appearance at dinner in a Swiss hotel, an evening dress occasion. Sonia Keppel recalls 'a black velvet, low-cut evening dress of mamma's with which she wore a huge, black, feathered hat'.

On a holiday visit to New York, to spend the Christmas of 1909 with Elsie de Wolfe (Lady Mendl) Lucile observed women in restaurants wearing 'copies of Paris models, but . . . their wearers had chosen them indiscriminately and without taste'. There were no good American designers, so Paris models had to be imported and copied. Lucile to the rescue – and soon there was a New York house in West Thirty Sixth Street for Lady Duff Gordon, 'first English swell to trade in New York', as the papers said. A copy of the London house, decorated in the same pale grey elegance, it was opened at the end of February 1910 with a parade of 150 models specially designed for the occasion and shown by four of her prettiest models from London. The clothes carried more alluring names than ever – 'The Wine of Life', 'Love will find out a way' among them. It was another triumph. 'Everyone who mattered in Society was there,' purrs its originator. 'I became the rage.' Personal consultations at 500 dollars a time were a useful side-line and were greatly in demand. Her triumphs continued, as will be shown later.

Unlike their successors later in the century, the London fashion houses of this time did not borrow the French description 'couturier', but were usually known as Court dressmakers. Round the perimeter of the top names there had grown a very large number of firms using this description. They included many who had started as private dressmakers and whose individual skills had won them a distinguished clientèle. On the strength of this they had expanded and set up fashionable businesses under this name. It gave the right tone at the time. It indicated that the standards and expertise of those concerned were up to what was expected in Court circles, but even though such circles covered a much larger field of social and therefore of fashion activity than today, all the clothes made by the Court dressmakers could not have been worn on Royal occasions. Many such dressmakers had no claim to be original creators; their most usual practice was to buy models in Paris and adapt

32   An evening dress with hat of 1908

or copy them, or else to ring the changes on prevailing styles as seen in the fashion journals.

Somewhat lower down in the social scale of the very class-conscious world of fashion were considerable numbers of other dressmakers, many of whom had been apprenticed in the craft in the workrooms of Court or other categories of dressmakers and who had risen above the description 'little' to the extent of setting up their own premises. Sometimes these were part of a private house, at others a shop where they combined the business of dressmaking with drapery. They would sell haberdashery, ribbons, laces, trimmings and dress accessories, and in addition would do dressmaking of the made-to-measure kind then greatly in demand. Sometimes mother and daughters would work together in this kind of enterprise. Sometimes a few apprentices were taken on for training, thus continuing the tradition. They were a boon to middle class families of restricted means but the historical significance of this source of fashion is that from many such shops developed the later 'madam shops' – the specialist fashion shops which in years to come were to be an important outlet for the top end of the wholesale manufacturing fashion trade that was to develop.

2

A main source of the expanding world of fashion in the early years of the present century was the department store. This was a force which was bringing fashion out of its previous narrow, exclusive confines. Its growth ran parallel with the growth of the middle-classes, whose main source of fashion it became – and to a large degree still remains.

In terms of bricks and mortar the store had in most cases been in existence for a long time, because nearly every big store in Britain started as a small shop, sometimes as early as the eighteenth century. Fortnum and Mason began as grocers in 1707; Browns of Chester opened in 1780; Dickins and Smith, later to be Dickins and Jones, dated from 1790. Clark and Debenham, later Debenham and Freebody, was established by 1791, with records of the haberdashery shop of William Franks on the same site as early as 1778. Swan and Edgar's starting date was 1812; Peter Robinson's 1833; Marshall and Wilson, which became Marshall and Snelgrove, began in 1837, and Harrods opened as a grocer in 1849.

Many well-known American stores started business in the mid-nineteenth century, though some kind of family tree can be claimed with the trading posts and general shops set up by immigrants from Europe from the seventeenth century onwards. The big developments, as in Britain, took place in the second half of the nineteenth century and after that. As in Britain, each store developed in its own way. The original Gimbel started life as a travelling pedler and opened his first shop in 1842 in Vincennes, Alabama. Lord and Taylor started as a dry goods store in 1826. Macy's was founded in 1858. Bergdorf Goodman was born at the turn of this century, when a tailor called Herman Bergdorf designed and made a costume for his daughter, a career girl who was social secretary to a prominent socialite. Friends of the latter wanted similar costumes and this was the foundation of a business which grew rapidly. Bergdorf engaged as assistant a young man called Edwin Goodman. He sold the shop to the newcomer and returned to his native Alsace, but the name remained and the store became very fashion-conscious, with Goodman going to Paris with his buyers, seeing wholesalers as they came into the fashion world, training assistants, even helping with the tailoring and fitting. Ohrbachs' founder, born in Vienna in 1850, came to America and started his career sweeping out a wholesale warehouse. At 17 he became a travelling salesman, started small shops and then a big one, based initially on job lots and odd lots sold at cut prices, but up-graded steadily to such a degree that although it had a bargain element it attracted film stars and other celebrities, as well as ordinary housewives. Neiman Marcus, founded in 1907 by Herbert Marcus, and his sister and brother-in-law Mr. and Mrs. Neiman, was continued by the next generation and brought fashion to the big-spending oil land of Texas. By the close of the nineteenth century a few exclusive U.S. stores, among them Marshall Field, John Wannamaker and B. Altman, were producing custom-made fashion, usually based on Paris originals, just as British stores were doing.

The early stages of growth in most cases led to these original shops becoming medium-sized drapers, and this happened mainly in the first half of the nineteenth century. There was, however, no concerted or set pattern. 'The history of the department store is a collection of highly personal success stories', says Dorothy Davis in *A History of Shopping*, and although she refers to Britain it was the same across the Atlantic. The rate of progress in each case and the point at which the draper's shop began to rate as a department store is difficult to assess in modern terms. Alison Adburgham, in her *Shops and Shopping*, gives priority in this respect in Britain to Kendal Milne's of Manchester and Bainbridge's of Newcastle, and ascribes this to a date before

1850. James Jefferys, in *Retail Trading in Britain 1850-1950*, considers that in the mid-nineteenth century no departmental store existed in the modern sense and that the years 1850-1875 were the crucial ones in their emergence. During this period there was rapid development, both in London and throughout Britain and also in America. William Whiteley, a recent arrival on the London shopping scene, claimed that when he started his big expansion into Queens Road in 1872 and called himself 'the Universal Provider', his was Britain's first department store, capable of supplying everything 'from a pin to an elephant'.

That women's apparel and, increasingly, women's fashions should become a main part of the retail store's activity stemmed naturally from the starting point in drapery. From selling clothing materials, accessories and trimmings it was an obvious step, at a time when there was no organised method of fashion manufacture and no system of wholesale production, for the store to start making-up as well as selling dress lengths (six or seven yards, double width, incidentally at the start of this century), blouse lengths, costume lengths and so forth. From quite early in the nineteenth century ready-to-wear mantles, cloaks and shawls had been on sale in shops, and ready-made underwear had also been made for a considerable time. But other clothes which demanded sizing and fitting were slower to move out of the made-to-measure category so far as any claim to fashion was concerned. So important was the part played by the private dressmakers that ready-made meant something cheap and rather makeshift until after World War I and the description did not really come into repute fashion-wise till well after that. At the end of the nineteenth century Debenham and Freebody offered private dressmakers facilities for buying short lengths of material at trade prices, instead of limiting this concession to bulk purchasers. They also provided matching services for trimmings and loaned lengths of fabrics for such dressmakers to show their customers.

Most leading stores in Britain had set up their own workrooms for making bespoke women's fashions on a large scale during the later nineteenth century, doing very substantial business in high quality clothes which became second only to the products of Paris or the Court dressmaker. Debenham and Freebody described themselves as Court dressmakers in the early 1900's. In general the status of stores, many of which had been cheap and addicted to price-cutting in their earlier days, had risen very considerably by the start of the twentieth century. Their aim was to attract the upper end of the middle classes, including 'carriage trade', and they provided very comprehensive services to their customers in the shape of patterns of materials, elaborate sketches of clothes, sometimes coloured, and measurement forms, all sent by post to any part of the country. In addition to their own designs they offered copies of Paris models from originals bought in Paris by their buyers for this purpose. They even kept customers' own patterns and size details on file for reference. These were for clothes made in their own workrooms, and by this means the stores became to a large degree the first manufacturers of fashion.

From this high-class business in made-to-order clothes many stores began to make their own ready-to-wear, using their workrooms for this purpose at slack times, so as to keep them operating profitably and starting, last century, with mantles, aprons, cloaks and similar loose-fitting or non-fitting garments. In addition, they began to sell partially made clothes.

From quite early in the nineteenth century until about 1908, references to buying a dress could mean material to make one, not the completed garment. Up to the end of this period, descriptions of dresses in store catalogues often meant a made-up skirt and material for the bodice. Marshall and Snelgrove included many items of this kind in their catalogues. A 1906 catalogue offered a 'handsome lace robe in écru or ivory, including full material for bodice' and also a 'handsome sequin-embroidered net robe, with bodice piece, in Brown, Turquoise, Helio, Grey, Red, Iridescent and Black'. Swan and Edgar's catalogues of about 1907 featured a 'Smart Silk Robe (unmade), easily adapted to any figure', and various other similar items, all

33   Swan and Edgars as it was in 1927

34 *'Robes' (unmade) in 1904*

described as 'easily fitted', but in appearance dauntingly complicated. Peter Robinson also did this and varied the procedure by advertising dresses that could be completed by the sewing up of the back seam, which was left undone to accommodate the wearer's measurements. Skirts were also sold with the back seam left open. This was necessary because at this time, and for many years to come, sizing was very rudimentary and haphazard. 'Stock' size and no other persisted quite generally until the 1920's; often size was not mentioned in catalogues. Sometimes, in the early years of this century, two or three sizes were achieved, one smaller and one larger than the stock one. They were usually produced by the cutter adding or subtracting an inch all round the pattern – which produced a hit-or-miss result, as sizes do not work that way. As sizing is all-important to successful ready-to-wear fashion no relief from the tedium of fittings for made-to-order garments could come to the fashion-conscious until it had been tackled and achieved.

In the U.S.A. the story of shopping began at a different level from that in Britain, though it developed more rapidly. Ready-made clothing was sold first, before sewing machine days, to

sailors at leading ports and it gained a considerable impetus at
the time of the gold rush, when money suddenly became
plentiful but time was scarce. The first report on the women's
clothing industry in the U.S.A. appeared in the 1860 census and
it covered hoops, skirts, cloaks and mantles. From then progress
was rapid. A Report on the Dress Industry produced in 1948 by
the Market Planning Service of the National Credit Office of the
U.S.A. stated that between 1860 and 1880 the dress trade's
annual production rose in value from 2 million to 35 million
dollars. Manufacturers increased from 96 to 562, employees
from 5739 to 25,192. Fashion was, however, still in its infancy in
the manufacturing sector and real growth did not take place
until between 1890 and 1910. At first shops found fashion difficult
to cope with, through lack of knowledge of it, and many of them
found it unprofitable for some time.

An on-the-spot picture of fashion in a leading London store
at the turn of the century is, by a happy chance, recorded in
Somerset Maugham's novel *Of Human Bondage*, three chapters
of which describe the experiences of his hero, Philip Carey, at a
store called Lynn and Sedley. The material was supplied to
Maugham by Gilbert Clarke, a floor walker at Swan and Edgar's
who, Alison Adburgham records in *Shops and Shopping*, was
paid 30 guineas for a written account of the set-up as he found
it and who said that 'Willie used my stuff practically word for
word' – though the novel was not published until 1915. It all
shows how blissfully haphazard fashion was early in this century.
The shop it is said, 'received fashion papers from Paris once a
week and adapted the costumes illustrated in them to the needs
of their customers'. The buyer of costumes, a man, says: 'I go
over to Paris myself occasionally.' Philip had been an art student
in Paris and when he was seeking a job at Lynn and Sedleys this
was a strong point in his favour. The friend who was recom-
mending him assured him that 'with his training in Paris . . . he
was bound to get a well-paid job to design costumes and draw
posters'. It was the Paris mystique again. Starting at six shillings
a week as a floor-walker and living in, Philip did in fact find that
Paris was a magic word. 'As good as Paquin and half the price,'
was the buyer's recommendation for the store's fashions. And
again: 'What is the good of throwing good money away when
you can get a coat and skirt at Lynns that nobody knows don't
come from Paris?' In short: 'What you can get in Paris you can
get here.' Philip launched into fashion with a frankly imitative
intent; 'he remembered some of the costumes he had seen in
Paris and he adapted one of them'. He continued to do so – and

his pay rose to 12s. a week as he 'acquired quickness in the adaptation of French fashions to the English market'. He prospered: from Alison Adburgham comes the information that he subsequently went to Paris, New York and Chicago as a protegé of Lucile and eventually became chief designer for M.G.M.

At 90 Mrs. Ann Cheriton does beautiful patchwork, joining up with small, firm, even stitches the bundles of scraps of dress materials sent to her by Swan and Edgar, in whose workrooms she was employed early in this century, about the same time as Gilbert Clarke. Her story is part of the patchwork that made up the fashion trade of her time – the story of hundreds, perhaps thousands of girls like herself.

What did a girl do when she left school then? In Ann Cheriton's circle it was dressmaking or domestic service. So at 15, in 1897, she started a two-year apprenticeship to a Court dressmaker in Plumstead, where she had always lived (yes, there were Court dressmakers there, making presentation gowns for débutantes and other clothes for wealthy families in Essex and Kent). She received no pay during that time, and when it was over her employer wanted her to stay on as a trained worker at half a crown a week. This did not seem fair to Ann, so, overcoming her father's scruples, she found a job in London, in Peter Robinson's workrooms, at 7s. 6d. a week. Then she moved to Stagg & Russell as chief bodice hand, and one of the high spots of her career was making the bodice of a dress for Billie Burke to wear in the famous musical *Blue Moon*. It was a dream of pale blue, gold and pink chiffon. Then she went to Swan and Edgar, to work with six or seven other girls as a bodice hand in their workrooms for 12s. 6d. a week, later raised to 15s. and then 17s. 6d. – no holiday pay and 'we lived at home, otherwise we could not have managed', she explains.

Working hours were from 9 a.m. to 7.30 p.m. but to save money the girls (there were quite a lot of them in her area doing this kind of work) travelled up to Charing Cross on the last workman's morning train so as to get the 4d. cheap return fare. Arriving at 8, they filled in the gap by wandering round Covent Garden. Lunch was sandwiches brought from home, but the firm provided tea and bread and butter. At 7.30 there was a stampede as they raced all the way from Piccadilly Circus to Charing Cross to catch the 7·40 p.m. train – encumbered by their long skirts and flannel and cotton petticoats, but smart in their buttoned boots with patent toecaps and, of course, hats perched on the padded-out hair drawn up to what was called a 'teapot handle' on top. The ticket collector held the gates open for them and they often sang all the way home – they were all members of church choirs.

Swans at this time had a bodice room, a skirt room, a sleeve room (sleeves were very elaborate) and a tailor's room. All the work Ann did was on made-to-measure dresses, and nearly all the sewing was done by hand. A dressmaker did not do machine stitching. That was used mainly for linings and was done by a machinist whose job it was. Bodices were boned when Ann started work, with whalebone sewn in at the back, underarm and shoulder seams, and at the side and centre fronts. Boned waistbands and boned neckbands were also part of fashion's armoury. Work was done at long tables covered with white sheeting, which was folded over at night, and the girls wore white overalls.

The only dresses which were ready-made were those produced for window display. On one occasion there was a competition between two teams of workers to make two dresses for this purpose, with a prize for the best. Mrs. Cheriton's team was the winner, and the dress of emerald green chiffon, with panels of blue panne velvet, was bought by the famous music hall star,

35 Harrods was a famous name in fashion in the early years of this century, and drew elegant women to it in 1909

36 'People shopped for pleasure', about 1910

37 A departmental display of laces and other fashion accessories at Harrods in 1909

Marie Lloyd, for 60 guineas. The prize for the girls concerned was a note enabling them to go to the glove department and choose a pair of gloves apiece.

The big workrooms at the stores went on for many years after Ann Cheriton had stopped rushing for the 7·40 p.m. train and had settled down with the first of her two husbands. Miss G. L. Bennett, now in her sixties, who has been at Swans for most of her life, remembers the time when there were more than 70 people working there. Her mother was in the workrooms before her and as recently as the late nineteen-fifties there were still 36 employees. Now there are ten and all they do is alterations – which are becoming fewer and fewer as manufacturers' sizes become more detailed and accurate and clothes less given to having waistlines that have to be raised or lowered. Workroom staff are usually long-term employees – two who left recently had each seen 47 years' service.

By the latter part of the first decade of this century department stores had not only developed into large-scale and comprehensive purveyors of fashion but had also become luxurious and splendid places in which to shop. Shopping was a serious business. 'In Victorian and even Edwardian times,' says Susan Tweedsmuir, 'women shopped with enormous care, and often a dress had to last for many years, and be handed down, with alterations, for a daughter.'

When Harrods was celebrating its centenary, in 1949, it was stated that the store then 'was very largely in being, in much the same form, forty years ago'. The amenities included the luxurious atmosphere, air conditioning, special heating, staircases, lifts and 'an electric staircase which is particularly attractive to juvenile visitors'. This, Britain's first moving staircase, was installed in November 1898, running on a conveyor belt from the ground to the first floor. At the top 'an attendant was posted to administer brandy or sal volatile to any ascending customer who might be overcome by the experience, but no one seemed to need the treatment'.

When Debenham and Freebody rebuilt their premises in Wigmore Street in 1907, the *Tribune* called the new building 'A Modern Drapery Palace' and declared that the structure of Doulton Carrara, with massive interior columns of the finest Italian marble, embellished with bronze, made it 'one of the finest business premises in the world'. Much later, Sir John Betjeman agreed.

The amenities were on an appropriate scale. 'The comfort and convenience of our customers and the value of our goods,' the company declared, 'are the prime consideration.' They offered catalogues, sketches, patterns, estimates for fashions and drew attention to 'the large and varied selection of the newest Paris models in our millinery Salon'. Lingerie too came from Paris, bought by an expert, and 'a full set of garments will readily be submitted for approval or, if preferred, a competent assistant will wait on customers at their residence, in either town or country'. This was shopping in the grand manner for the well-heeled and it was for them that most of the stores catered at this time. It was an extension of fashion, but a limited one, and for those of less ample means fashion meant a struggle.

Prompt to grasp a different kind of approach at this time – the need of the new woman for clothing that kept pace with her new activities – was Thomas Burberry. A country draper born at Brookham Green, near Dorking, in 1835, he moved to Basingstoke and started his own business. His expansion into clothing and into fashion was somewhat different from the usual pattern followed by so many other drapers. It was founded on his secret formula for 'gabardine' weatherproof cloth, and he had his own mill and proofed his materials both before and after weaving as well as making up. He also achieved the unique drapery distinction of giving his name to his invention so authoritatively that it is included in the Oxford Dictionary as a description of his cloth.

His great service to fashion was his production of special clothes for the woman motorist at the start of this century. His

38   Burberry's great invention for the woman golfer—the free-stroke coat with pivot sleeve and adjustable skirt, 1904

son, Arthur, was established in the Haymarket by 1891, and by 1904 the firm was producing a large range of equipment for women. Full details are given in a precious copy of the catalogue of that year, which still exists. Three-quarters of an inch thick and running to 254 pages, it caters for all sorts of sports and out-door activities as well as Service needs, but it is outstanding in the prominent and pioneering place it gives to women's require-ments. For the woman motorist there is offered a dust wrapper – 'a long light and loose Overall, sufficiently large to go easily over any thickness of underwear, yet fitting at extremities to exclude dust'. It had been made since 1901 and many other versions of the motoring coat (affording full protection against dust and weather) are also shown. Further aids to the woman motorist are Skirt Sacs, which 'envelope a lady's skirts in a rug formed like a sac, and fitted with a rubber foot-board, with a Camel Fleece lining'.

An even greater step towards emancipation was Burberry's golfing invention – the 'ladies Free-stroke Coat with patent *Pivot* Sleeve and adjustable skirt. Probably the most freedom-affording suit ever invented'. The pivot sleeve, unlike any other design of the time, permitted 'perfect arm swing, upward, backward and forward movements being equally well provided for'. The pockets were shaped to keep out the wet and 'the skirt loops up by a simple contrivance and shortens its length some six to eight inches'. The accompanying action picture shows the lady achieving a powerful swing – and revealing several inches of ankle and leg above a practical laced shoe. At this time the struggle between the new woman's enthusiasm for golf and her hampering clothes had become so acute that it had led to special courses being laid out with short holes to accommodate her inability to achieve a normally long drive in her inhibiting, tightly cut jacket. 'No other sleeve is fit to golf in, or will ever be used again after this,' the catalogue claims. It may have been over-bold, but Burberry's pivot sleeve was certainly a great boon until the knitted golfing jacket appeared in the second decade of the century, and it made its contribution to the new sportswoman.

The Burberry coat and skirt, for more general wear, also struck a note of freedom that was rare in 1904 fashion, with a jacket that had Norfolk-style expanding pleats in its upper part, plus a fashionable neat waist and a fitted basque. There was a ladies' Weather-all, 'useful for Coaching, Yachting, Racing'. There was a forward-looking style in the *Amazon*, 'a modifica-tion – to suit the female figure – of the New Regulation sealed

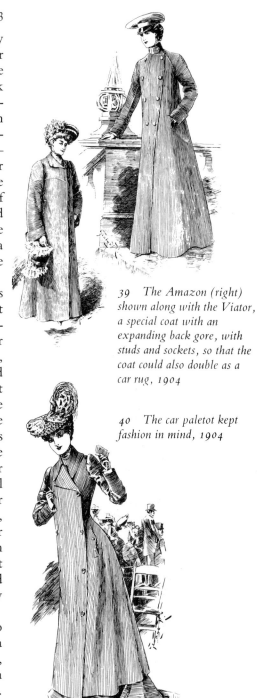

39   *The Amazon (right) shown along with the Viator, a special coat with an expanding back gore, with studs and sockets, so that the coat could also double as a car rug, 1904*

40   *The car paletot kept fashion in mind, 1904*

pattern Service Great Coat for Officers of all Arms', which Burberrys designed for the War Office.

Fashion was not forgotten; the ladies' Car Paletot was 'the only style of overcoat in which the art of the corsetière is allowed proper recognition'. It fitted closely to the waist and 'on a svelte figure is a picture of elegance, in which the natural lines of feminine beauty are emphasised'.

The new look that was coming into feminine headgear was also part of the Burberry sporting scene. Homburgs and peaked caps were featured, as was a kind of veldt hat caught up at one side. Dust-proof motor veils varied from the orthodox kind,

ARUNDEL   FORAGE   HOMBURG

DUST-PROOF   MOTOR VEILS

SCAPHANDRINE

MICA HOOD   ADJUSTABLE VEIL (Closed)

ADJUSTABLE VEIL (Open)

41 How fashion went to the head in 1904 sportswear

LADIES' MEASURE FORM

With which it is advisable to send a well fitting Bodice.

COAT OR BODICE

2 Collar Seam to Waist 5... ... . continue to
full coat length 6............... ......

Centre of Back to 1............to Elbow 3..........
to full sleeve 1............. ....

Round Collar, 8......... ....

Round Bust and Arms at 10........ ....

Round Bust, 11...................

Round Waist, 12...............

Round Hips, 13..................... Collar Seam, 9 to
Waist, 12............ continue full skirt length
11.......... skirt length back 5 to 7..............

CAPES

Round Chest 11...... ....

Length behind from Collar 2.............

*All Measures and Instructions are registered
for future orders.*

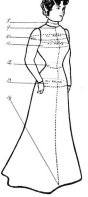

Order Form Overleaf.

42 *No ready to wear yet. How you ordered
the 1904 fashions*

43 *Invitation to the new Selfridges in March 1909*

worn over the hat and tied under the chin, to a 'motor cap with curtain at back to keep dust out of hair' and all-enveloping Klu Klux Klan contrivances with only a slit for the eyes and, in one case, no opening at all – just a complete bag!

The younger generation was not forgotten and 'Two-Garment Suits for youths and maids' were included in the catalogue. These were ready to wear and 'kept ready for immediate dispatch'. The women's clothes were made to order and the catalogue carried at the back detailed back and front figure diagrams requiring more than a dozen measurements to be supplied, 'with which it is advisable to send a well-fitting bodice'.

Details of how these early Burberry fashions were made are not known to the firm, but if they were in line with Thomas Burberry's starting point at his own factory and also with the firm's present-day procedure, they would have been made within it.

The climax of British store development, which had been progressively extending its scope and variety, came in 1909, when the American Gordon Selfridge opened his Oxford Street store. Born in Chicago in 1858 and a member of a family which traced its roots back to Ulster more than 150 years previously, he had been with Marshall Field in Chicago for 25 years and had bought and sold a store at the rear of that great company's premises before coming to London for the first time in 1903. In 1906 he decided on the big venture of building and running a store in London and when it opened on March 15, 1909, he had with him two American associates and a British staff of 1200, all engaged two months previously. His was the first London store to start from scratch – a completely new store purpose-built from its foundations and not the culmination of a long history of development from a small shop.

He opened with a fanfare of new-style advertising such as had never been seen before in Britain, with 104 full-page advertisements in 18 national newspapers and a host of half and quarter pages in other publications. Thirty-eight outstanding British artists were commissioned to provide drawings for this purpose. None of the advertisements was of the hard-selling type, instead they were all angled on goodwill to Britain and on the high business principles of the new store.

44 Selfridges in 1931, when new stages of building had been completed

This building carries no signs —It is assumed that every one knows it is Selfridge's

Soft lights, a profusion of flowers and a hidden string orchestra were part of an opulent opening scene, which created a great stir. In the first five days a million people visited the store. The windows marked a new stage in display, with Watteau and Fragonard backcloths to fashion tableaux, and they were illuminated till after midnight – a new venture for London. For the first time special window dressers and display staff were employed.

Open displays, where customers could inspect everything, were another new feature, as was an open door policy of encouraging the public to come in and walk round, even to spend a day at Selfridges, where a lounge, reception room, reading room, winter garden and aerial garden were among the many attractions. The main new feature, however, was that this was a store for the masses, aimed at appealing specially to them and free from the lingering Victorian class-consciousness that still clung to many stores. Selfridges brought luxury to the ordinary man and woman – but it also brought a bargain basement, the first ever in a British store.

Gordon Selfridge retired in October 1939 at the age of 81, but he became president and continued to visit the store. In his later years he was full of plans for a nation-wide chain of stores to cater exclusively for the mass trade in women's clothing – stores so planned that 'behind us there will be factories which we shall control, turning out the vast quantities of goods we shall need. We shall have full power all along the line, from production to sales. Our pricings will be exceptionally fixed to catch the widest possible range of customer. Our shops must be entirely new in design and layout, giving more freedom of movement than women shoppers have had before. There *must* be space as well as air, light and colour.' He dreamed of this right through the Second World War and until his death on May 8, 1947, at the age of 89. His dream was almost a blue-print of what Marks and Spencer, also under American inspiration, were already doing and were to continue to do with ever-growing enterprise through the years to come.

3 Manufacture grows, but sweated labour casts a shadow, 1900–1908

When in 1851 in America Isaac Merrit Singer successfully introduced his famous sewing machine and thereby crowned efforts which had been made by a number of people and had been proceeding sporadically for nearly a century in Britain, America and France, it seemed that a great break-through in clothing production would speedily result. Almost simultaneously, too, further versions of practical sewing machines created by Wheeler and Wilson of Michigan and Wilcox and Gibbs of Virginia, came on to the American market. 'The sewing machine,' say Margaret Stewart and Leslie Hunter in their study of the clothing trade, *The Needle is Threaded*, 'would lead to a revolution in tailoring as inevitably as the electric telegraph revolutionised communications and the steam engine travel.' It was as new in human history as these and other major technical inventions of the nineteenth and twentieth centuries, and in the area it covered – that of clothing and other wearing apparel, including footwear, and household and other textiles – its effect was to be comparable to other major inventions, vast, new and continually developing.

Revolution there certainly was, but it took an astonishingly long time for it to make significant inroads into fashion-making and it was by no means either the simple, happy liberation from the previous toil and trouble of clothing production or the smooth contribution to progress that first reflections might expect.

Clothing factories soon came into existence, spread and grew. John Barran of Leeds, still in existence, are generally credited with being the first to use the new sewing machines for outerwear in Britain by introducing between 20 and 30 of them into their factory in 1856. Although they did not embark on the manufacture of women's clothes until 1927, they were pioneers of high grade men's tailoring manufacture and among the first to bring into the Leeds clothing industry the Jewish labour which was to be the basis of future clothing manufacture of all kinds. They were also among the first to use the conveyor belt system for women's outerwear.

Symington's of Market Harborough, the corset manufacturers, claim to have brought the first sewing machines into Britain when a son of the family came back from seeking his fortune in America with three Singer machines in 1856, which were installed in the workroom of the family firm. The persuasions of his mother, a trained corset-maker, who presided over the busy workroom, won over her seamstresses to use the fearsome new contraptions and overcame their fear that this means of speeding up work would put them out of work. There was also the uncomfortable fact that you had to stand in order to operate the early treadle machines. Nevertheless, the machines came into use and notched up for Symingtons a definite first for their application to women's wear and either a first or a dead-heat for their use by the British clothing industry.

Sélincourt and Colman were pioneers in the factory manufacture of women's clothing when their business was set up in 1857 by Mr. C. de Sélincourt, a member of a Huguenot family, and Mr. F. Colman. Their premises were at 16, Cannon Street, in the City of London, and they began by making coats, mantles and fur garments, extending later to dresses, which were made in a separate factory in Pimlico. In the early days there was little equipment except the basic hand or treadle sewing machine, and work started every day with prayers. The firm specialised in embroidery and it is notable in the story of fashion because, unlike many other early manufacturers, from the start it made clothes of good quality with fashion appeal. Records show that leading stores bought made-up coats and mantles from Sélincourt and Colman from their earliest days. Although the structure and activities of the firm have changed, Selincourt is one of the fashion giants of today. In a centenary booklet produced in May, 1957, the directors recorded that 'the House of Selincourt still enjoys the support of customers who first traded with the original partners 100 years ago'. Sélincourt and Colman were also early exporters of women's clothes, doing business with Australia and New Zealand from the first years of this century, in the old steam ships.

Early factory production of clothes, however, developed mainly on the men's side. Being more uniform and standardised and free from fashion's quirks and changes, men's clothing lent

45 & 46   Selincourt have been manufacturing ready to wear fashions since 1857 and until about 1960 used their own name. Now they are a holding company, owning eight leading fashion houses. Here are styles from their 1923 catalogues

47   The kind of fashions which could not be mass produced: a 1909 summer coat and skirt in linen, embroidered with mercerised cotton, trimmed with lace and worn with an elaborate muslin blouse

itself much more readily than women's to factory production with its dominant benefits of bulk cutting, long runs, and mechanisation. Developments on these lines proceeded apace. John Barran were using a kind of band-knife for cutting by 1859 and the invention of the oscillating shuttle in 1871 made it possible for the sewing machine to be power-operated, at first by steam, then, at the turn of the century, by gas or petrol and later by electricity. New developments in cutting, pressing and sewing followed fast upon one another, but for many years they were mainly used in the men's trade.

Progress in women's fashions continued to be centred in the department stores during the early years of this century, and their own workrooms were normally the main source of supply. 'Made in our own workrooms' occurs continually in fashion catalogues and advertisements as an assurance of quality. The bulk production of women's clothes in the early stages of the industry was largely in the cheaper grades, except for underwear and some loose cloaks, capes and coats, where fitting was not crucial. Most of the ready-to-wear was not fashion, just body coverings.

The slowness in developing mechanisation and other new techniques in the manufacture of women's fashions is not difficult to explain. One needs do no more than look at the fashions of the years from the mid-nineteenth century until the first World War. The persistence of elaborately fitted bodices, of skirts that moved from the crinoline to the bustle and to a series of other styles which fitted closely and intricately over the waist and hips and flowed elaborately on the ground, and also of a perfect razz-ma-tazz of braid and other trimmings defied the aspiring manufacturer to wrest the making of fashion from the made-to-order world of couturier, Court dressmaker, store or the pervasive 'little dressmaker', still to be found in her thousands from city to village.

The foundations of the future large-scale manufacture of fashion were, however, being laid in the early years of this century. What had been an age-long craft was being transformed into an industry not only by the sewing machine but also by the vast numbers of Jewish immigrants flocking into Britain and America from Central Europe as a result of the persecutions which drove them from their homes. The Jews were the traditional tailors of Europe, probably largely because the waves of anti-Semitism which swept through many countries century after century banned their entry into established professions and many newer, progressive occupations. Tailoring needed no tools or capital investment and little equipment. It could be pursued even in the ghettos and was always needed, for the worker himself and his family to start with. It could, too, be practised usefully wherever the immigrant might settle when harried across the world. Immense numbers of these Jewish exiles arrived in America and Britain from the start of the Russian pogroms in 1881. They took up their time-honoured occupation of tailoring, and clothes-making, sometimes on their own, sometimes as outworkers for a contractor (who might be one of themselves), at others finding employment in small factories or workrooms or setting up their own units, often family ones. In all these capacities their services came to be used by every section of the expanding clothing trade, from high class tailors to stores, whose workroom capacity for bespoke clothes was extended by this supplementary labour; from fashionable dressmakers to wholesalers seeking cheap ready-to-wear clothes for shops or market stalls catering for working classes.

All these types of workers still exist in great numbers and from them have emerged some of the top personalities in the fashion world – men whose modest beginnings have led to the establishment of companies which are among the giants of today, and who have taken a worthy place in public life as well as being the mainstay of large-scale fashion manufacture.

About 1890 Charles Green arrived in Britain at the age of 12 from Poland, where his father had been in the tailoring trade, specialising in uniforms for army officers. Charles Green went into the clothing trade in London and when he was 20 started in the women's fashion business with two friends under the name Green, Hearn & Co. This company was possibly the first and certainly one of the first to manufacture women's fashions on a large scale in Britain, starting about 1910. From the partnership developed the Harella company, taken over and developed by Green's brother-in-law, Louis Harris, who had been one of his partners. Two of Charles Green's sons later started to manufacture on their own and established the Windsmoor company, one of the leading fashion manufacturers of today.

Alexander Steinberg, who was a friend of Charles Green, arrived in England in 1898 at the age of 13 and likewise entered the clothing trade. Four years later he set up his own business with two pieces of cloth from which he produced his first samples as a master tailor. Within a few years he had 40 operatives on his pay roll and was set on the course of expansion in the women's fashion trade which has proceeded ever since. He was an expert craftsman, a keen salesman and an adept in business matters. When he died in 1959 at the age of 74 his company, Steinbergs, was one of the largest in the fashion world, continuing its success in the hands of his two sons. Another link between the beginnings of large-scale fashion manufacture and its immense developments was the fact that the father of Lou Ritter, founder of the famous Dereta firm and notable in the later development of fashion manufacture, worked for Charles Green in his early days.

In America the immigrant clothing workers landed in New York and crowded into the slums, mostly on the East side, though eventually they were instrumental in establishing the great garment-making centre of Seventh Avenue. In Britain the main ports of arrival were Hull and London, which led to their gravitating to the two great manufacturing centres of Leeds and the East End of London, near to the docks. As they were poor and their craft was wholly unorganised, the immigrants were open to exploitation by those for whom they worked and ruthless exploitation was still prevalent in both countries in the early years of this century. An 84-hour week for an average wage of between six and ten dollars a week was a commonplace, says Edna Woolman Chase in *Always in Vogue*, when summarising the gloomy background of the fashion trade as she found it in her early working life on American *Vogue* at the beginning of this century. In Britain things were much the same. 'Side by side with the factories there was growing up that army of underpaid, overworked men, women and children, whose existence came with such a shock to the pioneer reformers of the 'eighties, when the "sweating problem" was first heard of,' says S. P. Dobbs in *The Clothing Workers of Great Britain*. 'Sweated workers,' he continues, 'were engaged in a great variety of occupations, but chief among them was the manufacture of clothing.'

There were various reasons for this state of affairs in the clothing trade, which was becoming increasingly associated with fashion. The immigrant workers were unable to protect themselves from exploitation because they were struggling for the bare means of existence. The long tradition of craftsmanship in clothing led to a clinging to the small workshop or the outworker system which made united protest difficult. The seasonal nature of fashion and the vagaries in demand for this or that type of garment made it difficult for stability to be achieved even in factory production, especially where women's clothes were concerned. It was easier for the manufacturer of this time, probably operating on a small scale with little capital, to off-load work at peak times by passing it on to contractors or outworkers, rather than try to maintain a factory which might not be fully operative all the year round. It was the spirit of the times to pay the worker as little as possible. Attempts to secure a measure of protection were made by the outworkers and contractors and in 1904 a group of immigrant clothing contractors established a Master Ladies' Tailors organisation, with the purpose of achieving a united front in negotiations with the manufacturers for whom they worked, on such matters as prices and wages. It was, however, not until after the 1914–1918 war that the contractors grew strong enough to defend themselves to any degree against exploitation. Early factory legislation, designed to protect the workers, often produced the opposite effect in the clothing trade by encouraging the increased use of home workers who could not be supervised or protected from injustices by the authorities. They became a kind of underground movement and in the unorganised state of the trade it would be difficult to blame them for undercutting the factory workers in the struggle for existence.

The first strong move against sweating, which continued to be particularly prevalent in the clothing trade, was the *Daily News* Anti-Sweating Exhibition of 1906, organised by J. J. Mallon and A. G. Gardiner, editor of the *Daily News*, with the support of the Cadbury family, the paper's owners. During the six weeks after it was opened by Princess Henry of Battenburg, it drew attendances of 30,000 people to the Queen's Hall, the large and famous London hall in Langham Place which was destroyed in the Blitz of the second World War; 20,000 copies of the very detailed catalogue were sold and the event led to the formation of the National Anti-Sweating League, aimed at the establishment by law of minimum wages by means of Wages Boards. After House of Commons discussions in 1907–1908 a Select Committee was set up to enquire into home work in the clothing trade.

2

It was evident at this point that detailed investigation into conditions in the clothing trade was urgently called for. A voluntary effort of this kind, begun on January 30, 1908, resulted in the publication, in the following year, of what has become a unique and invaluable 'human document' constituting a factual, independent, on-the-spot survey of the conditions in which much of fashion was being produced in London, a main manufacturing area, at a critical stage in its slow development from a handicraft product into a large industry. This book is *Makers of our Clothes*, by Mrs. Carl Meyer and Clementina Black, who were the instigators of the enquiry. Clothing trade employees, forewomen, factory and home workers all over London were located with the aid of every kind of local social, religious and welfare organisation. They were visited by members of a committee appointed for this purpose and thereby hard facts were obtained on the conditions in which clothes were being made and, in particular, how a large part of the growing market for ready-made and, to some extent also, bespoke women's fashions was being supplied.

The authors note that 'the great characteristic of women's clothing in our own day has been the development of the ready-made garment' and they proceed to particularise: 'Mantles and coats have long been "stock" articles, the "coat and skirt" is of more recent growth, and the "costume" of later date still.' They describe the main categories of manufacture – bespoke, mail-order, made-to-measure and ready-made – and in all of these they find that the factory, the small workshop and the home worker have some share. Even the highest classes of fashion

48   Sweated workers in the fashion industry in 1906 make skirts in cramped conditions where poor pay and long hours were the general rule

49 *Fashionable Edwardian clothes were decorated with pom-poms, made by home workers in squalid conditions*

manufacturers and retailers call in the help of these ancillary sources of production.

Case histories add up to a picture of a bad situation. A 17-year-old girl in 'one of the smartest houses in London' has advanced in a year from being a 'trotter' to becoming a hand in a skirt room where 50 hands are employed – presumably on high quality bespoke work. Her wages, decided by the fitter, are 4s. 6d. a week. A fully competent skirt hand in another house earns 16s. weekly. Other workers in the workrooms of 'well-known shops' earn from 13s. to 22s. a week (the latter for the first hand) and work from 8.45 to 7.30, with overtime at 6d. an hour. Dresses are elaborate and the making of them is divided between workshops, factories and the workrooms of the shops where they are to be sold. In the shops wages are low – 16s. or 18s. a week for a full hand in the West End, a little less in the suburbs.

A home worker, making skirts for a West End shop, had earned 12s. for 'a seven-seamed skirt, forty-five inches long, which had four rows of stitching at each seam and twelve rows at the foot. The skirt was four yards round, so that there was about eighty three yards of machine stitching to do, apart from finishing'. For a cheap coat a piece worker received 1s. 6d. – and it took two or three hours' work. Another worker was paid 5½d. each for 'light alpaca coats of full length, with gauntlet

cuffs, a collar and two rows of stitching at the seams and hem'. She made two and a half in a day. A costume taking two and a half hours to make earned the worker 1s. 2d. and voile costumes with silk strappings were made for 4s. 6d. each. Often the workers had to pay for thread as well as the hire or purchase of their machines.

The beautiful blouse was the most distinctive new elegancy of Edwardian fashions and one which has retained its prominent place in fashion ever since. It should have had a beautiful start, but the story behind it is far from that. Fashion publications and department store catalogues extolled it in the early 1900's and illustrated it in all its exquisite intricacies, but, say Mrs. Meyer and Miss Black, 'many blouses of handsome material and of excellent workmanship are made . . . by girls who are paid considerably less than 10s. a week. A silk blouse was shown to one of us for the making of which 10d. had been paid. Back and front were composed entirely of small tucks and of insertions of lace. The retail price of the garment would have been from 18s. to 25s. The worker, a skilled young woman, could not make two such blouses in a day.' It was in such conditions that blouses came into the ready-to-wear fashion market, but they continued also to be made to order.

Some factories specialised in blouses only, so important a fashion were they at this time, but sometimes they were made along with dresses and fine underwear. Power machines and many-needled machines were used to help with the fine workmanship, as were hem-stitching machines, showing that for the time manufacturing methods were well advanced. In some factories the rates of pay worked out at the recurrent £1 a week, but when, as often happened, the blouses were made by home workers the price paid for a beautiful fashion was sadly low. Japanese silk blouses, with lattice-work tucks and four rows of insertion in front, and with backs, sleeves, collars and cuffs all tucked, were paid for at the rate of 4s. a dozen. The home worker concerned could make only three in a day. Plainer blouses were made for 3s. and even for 1s. 2d. a dozen. Factory piece rates were 5d. each for plain blouses (one an hour), 1s. 8d. for handker-

51 Rustling silk petticoats were also an important part of fashion at this time

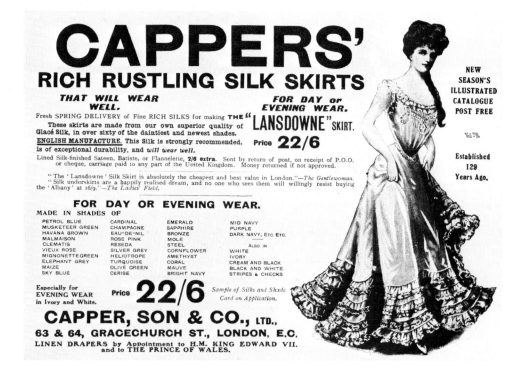

chief blouses (two a day), and 2s. or 2s. 3d. for lace blouses (one a day). Many of these were sold at high prices in good shops. The investigation adds that 'blouse-makers employed even in first-rate West End establishments are sometimes no better paid'. A girl of 19 working in a most expensive place (from the customer's point of view) received only 8s. weekly wages. In the suburbs a woman made blouses for 1¾d. and 2½d. each, taking an hour to make each one. The general conclusion, from these and many other similar cases, is that 'on the whole blouse-making seems to be worse paid than dressmaking proper . . . and the proportion of those who earn, when all deductions are made, less than 2d. an hour, seems considerably larger'.

Underwear made for private customers earned the worker 3d. or 4d. an hour and hand-made undergarments were paid for at 1s. 3d. for combinations with lace and trimming and 1s. 6d. for chemises, which took two days and one and a half days respectively to make. Factories and workshops also made underwear and one West End shop employed 300 hands in its underwear department, paying wages of 15s. weekly to competent machinists. Other evidence records that underwear rates for home workers and factory workers at piece rates were 2s. 6d. a dozen for chemises and 4s. 4d. a dozen for petticoats. The frilled petticoats which were such a delectable feature of the fashions of the time must have given out many a sigh in their elegant, whispering frou-frous and rustling. Lawn ones, with elaborate frills of lace and insertion, were made for 3s. 6d. a dozen. In silk, they earned the workers in a West End house 5½d. or 6d. each for the making, which meant a weekly wage of 12s. or 13s. The popular moirette and medium quality silk versions were paid for at 5d., 6d. or 7d. apiece and took from half to over an hour to make. The fivepenny ones were sold at 10s. 11d. and 12s. 11d. Silk underskirts, with 18 rows of tucks, were made for 1s. 3d. and sold for 21s.

The grim fact behind Edwardian glamour and behind the new woman's growing self-assertion and claim to her 'rights' was that, in the making of fashions which she no longer wished or had time to produce at home, 'for the great majority of indoor as of outdoor workers life is a steady round of work at high pressure combined with a ceaseless effort to make a weekly ten shillings equal to a pound. The spectre of slack times and the more dreadful spectre of unemployment are always lurking in the background.'

In conclusion, the authors sum up the position: 'Looking back upon an assemblage of facts, the word that rises in our minds is chaos. . . . In no two factories is there an identity of conditions. In very few is there parity of payments. . . . Individualism run riot, a lack of co-ordination, a welter of persons all striving separately, this is the spectacle presented.' Bespoke tailoring and high class dressmaking, they add, showed 'traces of a customary wage for "full hands"', but even this was being broken down. Hours were longer than in most industries – 8 to 8 on five days a week and 8 to 4 on one day, with overtime not unusual at peak times.

A concluding plea for trade schools, where workers could be trained proficiently, was to be fulfilled later in the century, but already, in 1909, the Borough Polytechnic was doing good work in this direction. The time when the making of women's fashions was to be a creditable and attractive trade was, however, not yet showing even a glimmer of a rosy dawn so far as the workers were concerned.

Wages must, of course, be seen in the context of what prevailed at the time, both for women and men. Other evidence shows that, although the clothing trade was a bad example of sweated labour, overwork and poor pay, the situation was similar in many other industries. In a survey of women's employment carried out in Birmingham by Edward Cadbury and others and published in 1906 it was shown that in, for instance, some of the metal industries, women were paid as little as 6s. a week and never more than 24s. When they replaced men the pay was always less and a general average was 10s. or 12s. 6d. a week – 'a woman would get from one third to half the wages of a man'.

Between 1900 and 1914, when neither trade nor conditions in the labour market changed to any substantial extent, 'the average wage of the British working man was about 30s., but the skilled and relatively privileged woman textile worker averaged no more than 18s. 8d.', says Vera Brittain in *Lady into Woman*. Further figures which she quotes from a 1919 report by the Women's Employment Committee are that the average weekly wages for women in the linen and silk trades – part of fashion – in 1906 were 9s. 9d, and in other trades much the same. Women carding hooks and eyes were paid 1d. for 384 and by working 18 hours a day could earn only about 5s. a week, 'yet no second Thomas Hood rose to challenge, with a new *Song of the Shirt*, the wealthy indifference of Edwardian England'. Trade Unionism offered little hope at this time, for it was notoriously weak among women workers. When Mary MacArthur founded the National Federation of Women Workers in 1906 the women's trade union movement had only 107,000 members. This rose to 878,000 by 1913, with two-fifths of them from the textile unions. But this was a mere fraction of the whole. In 1914 there were nearly five million women at work, including 612,000 in clothing and 86,000 in textiles, and nearly two million in poorly paid domestic service, earning about £20 a year and often grossly overworked.

In America in the latter part of the nineteenth century progress in the organisation of fashion manufacture, in which that country was subsequently to show Britain a powerful lead, was not far ahead of Britain. There was, however, an earlier success in the effort of the workers to organize themselves in order to strive for better conditions of work and pay. The International Ladies Garment Workers' Union was launched in 1900, when, says Edna Woolman Chase, 'eleven men, sober and dedicated, emerged from the maelstrom. They were delegates representing about 2000 organised members, and they voted in favour of a national union of all the workers in the women's garment industry . . . and the International Ladies' Garment Workers' Union was launched with thirty dollars in the kitty.' Thousands joined and as a result, she says, 'at the beginning of the century success and prosperity were in the air and the creative side of the industry as well as its politics, was on the march. Many smart women whose clothes had always been made by private dress-makers or at home, began discovering the ready-to-wear, which, as it gained a more fashionable clientèle, improved its output, grading the merchandise as cheap, medium, better and high.'

Wages, however, were not thus graded in America any more than in Britain. In both countries the women who bought ready-made clothes were enjoying the products of an industry in which bad conditions and poor rates of pay still persisted. In 1909 20,000 workers in the New York clothing industry went on strike, among them being enough women and girls to make this the biggest strike of female labour ever known in the U.S.A. up to that time. It took a further strike in 1910 to achieve an agreement with the clothing manufacturers which represented a real advance for the workers. It was not until after World War I that the American women's fashion industry reached the state when it became a model to the world and provided a blue-print for Britain to follow in the transformation of her own fashion industry.

For the moment, about the close of the first decade of this century, the new woman in America, as in Britain, was making a stand against the frustration of interminable fittings and the tyranny of fashion produced in the traditional terms of craftsmanship. She was seeking fashion increasingly in the retail stores which, Alison Adburgham says in dealing with Britain, 'with their variety of ready-made clothes and accessories at reasonable prices, played an important part in the emancipation of women'. At this stage it was, however, the incomplete emancipation of one section at the cost of the continued oppression of another. That was no new problem. It has been indigenous in all civilisations of the past and has been accepted. It is not accepted today, and it was a problem that fashion was soon to tackle, just as the larger world was to tackle it – but not in one stage and not instantly.

It was, however, at this stage that one clothing firm brought an early measure of sex equality into its fashions. Britain's Aquascutum, which had been making men's clothes under that name since the year of the Great Exhibition, 1851, launched out into a range of women's fashions for the first time in 1909. They included special styles for golf, motoring and country sports; 'Coats for women,' they said, 'leading naturally to votes for women.' They went a step further after the 1914–1918 war when their trench coat, specially designed for the kind of warfare that developed in the trenches, was produced for civilian use for women as well as men. It is still going strong, and is probably the longest-living fashion ever created.

4 The start of modern fashion and the effect of World War I, 1907–1918

52   A day dress by Paul Poiret with the new, straight line. 1908

For most of the first decade of this century fashion, visually, showed seasonal modifications rather than any basic changes or new thinking. 'The essential lines of female costume,' says James Laver, 'remained the same from the beginning of the century until 1908, and in some particulars even until 1910.' Writing in 1955 of the fashions of the years before 1914, Christian Dior expressed the same view: 'Unlike today, the actual design of the dress might remain virtually unchanged for several seasons. . . . This system also meant that at the beginning of this century fashions varied little from house to house; and in order to introduce some variety into the dresses, they were often loaded with trimmings of exquisite craftsmanship. Braid, beads, embroidery, lace and frills, all helped to differentiate models which cut alone would not have distinguished one from the other.'

But about 1908 a new look as riveting as anything in the whole story of fashion began to transform the scene. It could be called the start of modern fashion because the concept upon which it was built has, in various ways, been basic to fashion ever since that time. This concept was the natural figure. For the first time in fashion history, with the partial exception of the brief Regency period vogue for straight shifts among the young and the *avant garde*, women were to acquire and retain an upright, unshackled stance, based on the way nature made them, instead of assuming an unnatural shape dictated by fashion's artifices. They were to discount Baudelaire's claim that 'Fashion is a sublime distortion of nature, or rather a constantly repeated attempt to reform nature'. But they were to take a long time to complete the process.

The man who was mainly responsible for this revolution in a fashion world that still took its unquestioned lead from Paris was Paul Poiret. Dior, pursuing his historical theme, says of him that 'this great artist excelled at creation and decoration. His models were vigorous sketches, whereas the fussy toilettes of his predecessors had been carefully painted miniatures.' Poiret was a paradox in that he was at once the first of the modern couturiers and the last of the traditionalists. He was a modern in his great fashion change, which was to banish the elaborately corseted and unnaturally curved 'S'-shaped figure and to bring into fashion the natural line. 'It was,' he declared in *My First Fifty Years*, 'in the name of Liberty that I proclaimed the fall of the corset and the adoption of the brassière which, since then, has won the day. Yes, I freed the bust, but I shackled the legs' – a reference to the 'hobble' skirt, which was an outstanding and contradictory feature of his innovation.

53 *The new-style corset for the straight figure. The advertisement states that on request all corset styles can be made less long for ladies fearing to be hampered by the great length. 1908–9*

He did not, of course, really banish the corset, but only one version of it, nor was he, in strict accuracy, the originator of the brassière. But he did get rid of the 'S' shape which had been distorting women's figures for years and his rise to fame coincided with the introduction and growing adoption of the brassière, first mentioned in American *Vogue* in 1907 but preceded by many kinds of bust bodices and bust 'improvers' since the 1880's. What Poiret did do, beyond controversy, was to loosen the constricted waist, an almost constant feature of all previous fashions, and relieve the pressure of the 'S'-shaped corset on the stomach, thereby getting rid of the exaggeratedly curved hips and producing a natural or near-natural figure. The narrowed hips were in his day part of the effect of a new style of corset that was lower in the bust (therefore the need for the brassière) and easy fitting at the waist, from which it descended in a much straighter line to the hips, minimising curves instead of exaggerating them. It does not look a very comfortable garment or even a very natural one by today's standards, but it was so in comparison with previous styles. To start with, the new corsets were so sedulously faithful to the new up-and-down figure that they reached almost to the knees and made sitting down something of a problem. This was soon modified and the fashionable woman, usually corseted in comparative comfort, not only stood erect but also began to stand free – and has continued to do so ever since to an increasing extent. Anything else would be absurd now, but it had been an accepted part of fashion up to that time that it should improve on nature by reshaping it with scant regard to comfort or anatomy.

To attribute all this to one man is only symbolically true, but in the history of fashion, as in all arts, great and small, individuals

54   *The hobble skirt persisted for some years.*
1912

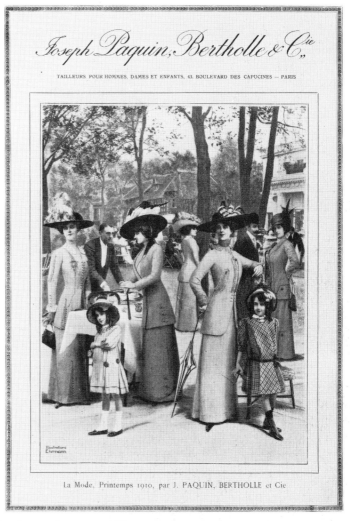

Joseph Paquin, Bertholle & Cie

TAILLEURS POUR HOMMES, DAMES ET ENFANTS, 43, BOULEVARD DES CAPUCINES — PARIS

La Mode, Printemps 1910, par J. PAQUIN, BERTHOLLE et Cie

become identified as such symbols. Poiret's creations were 'the glass of fashion and the mould of form' of his time, expressing a decisive change in women's attitudes which was coming to the surface. They coincided with the rise of the militant – and also the larger non-militant – suffragette movement, more explicit in Britain and America than in France, but part of the widespread change in the status of women. Women's education was better, their part in the community was increasing and they were entering a growing variety of careers, with consequent independence and new ways of living. The connection between fashion's changes and social change has never been more emphatic than at the end of the Edwardian era and in the following years.

The new line meant the end of the famous Edwardian petticoats, with all their frills and flounces. It also meant that underwear in general became much simpler, with straight, clinging
slips, and there was progressively much less of it from this time
onwards. Liberty was not, however, complete. What of Poiret's
claim to have 'shackled the legs'? The hobble skirt, which he
introduced, could, at its most extreme, almost immobilise the
wearer. Perhaps it was part of the *mystique* of Poiret that, though
he was a modern in his general conception of clothes, he was also
an aristocrat of fashion, still interested in the great and privileged
and scorning the masses. He created a line which was basically
revolutionary. It could be seen as the line of a man's suit, except
that it had one trouser leg instead of two, but he made it a
hampering line, a fashion which, as in the past, was only for the
leisured and privileged and which proclaimed that fact – it was
impossible to wear it and demean oneself by being other than
decorative.

Fashion was by now being disseminated widely and with
increasing speed. Newspapers as well as magazines were dealing
with it regularly and manufacture was improving in scope,
efficiency and working conditions, assisted by Trade Boards,
first set up in Britain in 1909 and applied to the clothing trade in
1911. The hobble skirt was easy to make. It caught on quickly
and became a widely worn fashion. But it was liberated by
various expedients to meet the needs of the middle class fashion-
makers, the busy, active women. Flat, almost invisible pleats
were inserted in it near the hem to make walking and movement
in general more free. A slit or slits at the front or sides of the skirt
also brought liberation. The contradiction between freedom and
captivity thus achieved was perhaps an epitome of the time.
Women were on the verge of emancipation, but they were not
yet quite ready to come out into the open about it. The tradition
of being sheltered and in need of protection by the dominant
man still lingered on.

Poiret did, however, lead the way to the modern tailored
costume, which was a considerable liberation in fashion. With
the new, comfortable, loose-waisted jacket and the straight, off-
the-ground skirt – the 'trotteur' or walking skirt of above ankle
length – this rapidly became a classic. Englishwomen followed
fast on the heels of Paris in adopting it and the rest of the new
fashions, though they did not take to such extremes as the harem
skirt, which had a certain vogue in the French capital and was the
first move since Bloomer days towards the wearing of trousers
by women. There was, however, an uproar when, in 1909, Mrs.

*56   Pleats broke up the rigidity of the hobble
skirt for the active woman. A tailored suit of
1909*

57 A slit at the foot of the skirt also brought freedom. 1911

58 The off-the-ground walking skirt came into favour. For summer 1910 a foulard gown (l) is a copy of a French model, the other (r) a smart style in striped cotton voile

Asquith, later Lady Oxford and at the time wife of the Prime Minister of Britain, brought Poiret over to London to show his collection at a special presentation at 10, Downing Street. This was seen as a body-blow to British fashion and led to a violently hostile press, questions in Parliament and diatribes from all sides on the insult to British trade and the ignominy of the nationally-maintained residence of the Prime Minister being used for the presentation of fashions that threatened British fashion. Mrs. Asquith had hastily to give her fashion patronage to leading London houses and became a customer and friend of Lucile. A similar situation was to rise in America more than half a century later when Mrs. Jackie Kennedy, when wife of the President and an international fashion-leader, gave her custom to Paris houses instead of to American dress designers. She too had hastily to recant and identify herself with home-bred fashion, thereby bringing her chosen designer Oleg Cassini into the limelight.

Poiret, the son of a bourgeois cloth dealer, had first made his way into fashion by dressing dolls given him by his sisters and

59   An evening dress of 1909 by Worth in satin trimmed with chiffon, vividly embroidered and with Empire waistline

showing sketches of the results to leading couturiers of the time. Doucet bought some of his sketches, had a big success with the first models to be made up from them and took the young man onto his staff in 1896. A few years later, after doing his military service, Poiret went to the reigning house of Worth, but he was too much a modernist for that citadel of the Establishment, which before long was immersed in making robes for the Coronation of Edward VII – something not at all to his taste. (There was a London Worth, so patriotism presumably was satisfied.) In 1904 he opened his own house, with eight employees and a small capital of 50,000 francs, and proceeded to launch his ideas of fashion with such success that in a few years he was dominating the scene.

Almost as important as his new slim line was his introduction of strong, startling, vibrant colours as different as anything could be from the sugar-almond, sweet-pea colours of the time and also from the neutral greys and browns of more practical fashion. In doing so, he drew on new elements which had never before exercised anything like the effect they were to have on fashion in the following years.

The start of this new trend came from outside fashion. Its origins lay in the first exhibition of the painters known as Les Fauves in Paris in 1905 and the fashion colours that now became all the rage were those first seen in their paintings. Further impetus had come from the immensely colourful 1906 exhibition of Russian art organised by Serge Diaghilev at the Salon d'Automne, but the new fashion look was really launched when Diaghilev presented his famous Ballets Russes for the first time in Paris at the Châtelet Theatre in 1909, with Pavlova and Ida Rubenstein among the dancers, and costumes and décor by Bakst in the new dazzling Oriental colours. Poiret claimed to have anticipated Bakst in this colour-craze, but it was on the wave of enthusiasm for all this exotic spectacle that he set the fashion scene. Soon he ruled supreme, with clothes that fairly sizzled with the new tones of blue, green, violet, orange and yellow.

The age of Worth had been succeeded by the age of Poiret. It was in many ways a curious age, admitting to fashion disparate influences the full implication of which only the future was to show. Negro sculpture, South Sea Island painting, Oriental art were all involved. Artist Raoul Dufy was set up in a studio to design fabrics for Poiret and fashion was regarded as an art. The new mood of fashion crossed the Channel in great force in 1911, when Sir Thomas Beecham brought Diaghilev's ballets over from Paris to give an extra fillip to the Coronation scene of George V. 'They burst on London,' says J. B. Priestley, 'like a bomb filled with silks and coloured lights.' The fashionable world was dazzled. Though Russian ballerina Tamara Karsavina had appeared in variety at the Coliseum in 1909 and Pavlova, after leaving the Russian ballet, at the Palace Theatre in 1910, there had never been anything like this. Lady Diana Cooper recalls it vividly: 'There was,' she says, 'a general new look in everything in those last years before the first war – a Poiret–Bakst blazon and a budding freedom of behaviour that was breaking out at the long last end of Victorianism.' Recalling Chaliapin's appearance in the Russian opera which followed the ballet in 1912, she declares: 'Never since, I think, have we in England had our eyes so dazzled with new light. The comets whizzed across the unfamiliar sky, the stars danced.'

The Eastern influence was pervasive and it continued until 1914. Oriental satins were advertised by London stores as early as 1908, so were kimonos. The new fashion spread into the furnishing of typically English houses, says Sonia Keppel, describing Eastern décor, armchairs replaced by cushions, walls painted black or midnight blue and hung with brilliantly patterned draperies, while incense burned and people dressed up in Oriental attire.

The new fashions did not stand still and the years before the 1914 war saw a speeding up of the tempo that was symptomatic of the greater rapidity with which new ideas were being followed by an increasing number of people. By 1912 the straight line had become too stereotyped to be acceptable to the leaders of fashion and it was too easily copied for any obvious variations of it to be exclusive – as fashion still wanted to be. Ready-made clothes were also increasing in their appeal as they became much simpler to make and as the difference between them and couture styles therefore became less pronounced. They were in growing demand and fashion for the ordinary woman took a step forward as the new line gained acceptance.

To satisfy the still powerful class-consciousness that invested clothes, new variations came into top fashion, with Poiret in the lead. His skirts were draped closely round the figure in subtle folds. Bodices had for a time a high-waisted, Empire look that recalled the styles of almost exactly a century before. By 1912 floating panels and panniers were also appearing on skirts to vary the line and this led to a fashion for wide tunics, worn over tube-like skirts. For evening-wear these tunics were made of lace and other filmy materials, often embroidered with silver or gold.

60   The straight line became stereotyped. Here, in a chiffon evening dress of 1911–12, made over a charmeuse slip and trimmed with pearls and satin ribbon, a tunic effect provides variety. By Mascotte

61 The slim line broken up again by a tunic in an evening dress of 1911

62 For the ordinary woman, Butterick Patterns present two simple dresses for summer wear. 1909

The lampshade tunic, wired all round for this effect, was very fashionable.

Poiret, the fashion centre of all this, went from strength to strength in these pre-war years, famous not only for his fashions but also for the splendour in which he lived and for the magnificence of his fancy dress balls and elaborate parties. He was the first couturier to launch his own perfume, Rosine, named after his second daughter. He started a new chapter in international fashion by taking a team of nine mannequins in two cars on a tour of all Europe's capitals, showing his latest models and giving lectures on fashion. This had never been done before and, although it was carried out in an ambience of elegance and wealth, it showed the immense flair for publicity which Poiret was bringing to the fashion scene. It was the forerunner of things to come in the international dissemination of fashion by personal public relations enterprise. Later Poiret went to the U.S.A. with one of his own mannequins to give the Americans lessons in Parisian taste in fashion. During this visit he was enraged at finding copies of his own models on sale in American stores at 15 dollars. He returned home determined to fight this piracy – a fight which has proceeded ever since then without ever being resolved completely.

63 Tunics in various styles were in favour in 1914

64 (opposite) The elaborately draped skirt and the new ankle-length 'trotteur' skirt, both seen at Longchamps races in 1910

It was at this time that American wholesale manufacturers, growing rapidly and developing the expertise that was to give a lead to the rest of the world, became seriously interested in buying Paris models for copying on Seventh Avenue, the centre of ready-to-wear, so as to keep up with top stores, private dressmakers and rich women who had been buying from Paris for many years. By 1911 American business had become sufficiently important for the Chambre Syndicale de la Couture Parisienne, established in 1867, to reconstitute itself and set up the system of regular seasonal showings for the benefit of overseas buyers, whose purchases of models for copying were becoming big business to the Paris houses. American stores also began to pay increasing attention to Paris. Garfinkels bought there from 1913 and in the summer of 1914 John Wannamaker sent his top buyer to bring back a Paris collection – and she did so, even although the Germans were by then advancing towards Compiègne. Fabric manufacturers also began to buy original models in Paris, allowing makers-up to use them in return for substantial purchases of materials.

In these respects America was ahead of Britain, for several reasons. For two women to be seen wearing the same dress was still – and was to be for many years to come – a social disaster, but in America it was much less likely to happen than in Britain because of the greater size of the country and therefore of the fashion market. The long production runs which were essential for a profitable ready-to-wear industry were possible for this reason. There was also a strong traditional link between America and Europe, while the lack of the background of fine craftsmanship in tailoring which existed in Britain encouraged speedier development in ready-to-wear manufacture. Paris fashions had been shown at the Chicago Fair of 1893 and American *Vogue* followed this course to some degree when it started in 1916 and for many years after that, angling its fashions strongly to Paris.

In one respect the 'liberation' which Poiret promised failed to materialise, at least for some time. Fashionable hats became bigger and bigger as skirts narrowed. They exceeded the width of the shoulders and were surmounted by even more towering masses of flowers and feathers than before. They were at first perched on top of elaborately padded hair styles. This feature of the Edwardian lady lingered on, but by 1913 it gave way to flatter, more natural coiffures, with the hair coiled and waved round the head, and hats became flatter too, but still remained large. They continued to be worn with country and even seaside outfits as well as with formal fashions. They were still apt to be

expensive, with 'elegant picture hats' costing some $20\frac{1}{2}$ guineas at Harrods, but you could also be in fashion with other versions at 55s. and 39s. 11d. in the millinery departments of the stores, if this suited your purse better.

Poiret started a change to more practical hats when one of his staff spent a week at London's Victoria and Albert Museum studying Oriental turbans and similar historical headgear for copying purposes. Soon afterwards hats became smaller and there was a vogue for the toque, the brimless hat which was worn with evening dress as well as by day.

It was from this time too that the modern handbag, indispensable to every woman, began to achieve some importance. The flowing Edwardian fashions could conceal essential pockets, but

66   Hats became bigger as skirts narrowed. A style for Autumn 1908 in saxe blue satin with deeper blue underbrim and blue ostrich feather mount with pale blue buckle

67 *For croquet in 1910 a degree of comfort
but still the formal hat*

68 *Golfing in 1910 in handicapping clothes*

the new narrow styles would reveal every bulge. The handbag
had up to now not been wholly approved of: 'Many women,'
said one fashion writer in 1902, 'seem unable to exist without a
satchel of some kind, be it of fine gold, silver, gun-metal, black
suède studded with jewels, or what you will. . . . Recollect that
a really good leather or suède handbag may not be particularly
smart, but it is never in bad style, while it has the advantage of
being useful.' The Edwardian handbag was not very prominent
and little purses, of silver or gold mesh, often sufficed, but now
and in the next few years make-up was to become more general,
women were to start smoking in public, to have their latch-keys
– and to be lost without a handbag, as they have been ever since.
Large, flat ones became fashionable at this time.

Another innovation was emancipation from the high, boned
neckline which had been as universal in daytime as the extreme
décolletage of evening wear. By 1908 necklines were descending

from the boned 'chokers' of past years. Round necklines were appearing, sometimes plain, sometimes decorated with a 'pie frill'. Poiret claimed this liberation and so did his sworn enemy Lucile, who asserted that she introduced the lower neckline and the Peter Pan collar into Paris shortly before the 1914–1918 war. This collar was, however, being worn before that – it is seen in blouses in store catalogues of 1910, and the general easing-up had started even earlier. 'V' necks of a restrained kind also appeared from this time for day wear, although they called forth diatribes from the pulpit and elsewhere and were denounced as sources of danger to both morals and health. Modesty vests came in to modify them – squares of lace or embroidered fabric pinned in at the neck line. In a few years, however, the 'V' necks were generally accepted, were much lower and acquired the sprightly popular description 'glad neck' for many years. It was the first time fashion had been treated as something to be enjoyed to the point of laughter by its wearers – an attitude that was to recur and reach a point when, half a century later, all fashion could be 'fun' and even the dignity of fur coats be undermined by a whole range of 'fun furs'.

69   *Mrs Sterry, tennis champion of 1909, in the tennis outfit she recommended*

Although women had been taking part in an increasing number of active sports since the 1880's, they had up to now done so in their usual hampering, cumbersome clothes. They went on walking tours, climbed mountains, rowed and sailed, played golf and tennis in the full, ground-length skirts of accepted fashion. Even on bicycles, their favourite form of transport, it was more usual to keep to long skirts than to break out into bloomers or any of the variations in breeches which the venturesome would don. Many of the carriageless middle classes even cycled to dinner parties, tucking up their trains as well as they could. When ski-ing, as many of them did, women early in the century went to the snow slopes in their long skirts, and the breeches they wore underneath were revealed only at the moment before they were due to go into action. Their male escorts then gallently carried the discarded skirts in knapsacks, brought for the purpose. Then for a time they wore skirts a few inches above the ankle. Trousers were not worn until the 'twenties. Lady Cynthia Asquith deplores the general inconvenience of long skirts and tells how 'even our lawn tennis dresses, usually like nursery maid's wear, made of white piqué, were so long that it was impossible to take a step back without treading on them'. In 1909 Mrs. Sterry, on becoming British ladies' champion for the fifth time, said: 'To my mind nothing looks smarter or more in keeping with the game than a nice clinging white skirt (about two inches off the ground), white blouse, white band, and a pale coloured silk tie and white collar.' Pictures of the time show such outfits, complete with the inevitable hat. Full liberation did not yet come, but by about 1910 'tub' dresses of a much simpler kind became fashionable and provided some measure of ease.

Golfing attire also relaxed from this time. The heavy tweed suit found an alternative in the knitted sports coat, a loose, rather long cardigan, often belted, which came in about 1909 and was widely worn on various informal occasions from that time onwards. Fashion catalogues were much given to showing the golfing girl, complete with golf bag or swinging a vigorous club and dressed in comparative comfort. Bathing attire was very elaborate all through Edwardian times, with below-knee serge dresses worn over matching bloomers and often accompanied by stockings and bathing shoes. In 1910 the one-piece bathing suit, in serge or woven wool, but still long and loose, first came into accepted wear, although the American swimmer, Annette Kellerman, had worn such a garment in 1900.

Other forces of various kinds were also helping to remove women's 'chains' at this time. As early as 1907 Isadora Duncan was dancing at the Théâtre Sarah Bernhardt in Paris in short, flowing classical robes designed for a new freedom of movement, and with bare feet. Maud Allan danced at the Palace Theatre in London in 1911 'in a wisp of chiffon and bare legs', says Lady Diana Cooper.

Another indication of changing times and changing fashions was the great vogue for the tango. It started in America in the spring of 1911 and in a year or two spread everywhere, drawing young and old, high and low, into its unrestrained and, for these times, almost wild abandonment. Its denunciation as an importation of low South American origin had no effect on its instant success even in high places. Tango teas and tango parties became all the rage well before 1914; they continued through the war and went on with increasing fervour in the 'twenties. The Poiret-inspired slinky dresses with their slit hems were ideally suited to the fashionable contortions of the new dance, for which the traditional tea-gown would have been utterly incongruous. Fast on the heels of the tango came other dances even more hectic, with the Turkey Trot and the Bunny Hug taking the lead in the importations from America which swept the world. Ragtime, also transatlantic in origin, appeared in Paris and London in 1912, and it too became all the rage, with the revue *Hullo Ragtime* presented at the Hippodrome in London

70   The sports coat was a liberating garment which came in about 1909. It took many forms and was the first 'casual' to appear on the fashion scene

Snapshots at Ascot   June 1914

In June, 1914, dress was elaborate and hampering. The long skirt, narrow at the hem and wide at the hips, with a swathed arrangement of its drapery, was about to be replaced by the short and wide skirt. The revolution of fashion is now bringing back the pegtop skirt, and a number of Paris dressmakers in their collections for spring, 1935, are showing skirts resembling those of the spring of 1914

71   A vanishing world: Royal Ascot 1914

72   Mr and Mrs Vernon
Castle at the height of their fame
in 1914

on December 21, 1912. The famous dancers, Mr. and Mrs. Vernon Castle, the very symbols of the new mood that had nothing in common with Edwardian high falutin' ways, went over from America to Paris and had an immense vogue there as thé dansants spread and night clubs were opened up – a new attraction which rapidly crossed the Channel to Britain. Mrs. Castle, with her bobbed hair dating from 1913 and her slim, lithe, boyish figure, set a new ideal for fashion. The 'vamp', dressed for choice by Poiret, described as 'the Sultan of Fashion', also became a quite new fashion symbol, her dress clinging sinuously to her long, svelte figure, her hair nearly covered by a turban crowned with an upstanding aigrette and drawn low over her brows and her black-pencilled eyes. She had deep red lips, for make-up was coming into use among the bolder spirits, and to complete the effect she flourished a long cigarette holder. She had a great vogue in the silent Hollywood films for many years, with Vilma Banky as her chief embodiment and the siren-call of her alluring wickedness sending shivers of delight through all viewers.

What all this amounted to was a clean break with everything that belonged to the sunlit Edwardian afternoon of the world. It all happened before 1914, although it was to be the blue-print of the 'twenties in manners and modes.

2

The 1914–1918 war had at first little effect on fashion. There was, to begin with, the great delusion that it would all be over victoriously in a few months, with little loss of life and much rejoicing. The early mood had a flag-waving, starry-eyed quality which had more in common with the old-time Crusades than with the horrors of modern warfare as this and the following 1939–1945 conflict were to reveal it. Women's efforts to be allowed to contribute to the struggle by taking over men's jobs or working in munition factories were rebuffed until 1915. Their mission in life was to be elegant and gracious; to soothe and inspire the tired warrior when he came home on leave.

The life of civilians in Britain was at first little disturbed by the conflict. In their spring catalogue of 1915 Marshall and Snelgrove say: 'Here is a word for the wise; Marshall's buy many model garments from well-known Paris houses, and they will copy them exactly for about half the price of the originals.' The French couture, after a few panic-struck months, resumed virtually normal production during the war, though daily life in the French capital had its rigours. French fashion pictures and reports reached British and American magazines more or less

73 Fashion was at first little affected by the 1914–1918 war. At the start of 1915 narrow skirts still prevailed, but this was the last of them

TEA & REST FROCKS

We have made a special study of Rest, Boudoir, and Tea Frocks, and have now in stock a wonderful variety of these dainty and useful garments. All these gowns are our own exclusive designs. They are adapted from Paris models, and are made by our own workers from materials that we can recommend with the utmost confidence. The value is quite exceptional.

DAINTY TEA FROCK in rich, heavy Crêpe de Chine Brocade, with dainty Old World Fichu of fine Paris lace and full silk swathe. In a variety of fashionable colourings.

98/6

CATALOGUE POST FREE

Debenham & Freebody.
(DEBENHAMS LIMITED)

Wigmore Street.
(Cavendish Square) London. W.

Famous for over a Century
for Taste, for Quality, for Value

74   *In Spring 1915 the tea gown, adapted from a Paris model, still kept alive the old traditions of fashion*

normally, just as French models were obtained for copying by both countries. At the start of the war, however, American *Vogue*, fearing isolation from Paris, organised a Fashion Fête of American designs in aid of French charities, to show that America could offer a lead to fashion, although it was a time when, admits Edna Woolman Chase, then editor of *Vogue*, 'New York had very few designers; we had importers and there were good dressmakers who subscribed to fashion magazines and copied models for their customers, but they did not aspire to be creators'. Nevertheless socialites and fashion leaders supported the venture, which was staged on 5 and 6 November 1914. The immediate result was consternation and despair in Paris, but peace was made and the French leadership and *amour propre* were restored by a French Fashion Fair, also sponsored by *Vogue*. This was presented in November, 1915 by Paul Poiret and other leading Paris designers. 'Long before the fête,' continues Mrs. Chase, 'feeling that the American dressmaking industry and French designers were inextricably bound together,' *Vogue* had decided to set up a fund to help the workers in the French couture, who were suffering materially under wartime conditions.

When the grim reality of the war was brought home to the British public and women became involved in it, the hobble skirt, which had already eased, quickly disappeared. A sudden change came early in 1915, dictated by the ordinary women's needs, not by fashion's *mystique*. The prevailing style of fashion, with narrow skirts either worn alone or under full tunics, was transformed by the tunic being lengthened and the inner tube dispensed with. The result was costumes and dresses with wide, even voluminous skirts, coming to a few inches above the ankle. Jackets also became loose and shapeless, with broad but slack belts at a rather low waist. Wide coats had floppy shawl collars. The great number of semi-evening dresses, tea frocks and even tea coats perhaps reflected a feminine world whose men were at war. But there remained a full range of everything that fashion could desire, including all the fanciful accessories of the time and elaborate crêpe de Chine underwear. By 1917 skirts were even fuller, but had risen to a further inch or two above the ankles. Clothes in general were shapeless, easy-fitting but cumbersome and bulky. They were, however, much freer than anything that had previously been worn. Freedom was necessary for the great number of women now working in factories and offices, and undertaking all sorts of unaccustomed activities, including driving vans, manning railway signal boxes and even sweeping

75   *A sudden change in 1915. Voluminous skirts, above the ankles, shown in a May magazine*

76   *Clothes were shapeless, easy fitting, but cumbersome in 1916*

77 *A woman munition worker wore a boiler suit, an innovation which was at first thought very daring*

78 *Women at war. Edinburgh tram conductresses in 1915, in the ankle length skirts of the time*

chimneys, as well as serving in the police force and in the women's services. Sometimes women wore trousers for the rougher tasks and land girls took to breeches.

Fashion, all in all, lacked creativeness, but it remained Paris-orientated. New Paris fashions continued to be advertised in the glossy magazines; a new Paris house announced the opening of a London salon. More significantly, Robinson and Cleaver advertised 'our new ready-to-wear coats and skirts' and Burberrys had both made-to-order and ready-made fashions. The new loose styles made it much easier than before to make – and sell – ready-made fashions and busy women needed them.

Lucile came into the fashion picture with some prominence at this time. About 1912 she had challenged Paris. 'People said: Paris will teach her a lesson. But instead it was I who taught Paris a lesson,' she proclaimed. Eight hundred people held up the traffic at her opening parade in an aura of mauve invitation

79   Ready to wear fashions flourished and the sports coat became increasingly popular. 1916

80   Paris continued to lead the fashion. Elaborate toilettes like these were shown in Spring 1916

81 Fashion could still be gay in 1917, with this evening dress in crepe de Chine, with gold or silver tissue trimming the bodice and a large tulle bow falling over the draped skirt

82 Boots and shoes were very elaborate in 1916

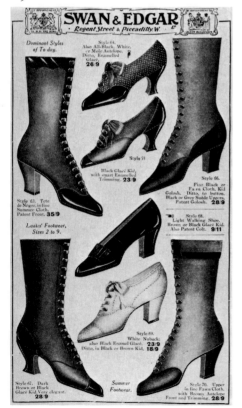

cards, purple carpets, flowers, tea, iced coffee, little cakes and the best orchestra in Paris. Before many months she had doubled her staff and the 'talented little group of designers' working with her now included Edward Molyneux, who had come over from the London house and who 'tells me he owes everything to me'.

During World War I she concentrated on developing the New York business, because 'without the lead of Paris, New York was lost sartorially, for the American designers . . . were turning out some frightful garments. . . . So I became an institution, the established leader of fashion in America.' However that may be, it is of note that the great impresario, Florenz Ziegfeld, went to one of her spectacular three-hour wartime fashion parades, held in theatres on several afternoons a week. He made the request that an Arabian-Nights-style scene included in the parade should be transferred to his famous Follies, complete with the mannequin, Dolores, who appeared in it. This was done. Dolores became a permanent member of the Follies and, appropriately, married a millionaire, as did many of Lucile's other girls. 'After that,' she recalls, 'I dressed many of Florenz Ziegfeld's productions.' Here she claims another 'first': Dolores' scene 'made theatrical history in one sense, for it introduced the "Show Girl" who was there simply to look beautiful'. Such show girls were to have a great future in the spectacular film musicals of the 'thirties. Lucile also dressed Irene Castle before the 1914–1918 war, adding this new, forward-looking figure to the Royalty, aristocracy, film stars (including Mary Pickford and Norma Talmadge) and other celebrities who had been her clients. Writing later, she said; 'Irene Castle and the dresses I designed for her brought in a new type of women's beauty. She was the first of the moderns. Her slim, boyish figure and her sleek bobbed head . . . set a new standard which other women imitated. It started in New York and spread to Europe. . . . I knew instinctively that here was the accepted type which the fashions of the next ten or fifteen years would follow. So I anticipated them a little.'

Lucile's clothes, softly coloured, infinitely gracious and decorative, were admired by thousands of women who could never hope to afford them. But she belonged to the vanishing world. After the 1914–1918 war 'the old standard of extravagant dressing had gone for ever', she lamented, and that was her standard. She sold her London house in 1918 and by then America was forging ahead in the cheaper, ready-to-wear market. She remained in Paris for some years and her post-war designs are elegant and beautiful. But although film stars and visiting tourists meant substantial business, her heart was not in the new world of short skirts, boyish looks and slim figures.

Wartime restrictions did not bite deeply into fashion, even in Britain. In 1917 Marshall and Snelgrove explained that 'owing to the restrictions on paper we are issuing a much abbreviated catalogue. . . . Our stock is, however, unusually well assorted.' Not till 1919 did a slight crunch come, in the shape of a catalogue of budget-priced fashions, with the explanation: 'This catalogue has been produced mainly in the interests of those of our customers whose incomes have been adversely affected by the War. It affords an opportunity of purchasing practically any necessary item of wearing apparel at prices which under present conditions are exceptionally moderate.' It was a sign of a trend towards less expensive fashions which were to be increasingly in demand in years to come.

But if such fashions were to be sought by those who had previously bought more expensively, that was nothing to the demand for them coming from those who, during the war, had their first taste of earning more than a bare subsistence wage and who therefore were having their first chance of being in fashion. Munition workers were rich by the standards of women's earnings at the time. One fashion-trade man whose recollections

83   River girls in 1916 get away from it all in gay summer frocks

" Muriel."
Dainty Gown in Cotton voile, printed in sprays of roses on black ground square medallions, finished at neck with Lawn Collar and bow of colored ribbon. Various colorings. **25/9**

"Peggy."
Chic piqué gown, suitable for boating or tennis, the coat and bands of skirt being carried out in colored stripe piqué. Various colorings. **16/11**

"Joan."
Useful gown in white voile, the foot of skirt, sailor collar and belt being carried out in navy voile. Various colorings. **25/9**

"Barbara."
Smart gown in plain voile, daintily tucked. Various colorings. **25/9**

"Dorothea."
Dainty gown in floral voile, organdi muslin collar. Various colorings. **21/9**

"Glawdys."
Useful gown in cotton-crêpe, the coatee and bands of skirt being carried out in navy and white check. Various colorings. **21/9**

go back to this time recalls that when he came home on leave the chief thing he noticed about women's appearance was that nearly every one of them was wearing a fur coat – not a mink or a sable, but a quite worthy musquash or seal. The ostentatious dressing of some of the munition workers was decried in many quarters, but, if it was somewhat untimely, it was a big step up in status and self-respect for the working girl or woman, an entry into a world which had hitherto been closed to her.

Apart from this, the war had helped the development of fashion in Britain. Though little had been produced that was of note at the time, it gave a strong impetus to manufacturing methods. Its outbreak had meant that there was a sudden demand in Britain for millions of uniforms to be made in a wide range of more or less standard sizes and to official specifications in style, quality and standard of production. Agreements had to be made with the textile and clothing industries on how this could be done. Manufacturers were called together from various regions to meet ministerial representatives. The industry's Trade Boards helped considerably in enabling it to gear itself up to the new needs. There was a certain irony in this, because the Boards had not been very successful in their original purpose of improving wages and working conditions, but they now provided a negotiating body for an industry which remained persistently fragmented in its structure.

The clothing industry's wartime responsibilities resulted in a substantial improvement in its structure and in the methods used in clothing manufacture. Service requirements meant that cutting had to be carried out in bulk. Mechanical cutters, power machines, all the existent labour-saving attachments had to be employed on a larger scale than ever before. Many sections of the trade which had been using very primitive methods were updated. In order to speed up work and make the best use of labour, for the first time in short supply, bigger factories were obviously better than small, isolated workrooms. During the war making up was, often for the first time, broken up into a series of consecutive operations, carried out by different workers, so as to make the best use of limited skills.

The Tailors and Garment Workers Union, set up in 1915, was a big step towards consolidating clothing manufacture in Britain. The authors of *The Needle is Threaded* declare that its establishment 'settled once and for all the question of whether or not all clothing workers should be organised on an industrial rather than a craft basis. There was no looking back.' It regulated apprenticeships, wages, conditions of work and hours of work;

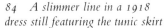

84   A slimmer line in a 1918 dress still featuring the tunic skirt

85   Elegance in velvet 1918

86   A product of the war, the coat frock was the first post-war fashion innovation to come to the fore. Here a 1925 version with the hip-line 'waist'

it had an education fund and a political fund. It was not, however, comprehensive in that many workers were not members of it, among them being a large proportion of those concerned with women's fashion. In this field small workshops and craft methods still had considerable advantages in view of changes in fashion, the great variety of styles that were required, the resultant short runs and the general lack of uniformity in standards and attitudes among women clothing workers. This meant that they were not easily brought into any union and there was still an immense way to go before fashion manufacture reached anything like a satisfactory structure for workers and wearers. But order was coming. Rules were being set up. Marshall and Snelgrove still have a yellowed booklet consisting of a series of sheets marked 'Form 338, an Overtime Register and Report. For use in Factories and Workshops, in which Overtime is worked in pursuance of a special exception.' Only one page has been filled up, for 'work to be continued in the Blouse Department from 8 p.m. to 10 p.m. on 16 July 1915, in the process of blouse-making'. This was, however, part of the growing movement against uncontrolled overtime.

To sum up, *The Needle is Threaded* concludes that 'the pattern of the modern clothing industry was definitely established during the war and inter-war years'. Max Radin, managing director of Ramar Dresses, with a lifetime's experience in fashion manufacture in London, says: 'Before World War I there was no such thing as a mass production industry. Soon after the War it began to take shape.' It was natural that the first effects of the wartime conscription of the industry should be felt in the men's sector and giants like Montagu Burton, Hepworths and Price's Fifty Shilling Tailors soon appeared. But fashion too showed the influence of the war years.

The coat frock was the first women's wartime and post-war fashion to be successfully manufactured by good-quality factory methods and it was a conspicuous item of dress during the early post-war years. This long-sleeved, one-piece, go-everywhere dress rated catalogues of its own from the stores, where it was shown with pleats, yokes, embroidery, braid and various other trimmings. It was fairly simple to make, and it lent itself to the tailoring techniques which had been stimulated by the war.

The biggest incentive to the coming production of fashions on a large scale by factory methods was, however, given by artificial silk, soon, by about 1926, more usually described as rayon. It came into general use in fashion in the 1920's, with America taking the lead and the rest of the world following rapidly. By the mid-twenties pretty, inexpensive, smart dresses with the look and some of the glamour of silk were being factory-made for the popular market on both sides of the Atlantic. The girl of limited means could now enjoy being in fashion to a degree hitherto impossible. It was a tremendous innovation. The fashion trade saw and took advantage of this opportunity.

To underwear too rayon brought a revolution. Pretty garments (by previous standards) in locknit, in a wide choice of colours, became available at modest prices and rapidly superseded the traditional boring white cotton still prevalent among those who could not afford the fashionable but expensive silk or crêpe de Chine. To the trade this was a mixed blessing, because the new garments could be made by semi-skilled or even unskilled labour, instead of the skilled seamstresses who had hitherto made them. But for the top end of the market hand-made lingerie was a fetish which lasted until the advent of nylon after World War II. Long after it could easily have been made by

ALL ARTIFICIAL SILK
KNITTED FABRIC

87   *Rayon was the greatest means of bringing fashion to the girl of limited means. A 1926 style typical of fashion trends.*

88 *With shorter skirts stockings in the new rayon became more important. A 1925 short evening dress with all the elegance of Paris and the contemporary fashionable earrings, slave bangle and ostrich feather fan*

machine, the hand-made undergarment was sought out by all who could afford it and was sold at prices which indicated a poorly paid army of workers.

Rayon had also an important effect on another item of wear which became increasingly important from the nineteen-twenties. Stockings had been mainly black for everyday wear for many years, with white for tennis and some summer wear. For special occasions and among the fashionable they had from Edwardian times often matched the dress and a large number of colours is detailed in store catalogues. Wool and cotton were used for the ordinary woman's everyday wear, with silk as an expensive but prized luxury. About 1921 there was a tentative fashion for beige, but the big break came in 1922, when flesh-coloured stockings began to be fashionable and popular among all classes in lisle, silk and, above all, in the new artificial silk. This yarn was to dominate the stocking market in a great variety of beige and skin tones for many years. As skirts of varying degrees of shortness were to be a continuous fashion from the 'twenties onwards, stockings, worn on legs revealed for the first time in fashion history, became a matter of considerable importance. Rayon remained unchallenged until nylon was invented in 1938. Limited supplies of nylon stockings became available in America from then, but in Britain women did not begin to enjoy the now universal 'nylons' until 1947, because the production of nylon, which started there in 1939, was concentrated on the war effort, being used for parachutes, ropes and service equipment.

3

Developments in fashion after 1918 were greatly influenced by the changing attitudes of women. The numbers of women at work had increased greatly during the war and they continued to be substantial and to grow still further as the century progressed. The new independent young woman with her career, her pay packet, her improved job prospects and her freedom to live her own life came to the fore. She took all forms and came from all classes. There was the 'flapper', flighty and gay, but she

89 End of war fashions for 1918

90 Skirts rose in the first year or two of the 'twenties

91 Ready to wear London coats and skirts. 1919

92 Skirts fell to near the ankles in 1923

93 The waist disappeared and belts were round the hips. A sleeveless jumper in georgette for wearing under tailored suits, 1924

would soon settle down. There were the 'surplus' women whose prospects of the traditional security of marriage had been reduced or destroyed by the war's death toll – Britain's losses amounted to 765,399 dead, the heaviest in any war and about three times as many as in World War II. They knew, these women, that they would probably have to be self-supporting for the rest of their lives. At the other extreme and outside the ranks of the workers, were the 'Bright Young Things' whose giddy parties, treasure hunts, night-clubbing and general wild pursuit of excitement caused a stir in the staid and rather exalted enclaves of society, from which they most of them derived, and who kept getting into the gossip columns and the newspapers round the mid-twenties.

To start with, post-war fashions were as voluminous as the later wartime ones and skirts ended somewhere between calves and ankles. They rose in the first year or two of the 'twenties, fell again to near the ankles in 1923 and then started resolutely to go up again. 'Dresses were very loose,' says Loelia, Duchess of Westminster, who 'came out' as a débutante in 1920. 'I think we were trying to be feminine after the war workers in trousers and uniforms, but the pendulum quickly swung back. Soon the heroine of every novel was described as "boyish".'

This was the start of a brief era when women sought to disguise their femininity as fervently as, a generation ago, they had tried to exaggerate it. The 'boyish' look was engendered by various factors, from the insistent 'equality' with men which was being demanded, to the psychological undercurrents created by

a world short of young men and also by the less complex but
pervasive emphasis on youth. It meant that a perfectly straight
figure, without a hint of a curve, became the ideal. The waist
disappeared and belts were worn round the hips. The brassière
reversed its rôle of booster and became a flattener – a straight,
firm band of material fastened round the body at bust level and
held up by shoulder straps. The corset was another straight band,
still usually made mainly of rigid materials, because elastic could
not yet be produced in the long lengths which made the 'roll-on'
the darling of the 'thirties. But it was often very short and bones
were disappearing. The corselette came in about 1920, first in
America, then Britain, and it too started as a flattener, made
in rigid materials and on occasion nearly as painful as a straight-
jacket.

These were all young fashions, and there was an increasing
emphasis on youth in the coming years. For a time fashion was
uncertain how it wanted to look. 'Hems went down nearly to
the ground in 1923,' says the Duchess of Westminster, 'but were
up to the knees by 1925, and the waistline wandered high and
low, but throughout the 'twenties bosoms and hips were
definitely *out*. A lovely figure meant a perfectly straight figure
and the slightest suggestion of a curve was scorned as *fat*. The
ideal woman's vital statistics would probably have been something like 30-30-30.'

The knee-length straight dress and the straight, boyish figure
without a curve are often regarded as the hallmark of the
'twenties as a whole and of every woman throughout the
decade. In fact they applied in their totality to only a small part
of the period – the years from about 1925–1926 to 1928–1929 –
and in their extreme form mainly to the young. Before that time
skirts were some way down the calf and in the early years they
were still quite full. By 1928 they began to go down again and
to be wider. The 1920's girl, as portrayed in hosts of later,
nostalgic drawings, plays and films, was something of a carica-
ture of reality. It was, however, fashionable to have a waistless,
bustless, hipless look throughout these years, with a belt round
the hips. This was the general aim, but it was interpreted, should
one say, loosely? The time had passed when those who were not
naturally like bean poles would torture themselves into fashionable shapes. The short skirts of the 'twenties were new to fashion
history, but never since then have daytime skirts of ground
length or anything approaching it become a general fashion.
The Dior 'New Look' of 1947 was always well above the ankles
and the dust-sweeping 'maxi' of the later 'sixties and early

*94   No suggestion of a curve in the 'twenties.
Styles of 1926 and 1927*

95   Skirts were still short in 1928

96 *Variety in daytime fashions. 1928*

'seventies was a minority movement and never became an accepted fashion.

The lengthening of skirts from knee-length started with evening dresses which, throughout most of the 'twenties, were the same length as day ones. Usually they were 'slinky' sheaths, clinging and made of chiffon, lace or soft silks, with shoe-string shoulder straps. This exiguous style was first modified about 1927 by means of skirts with handkerchief points, long sashes or floating panels extending beyond the normal hemline of the time. About 1928 fuller skirts came in for evening wear, and below straight, flat bodices evening dresses had uneven hems, nearly up to the knees in front but dipping almost to the ground at the back. By the following year this had become an ankle-length evening dress, quite distinct in length from daytime fashions, and the long evening dress has remained in fashion ever since. The ballet-length vogue of the 'fifties was an alternative, not a successor. In contrast, sports clothes stayed short. Suzanne Lenglen first appeared in her calf-length, one-piece sleeveless dress in 1919, and made it her uniform until 1929, when she retired after turning professional in 1926. Tennis skirts remained short and became shorter, ignoring fashion's lengthening hemlines. Mlle. Lenglen had established a new concept of tennis clothes by her example. In 1922 she said: 'If you wish to look neat in court, never wear a coloured skirt, always a white one. . . . I will briefly detail what I consider the ideal dress: a simple piqué dress, or one of drill or white linen, made in the old Grecian style, and fastened at the waist with a ribbon or leather belt. The sleeves should be short. A simple pair of canvas "gym" shoes are best.'

Short hair, a basic of 'boyish' fashions, is also an innovation that has persisted in various forms for nearly 60 years, since it first appeared before World War I, with Irene Castle adopting it in New York and Isadora Duncan adding short hair to short skirts in her dancing. The style was an obvious convenience for women doing war work, but it continued when other wartime fashions had disappeared, including that of having only the side sections of the hair cut short and either waved or wound into a 'Kiss curl' over each ear and against the cheek. The rest of the hair was then coiled into a 'bun' at the nape of the neck. The short 'bob' was succeeded by the even more boyish and much-talked of fashion for the 'shingle', the introduction of which was recorded for posterity by Michael Arlen in his novel *The Green*

97   Suzanne Lenglen brought in a revolution in tennis wear from the start of her triumphs in 1919

98   An embroidered knee-length evening dress. 1928

99   Signs of change Evening dress of 1929 with hem dipping at back

100   The late 'twenties fashion scene, with dipping hems, short skirts and lounging pyjamas at a poetry reading by 'Miss Edith Standish'

101   The cloche hat dominated the mid and late 'twenties and took many forms, but the basic form was always the same. Here a selection of 1925 styles

Hat, the famous best-seller of 1923. He was a top chronicler of fashionable life and his tempestuous heroine, Iris Storm, was cast in fashion's own mould. He describes how 'her hair was thick and tawny. . . . It was like a boy's hair, swept back from her forehead.' Then 'above her neck her hair died a very manly death, a more manly death than the "bobbed" hair was ever known to die, and so it comes about that Iris Storm was the first Englishwoman I ever saw, with "shingled" hair. This was in 1922.' A hybrid cut called the 'bingle' had a certain vogue after this and about 1926 the even more boyish 'Eton crop' appeared, but it too had a limited life. After a few years hair styles became softer, encouraged by the more feminine trend of clothes and by the growing popularity of the permanent wave, which, when introduced in America in 1906, had been as painful as going to the dentist', but which had lost its terrors by the early 'twenties and was fashionable in both America and Britain.

With the flat figure and short hair went a chemise type of dress which hung down straight and which from about 1925 to 1928–1929 reached only to the knees among the fashionable. It was a matter of distress to the fabric trade because it used so little material, but it was a blessing to the dress manufacturer, presenting few problems of size or fit and opening up a new world of fashion for the many. It was equally a gift to the home dress-maker. Writing of her début, the Duchess of Westminster recalls that 'as nothing had to fit, dressmaking was comparatively easy, and afterwards I made a lot of my own clothes'. At its simplest, but also often at its smartest, the dress of these years was made from a length of material twice the length you wanted, plus a few inches for the hem. You folded it from end to end, then across, cut out a rectangle from hem to where the armhole and sleeve should be, cut out a curved or right-angled piece for the neck, joined up the seams and hemmed the edges and there you were.

The 'cloche' hat came in at this time, closely covering the shorn head and worn low on the brow for some years. Its originator was Reboux of Paris, but every shop had it and it was in immense demand, for – again the Duchess is the historian – 'we wore hats all the year round, winter and summer, London or country, in the garden, playing games, always'. At least the cloche was fairly cheap: 'little round felt hats pulled down over the ears, cost 38s. 6d. at Fortnum and Masons and identical hats far less elsewhere'. For summer they were of straw, in the same shape, but occasionally big 'picture' styles appeared for special occasions.

Accessories took on a new look at this time and moved away from the traditional preference for real jewellery. There was a vogue for pearls, as big as pigeon's eggs and often worn as chokers or in long loops. Coloured glass was approved for necklaces, long dangling strings of beads, brooches and wide 'slave' bangles. There was a craze, which lasted for years, for diamanté clips, preferably a pair, which were worn with everything from sweaters to evening dress. Long drop earrings, nearly touching the shoulders, balanced the short shingles and Eton crops. Long cigarette holders were flourished in the 'twenties.

Make-up came into more general use among the fashionable. Eyebrows were plucked to a pencil-thin line, which was darkened with a special pencil. This went on into the 'thirties. Strong-coloured lipstick was worn – Iris Storm's 'painted mouth was purple in the dim light'.

A fashion which involved the paradox that it meant hours and hours of work for the busy young woman who, in her other fashions, was trying to get rid of inroads on her leisure, was the hand-knitted jumper. During the war every female, from schoolgirl to grandmother, had knitted mountains of navy, khaki or Flying Corps blue wool into comforts for the troops in the shape of mufflers, balaclavas, socks and gloves. There had been a few hand-knitted jumpers before 1914, but the fashion that put every woman into them dated from about 1918, when 'there was a positive craze for knitting jumpers' among all classes. The jumper, hand or machine-knitted, has remained in vogue ever since, beloved of women of all ages and classes, rising time and again into high fashion and increasing in popularity with the development of man-made fibres in recent years. It was and is, like most of fashion from this time onwards, classless in its appeal. In the 'twenties it was rather loose and shapeless, with a 'V' neck, and it usually went well down on the hips.

A new and potent influence came into fashion at this time. It was American films and it remained at its peak for nearly two decades. To look like their favourite film stars was the aim of the new young women, for films were the chief entertainment of the public everywhere in these pre-television days. The film influence was tremendous. It was universal as no previous influence could have been and, as cinemas sprang up everywhere, weekly or twice-weekly visits to the latest films became part of life, at a cost of 6d. a time in most cases. The chief creator of film fashions was the famous Adrian of Hollywood, who dressed innumerable successful films in the great cinema era of the 'twenties and 'thirties. Among the stars whose screen fashions

102 *Pearls were worn in all kinds of ways and in all sizes. They were in fashion in Paris by 1920, as seen in this advertisement. Note also the dangling earrings*

103   Greta Garbo's slouch hats and coats spread round the world from the late 1920's

were created by him were all the big names of those days – Greta Garbo, Joan Crawford, Norma Shearer, Rosalind Russell and many more, all idols beyond compare. Garbo's page-boy 'bob' and the slouch hats and coats which were almost non-fashions spread round the world. Fashion magazines featured the stars and 'lovely clothes from the silver screen' were given continuous attention on both sides of the Atlantic. Adrian left films in 1939, when the influence was past its peak. He moved on in fashion, presenting his first couture and ready-to-wear collections in Amerca in 1942. He retired ten years later and died in 1959 at the early age of 56.

Jazz also became very much the fashion at this time, affecting modes and manners and the whole pace of life. It too originated in America. The original Dixieland Jazz Band, formed in 1916 in New Orleans, had a big success in Chicago and New York. In 1919 it opened a three months' run at the Hammersmith Palais de Danse in London. It was the first band of its kind to play in Europe, and it made a great impact. The foxtrot, arriving from America in 1922, became an established favourite at every dance. In 1923 came the 'Blues', too extreme and neurotic for general acceptance, but in 1926 the Charleston, with its jerky, hotted-up rhythm, sent one and all jigging frantically. Night clubs, introduced before the war and flourishing during it, continued to be a high-spot of social gaiety. In this medley of new excitement fashion was young and gay as never before. Change was in the air.

5 New fashion makers and the new kinds of fashion, 1920–1930

I

To Paris the 1914–1918 war was a watershed in fashion. After it a new world had arrived. Poiret resisted the new attitudes, continuing at first on his former course, giving more of his famous parties which now prompted the comment that 'the difference between his creations and the costumes for his fancy dress balls was not very great'. He denounced the new mood of fashion, which looked to the average woman rather than the exalted few. He scorned the new designers, saying in 1931, in his book *En Habillant L'Epoque*: 'It has profited them considerably, but at the same time they have forfeited the title of couturier and fashion creator' and 'They have let the lights go out and they will never be relit'. In terms of past fashion he was right. He was in almost total eclipse by 1924 and after many years of poverty and obscurity died in a charity hospital in 1943. It was a tragic end for the man whom Edna Woolman Chase summed up in 1954 as 'still considered by many to have been the greatest originator of feminine fashion from the time of the Second Empire until about 1924. . . . The flaring, yet slim tunic and the modern silhouette were to a great extent his innovation. He abolished corsets and petticoats in a desire to conform to female anatomy as manufactured by Nature.' He set the course of future fashion, and then hated the way it was going.

Meantime, while all sorts of events and changes jostled with each other to influence fashion – work, sport, dancing, the motor car, American films – a new generation of couturiers rose in Paris, creating new kinds of clothes and ensuring that the French capital continued to hold its own as the generating force in fashion. The most significant new arrival was Gabrielle Chanel, whose influence has remained powerful for more than 50 years – an achievement unique in the history of fashion. She introduced

Part 2.

104 *Paris adapted to the new mood and remained a generating force in fashion. A look at 1920 in the* Gazette du Bon Ton *shows most of the trends of the decade*

an extreme simplicity into high fashion and all fashion and began in a small way before 1914 the fabulous career which, though interrupted by her 15 years' retirement from 1939 to 1954, she pursued with undimmed lustre until her death early in 1971, when her last collection was almost ready for presentation. Her house still goes on, with a team of designers headed by Guy Berthelot continuing her tradition with near-Chanel designs.

Chanel's real fashion career had its start when, during the war, she opened a shop in Deauville, adapting sailors' jackets and men's pullovers for women's wear with such success that they became the first examples of a new fashion trend. Established in Paris after the war, she soon achieved success with collections featuring jersey wool dresses, straight-line classic evening gowns, often beautifully beaded, and, above all, the simple wool suits with cardigan jackets and plain or pleated skirts which have remained in fashion ever since. The Chanel suit is more a way of life than just a fashion. She liked muted colours, chiefly grey and beige, and materials like flannel and the porridge-coloured wool jersey which had hitherto been used only for the stodgiest kind of underwear, but she also used strong, clear, even violent colours. She liked simplicity, to which she brought a matchless elegance. 'I make fashions women can live in, breathe in, feel comfortable in and look younger in,' she said. It was the antithesis of what high fashion had meant in the past. It was a 'poor look' of infinite chic. Her flair for fashion never deserted her. By 1930 she had 20 work-rooms and was employing more than 2400 people. She used jersey on such a large scale that in 1935 she opened her own factory for making it – and sold it freely to shops everywhere. She introduced the sweater line, the pleated skirt, the triangular scarf. She originated the fashion for chunky glass bead necklaces and many-stringed rows of fake pearls. Her perfume Chanel No. 5 (named after her 'lucky' day, her birthday on August 5, which also led to her fashion shows opening on the fifth of the month), was introduced in 1925 and it too had a lasting success and is still incomparable.

American buyers were captivated by Chanel and bought her models from the start, so that copies of them became part of American fashion. Chanel was won over to visit Hollywood, and did much there to promote the boyish 'garçonne' fashions in films during the 'twenties, thereby giving a new direction to fashion for all. The Chanel suit flourished in her hands and everywhere else, until 1939. Even during her 15 years out of business it continued to be worn and when, in 1954, she re-opened her house, she did so with a collection that was based on all her pre-war themes. After a shaky start accorded it by a baffled clientèle, unconvinced buyers and a deflated press, a second reign of non-stop success began and the Chanel suit got a new lease of life which still continues, with Britain's Wallis Shops injecting new life into it in the late 'sixties. Couture in her hands came to terms with the larger world, yet she kept her own impeccable identity. She brought to everything she produced an incomparable style and all the variations on her theme gave direction to the fashions women wore everywhere. She delighted in being copied, saying very pertinently: 'If there is no copying, how are you going to have fashion?'

Another powerful force in the growth of fashion from the late 'twenties was Vionnet, described as 'the architect among dress-makers', probably the greatest technician fashion has ever known and the between-the-wars aristocrat of couture, matchless in the elegance of her creations. She was the creator-in-chief of the bias cut. With its sleek, easy grace and its smooth comfort, it followed the lines of the body, making yet another contribution to the trend of fashion towards natural lines. She worked in dressmaking in London early in her career and then went to the Callot Soeurs and to Doucet in Paris, designing clothes of a deceptive simplicity which roused the scorn of the *vendeuses*. She opened her own house just before World War I, but closed it during the war and until 1919. From then she was a dominating

105 *Gabrielle Chanel in 1929, wearing the famous Chanel suit in jersey with the sweater she also introduced, and the multi-rows of pearls which were also part of her great contribution to fashion*

figure in fashion for the next 20 years, until she retired in 1939, handing over her house to her pupil, Mad Carpentier. She designed for the individual but, like Chanel, she influenced large-scale fashion by her masterly simplicity. The sinuous, body-clinging satin and crêpe de Chine dresses which were her chief hallmark were very much part of the new fashion scene of the 'twenties and, even more, the 'thirties. Unrestricting, easy to slip on and off and often free of all fastenings, so clever was the cut, they had everything to commend them. They were of the modern world; they could never have been worn over the old, heavy, stiff corsets but called for minimal underwear, with, at most, the new light, supple elastic girdles which helped considerably to put fashion on the lines it was now following.

New and practical links between couture and American ready-to-wear were forged in the 'twenties by another top Paris figure, Jean Patou. His first success had come early in 1914 when, recently established in modest premises, his entire collection was bought for America by a New York store. He at once planned to launch out on a scale that would enable him to compete with the top names in fashion, but the war intervened and for the next four years Patou was serving as a captain of the Zouaves.

He opened his salon again in 1919 and continued to add to his American conquests. It was pointed out to him by an American private customer that the difference in build between American and French women was so great that it was impossible to tell how clothes shown on small, round French model girls would look on tall, slim, long-legged Americans. He took prompt action over this, went to America to see the truth of it for himself and in December, 1924 brought back to Paris six American model girls to show his next collection there, along with the usual French girls. The idea paid off, and American wholesalers as well as private people bought lavishly.

Like Chanel, Patou brought a masterly new simplicity to couture fashion and it was probably inevitable that he should regard her as a rival. Another notable newcomer to the between-the-wars fashion scene was Edward Molyneux, the Englishman (or, to be exact, Irishman with some Hungarian blood) who became one of the most brilliant names in Paris fashion in its new mood, catering for the new kind of woman who travelled the world by air, sea and land instead of going the old round of the social season and of country house parties. Through these years the Paris influence remained strong in fashion. Michael Arlen has a reference, applying to 1922, to 'the women in those mad, barbaric colours which fashion, goaded on by Chanel and

106 Paris continued to exert a strong influence in the 'twenties. Worth's evening gown of 1922, while skirts were still long, has the new slim, waistless, curveless look

gallantly led by Captain Molyneux had flung as a challenge to our dark civilisation'.

In the post-war years the French domination of fashion was also shown by more direct means. In 1919 British *Vogue* had advertisements for French hats, available in Paris and described in French. Corsets from Paris were also advertised and Lucile took a full page to announce her Paris collection of 'robes, manteaux, lingerie'. In the mid-twenties many Paris houses, including Patou, Drécoll and Lelong, took full pages in the same fashion magazine to announce their Paris opening dates. The fashionable and wealthy could still spare time and energy to make visits to Paris and to endure the inevitable laborious fittings that followed the choice of new fashions there.

Stores also continued to make much of French fashions. In 1928 Debenham and Freebody announced that they had 'one of the finest collections of *ORIGINAL PARIS MODEL GOWNS* in London, as well as models designed by our own artists'. They explained that models can be copied 'by our own staff of highly

ORIGINAL PARIS MODELS
HALF PRICE
AND LESS

108 *Paris models were copied extensively by the stores*

Following our usual custom during the Sale, we shall clear all original models at half price and less. There are Evening Gowns, Two-piece Suits, Day Frocks, Reception Gowns and Creations for the smart occasion.

Included are Models by :

MAINBOCHER: LUCILLE PARAY: PAQUIN : LANVIN VIONNET, Etc., Etc.

Two examples :

On Right.
ORIGINAL PERIOD FROCK, of orange colour taffetta, with fichu and old-world petticoat, in ivory georgette embroidered with fine pearls. Original Price 75 gns.

Sale Price

35 Gns.

On Left.
AN ORIGINAL PARIS MODEL TWO-PIECE. The dress is in floral crêpe de chine, and the coat is embellished with rich fur trimming.
HALF PRICE.

skilled fitters and workers' much more cheaply than in Paris, and that their model-gown buyer visited Paris frequently throughout the season, so that 'we are continually receiving new models from Paris', which they would adapt and modify. In their spring catalogue of the same year they explained that 'the garments illustrated are exact reproductions and adaptations of models that have been produced for the coming season by leading Paris designers. These tailor-mades have been made in our own workrooms under the supervision of experts.' The tailor-mades included Chanel-type suits with cardigan jackets and others from Patou and Molyneux.

The tailored suit continued to be an important fashion, with considerable prestige attached to it, throughout the between-the-wars years. During the 'twenties and 'thirties it alone continued to a large degree to be made to measure by a man's bespoke tailor or by a store which had its special tailoring department. Ready-made suits, there were, especially of the softer type, but the classic tailor-made was the choice of the well-dressed woman and especially of the successful career woman, to whom it was almost a uniform. The woman executive was still something of a rare bird and as such she was psychologically a little unsure of herself at conferences and board meetings. The impeccable tailored suit, made to measure, was an effective specific for the inferiority complex, especially if it was in smooth black, with a *chic* hat, tailored white silk blouse, a row of pearls and spotless white gloves.

The Wall Street crash of 1929 dealt a severe blow to Paris fashion. Orders were cancelled in the economic panic, private customers dwindled and even store buyers had to reduce their commitments. *Haute couture* had been France's second highest export in 1925, but in 1933 it had fallen to twenty-seventh place. After the American disaster there were ten thousand workpeople unemployed in the Paris fashion business. Recovery came and new fashion achievements restored much of the lustre of Paris, but in terms of extravagant, magnificent fashion Paris never returned to her former grand manner. The new, more down-to-earth attitudes forced on the world did, however, offer great scope to the new simplicity and speeded Chanel in particular on her long course of success. Her intuitive grasp of the needs of the time served her well, as it always did.

In Britain too couture fashion was on the move in the 'twenties and through the 'thirties. It was more eclectic, and much smaller than Paris, but now the foundations were being laid for great changes in its character and scope. They were, however, rather slow to mature. Top fashion still held its elegant skirts away from any contact with the commercial and the wholesale. Madame Handley-Seymour, a long-established Court dressmaker, was chosen to make the Coronation gown of Queen Elizabeth (now Queen Elizabeth the Queen Mother), in 1937, but the first of the new generation of couturiers, Norman Hartnell, was entrusted with the dresses of the Maids of Honour.

Hartnell, who started a new era of expanding couture in Britain, had by this time achieved considerable eminence – by his own efforts and without, as usually happened in Paris, the leading reins of a ruling couturier. His 'discoverer' was Miss Minnie Hogg who, as Corisande, in the 1920's wrote a widely

109   The tailored suit could also be bought ready made. A 1932 version for the business woman. Alongside, a dress with the long 'thirties' look

read woman's page diary feature in the London *Evening Standard*. Seeing the clothes he had designed for a Cambridge Footlights Production, *The Bedder's Opera*, of which a special matinée was given at London's Daly's Theatre, she wrote that 'the frocks . . . set me thinking as to whether Mr. N. B. Hartnell wasn't contemplating conquering feminine London with original gowns'. Due to changing family circumstances Mr. N. B. Hartnell left Cambridge in mid-career and set about following Miss Hogg's suggestion. A brief job as a sketch artist at a fashion house folded on the first Christmas Eve. He tried C. B. Cochran, then established as an impresario, without success. Gordon Selfridge said: 'Go away, my boy, and learn to draw.' There was an unhappy episode with Lucile, ending in a lawsuit, which he won. Then in 1923, he started on his own in four small rooms at the top of a house in Bruton Street, with a small amount of capital borrowed from his sister and no practical knowledge of dressmaking – or business. In 1924 his first success came in the shape of an order for a gold and silver wedding gown for the Hon. Daphne Vivian on her marriage to the Earl of Weymouth.

By the early 'thirties Hartnell was installed in his present impressive premises in Bruton Street, and was prospering. One day a customer, after looking at one of his dresses, said: 'Whose model is it?' 'Mine,' replied Hartnell. 'Oh, is it not a Patou or a Lelong? Not a Paris model?' She departed, after saying evasively: 'I think I will consider it.' This made Hartnell decide to show his collections in Paris, and he did so, first with a moderate and, on the second occasion, with a big success at the Plaza Athenée. American buyers were particularly enthusiastic. New vistas were opened. In 1928 *Vogue* carried a full page advertisement for his house, in which it was announced that 'Mr. Hartnell had the same success at the recent openings in Paris, where he showed his models along with the *grands couturiers*, that he has already had with a chic clientèle in London'.

By the mid 'thirties he was dressing the kind of famous actresses whom all English women wanted to resemble, among them Gertrude Lawrence and Evelyn Laye. In 1937 the Duchess of Gloucester's wedding dress and those of her bridesmaids, who included the young Princesses, Elizabeth and Margaret, marked the beginning of a long association with Royalty. This was followed by a number of dresses for Queen Mary and then for the Duchess of York, now Queen Elizabeth the Queen Mother. One Royal incident that made fashion history occurred when King George VI showed Mr. Hartnell a number of pictures, including several Winterhalters, of Royal ladies in Victorian crinolines, among them the Empress Eugénie and the beautiful Empress Elizabeth of Austria. He indicated that he would like to see the grace of these gowns recaptured in some of the Queen's dresses. As a result Hartnell introduced 'picture' or crinoline-style gowns for great occasions, and these were worn faithfully by Royalty for many years to come, up to the late 'fifties. This theme was echoed by other couturiers and by their fashionable clients, and such dresses provided the grand finale of couture collections for years.

The between-the-wars era also saw the start of the careers of others who were to play an important part in the future of fashion. Digby Morton first became known as designer at the couture house of Lachasse, from its foundation in 1929, where he won quick and outstanding success by transforming the tailored suit from the strictly man-made town classic or the equally conventional country tweed suit, both long taken for granted by English women, into something as sensitive to fashion and as varied in style as any other item of wear. Suits for all occasions quickly became generally accepted and have remained so ever since. In 1933 Digby Morton left to start his own couture business and he was succeeded at Lachasse by Hardy Amies. Although his mother had been on the staff of the well-known Court dressmaker, Miss Gray, he had, after a short spell with a Paris silk firm, been working first in a German wall tile factory and then selling weighing machines. A description of a dress worn at a party by Miss Gray, by then Mrs. Shingleton, was sent by him in a letter to his aunt Louie, and, when shown to the wearer, led to her saying to her husband, the head of Lachasse: 'Get that boy into the business in Digby Morton's place.' So in 1934 Hardy Amies began his career in fashion in the showroom. After a hasty first collection contrived with the aid of a model girl who, as Digby Morton's clothes had been made on her for several seasons, 'had managed to think up some 20 or 30 suits and dresses which bore a reasonable resemblance to those of Morton's design', Hardy Amies was asked to take over the design side and did so successfully. After all, he had, through his mother, been brought up in fashion. Next he was appointed managing designer. By 1937 he was exporting to America and Canada and was progressing rapidly. He continued to design in the intervals of army service, at first for Lachasse, but he soon left that company. He made his first contact with the wholesale and retail trades when a collection of clothes wanted for South America for an export promotion was made in the workrooms

110 A graceful 1930 ensemble with natural waistline and longer skirt, with new off the brow hat

of Bourne and Hollingsworth with the co-operation of Madge Garland, who was then director of fashion for that store. The arrangement was that in return for the use of their workrooms the store could copy designs and sell them from its rails. This operation was carried through in brief spells of leave and on days off from Hampshire, where Hardy Amies was then stationed. The story of his establishment as a couturier on a new scale is, however, a post-war one.

2

While changes were going on in the structure of fashion between the 'twenties and 'thirties', fashion itself was also looking different as the new decade approached. Patou claimed credit for the longer skirts which came in suddenly at the end of the 'twenties. 'Patou bomb drops – skirts reach ankles,' said *Vogue*. By 1930 the 'boyish' look had completely disappeared. Women were women again. The waist was back in its normal place and,

111   Fashion's sudden change. By 1930 skirts were longer, with more shape, and the general look was more feminine

112   The waist returns to its natural place and hems drop further, 1931

113 The backless evening dress was a main innovation. An early style in georgette, with flaring, bias-cut skirt and spray of flowers on shoulder. 1930

114 Evening dresses from Paris, 1935 included backless designs and skirts flared to the hem from slim waist and hips

though there was no exaggeration of the figure at any point, curves were admitted to exist and allowed to be seen. Skirts were calf-length for day and full length for evening dress. They were fuller, but were shaped to the body at waist and hips. They often had gores and were also generally cut on the bias to give ease without bulk.

During most of the 'thirties there was no outstanding change from these natural proportions. Fashions were easy, graceful, rather softly shaped, even to the point of limpness. There was some elaboration in the shape of draped or cowl necklines, large folded collars, full sleeves and some fussy trimmings. For day-time summer wear the combination of a light woollen coat in a plain colour and a harmonising printed silk or rayon dress was much in favour. The coat would be straight, edge-to-edge and often collarless. The dress and jacket ensemble was also popular and silk suits were a favoured variation, derived from Molyneux.

The biggest innovation of the decade was the backless evening dress, fairly high in front but with a low back scooped out almost to the waist. Sometimes it had narrow shoulder straps, at others a halter neck line. It was sleeveless, with a skirt that flared

4699   4700   4701   4702

115   *Paris daytime styles for 1937*

from the hips. This low back had never appeared in fashion before and, especially when combined with back drapings on bodice and skirt, it had rather a back-to-the-front effect, as if the lady ought to enter the room backwards. Strings of beads swinging down the back and artificial flowers, very much in fashion at this time and often worn nestling on the spine instead of the corsage, added to this effect. Up to now it had usually been accepted that fashion's exposure of this or that part of the body had an aesthetic or sexual import – the submissive sloping shoulders, the alluring bosom, the intriguing ankle, even the legs of the 'twenties could be interpreted in this way, but the shoulder blades and spine seemed an aberration.

From now on evening dress was more distinct from day clothes than it had ever been. In the past, all through the history of fashion, the leisured and wealthy had set the style, so there had been no compulsion for daytime attire to be strictly practical and for the beautifully impractical to be reserved for evenings. The Edwardian lady had dressed up in all her glory for day events. But in a world where all kinds of women were leading busy, active lives, simple fashions were desirable for ordinary daily comings and goings, with the luxury of long, low-cut gowns reserved for evenings. At this time evening dress was worn very widely in Britain on a great variety of occasions and by the working girl and the middle class housewife as well as by the Duchess and the débutante.

Certain minor fashions of the 'thirties had an interest of their own, because of the extent to which they spread to one and all. There was a great vogue for carrying a huge, brightly coloured chiffon handkerchief in the evenings, not for any use but just to set off the dress as it drifted from the hand on the dance floor. A single ostrich feather made into a fan was also in favour and bigger and bigger sprays of artificial flowers were worn on the shoulders, at the corsage or at the waist of evening dresses. Beads of all kinds were seen on every occasion, often as long strings, and earrings became studs rather than the long drops of the previous decade. Fox furs were coming into great favour, with the entire animal – or, better still, two of them – draped round the shoulders or slung, like a sports scarf, round the neck, with the heads nose to nose on one shoulder and the beasts hanging grandly down back and front. Silver fox was the most sought-after, but the red, cross and blue varieties were also approved. Fox capes were worn with evening dress, and here the white fox was favoured.

Hats were of all kinds at this time, and the ubiquitous cloche

116   Fox furs came into great favour. Silver foxes slung round the shoulders were very fashionable in 1938

117   Fox fantasy. A design by Erté for a scene in the Palladium show 'Black Velvet' in 1938

of the immediate past had a host of successors. Most of them were flat and brimmed, and they were worn side-tilted, with one eye and one ear more or less concealed. Traffic hazards were a frequent source of comment. In the early 'thirties the Basque beret was in great favour, worn slantwise, so that half the head was bare, but supplemented with a brief veil tied round the forehead above the brows. Hatlessness was still unthinkable for the well-dressed woman in town. In *Present Laughter*, written in 1938 but not produced till 1942, Noel Coward, a reliable commentator on the modes of the moment, makes a shrewd, if acid, female character say of a young woman: 'That type's particularly idiotic and the woods are full of them; they go shambling about London without hats and making asses of themselves.'

Shoes in the 'twenties had not been very interesting, being limited for the most part to Louis-heeled styles with pointed toes and either laced or strapped fronts for best and heavier versions with flatter straight heels for tougher wear. Now there was more variety and court shoes became fashionable both for day and evening, with moderate heels and rounded toes. The day ones were of crocodile, lizard and snakeskin as well as coloured suède and various other leathers. For evening they were of satin, dyed to match dresses, brocade or gold or silver kid. Sandals began to come into fashion and were very varied, with open toes, sling-back heels and everything from very high heels to none at all. Platform soles also appeared, anticipating a style that was to be more characteristic of the 'forties.

The fashions called for a long, slim look, and dieting became popular. Corsets, except for those who needed strict control, became progressively lighter, prettier and, as elastic materials improved, they were made more and more of elastic and without the menacing bones of past history. Brassières were generally worn and also became very attractive. They did not exaggerate the bust, but improved its contours. Underwear increased in elegance as it diminished in quantity, and by the end of the 'twenties briefs were being worn by the young. Pretty, wide-legged French knickers (which did not need to come from France) were the choice of everyone who wanted to be in fashion. Slim bias-cut slips and cami-knickers were other fashionable items of lingerie, made in silk or satin for those who could afford it, and in rayon of ever-improving quality for the less expensive end of the market.

The backless evening dress, the outstanding fashion of the 'thirties, had less affinity with past fashion history than with a new factor which was coming into the picture. This was the sun-bathing cult. Short, knee-length skirts had lasted for only a few years in the 'twenties, but by the end of the decade exposure not only of the legs but also of a considerable part of the body was very much in fashion on the beaches of the Riviera and California. Sunburn was for the first time sought and admired. It even had snob-appeal, for in the days before jet travel and package holidays opened up the world's playgrounds to millions, to go to these favoured places in the sun was a distinction. In the late 'twenties soaking up the sun on the Riviera was new, but it caught on quickly and the South of France became a very fashionable international playground, drawing people from all over Europe and also a great number of Americans, with Maxine Elliott as a bright particular star. All the old cover-up ideas about bathing and the beach went by the board. Beaches strewn with sprawling brown, or would-be brown, bodies had been unthought of in the past, when clothes for the promenade or even the beach were almost garden party in style, but now they became usual everywhere at home and abroad.

When the change came, in the 'twenties, it was very complete. One-piece bathing suits of clinging jersey had by the end of the decade not only become briefer but also often had pieces scooped out of them at the sides and were completely backless, with

118   Beach pyjamas. 1931

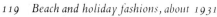
119   Beach and holiday fashions, about 1931

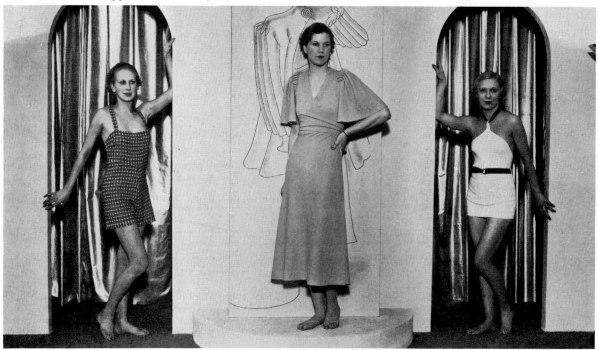

narrow shoulder straps or halter necks. Two-piece garments existed by 1929. Shorts were first worn in America but came over to Britain about this time, soon proving popular for cycling and on holiday. At first they were knee-length, but they soon became shorter. Beach pyjamas, with flaring legs, had been anticipated by slim lounging pyjamas, which Chanel was making in the early 'twenties and which were soon being worn by the fashionable. The beach ones, however, had a life of their own and were worn extensively on beaches everywhere, usually with backless sun-tops or sleeveless blouses. Sun dresses, bare-backed, also spread. It was the beginning of a new category of clothes, the start of the 'casuals' which were to have a great vogue in future years.

The new ideas brushed off on sports clothes, especially on the tennis courts. Alice Marble, the American player, introduced shorts at Wimbledon, where she wore them in 1933, five years after Lili de Alvarez, the brilliant Spanish player, had made her contribution to freedom in dress by wearing a just-below-the-knee culotte dress, designed by Schiaparelli.

Bare legs, also part of the sun-seekers' scene, also spread to tennis players. Joan Lycett appeared stockingless in 1929 and Eileen Fearnley Whittingstall was another early follower of this trend, which was soon generally adopted. Suzanne Lenglen wore a hat on her first appearance at Wimbledon in 1919, but from the following year she wore her famous bright coloured bandeaux. This style was very widely followed and the eye-shade, worn by Helen Wills from 1927, was also much copied for some years, until bare heads became general. Sunglasses were another part of the Riviera scene which spread elsewhere. They began along with the discarding of hats, another fashion which started in the South of France and California, but which took a long time to spread to towns and cities. The trouser suit, though it did not come into general fashion until a generation later, was worn by Marlene Dietrich in 1933 as a working outfit on the film set, and many other screen stars followed her lead.

With the 'thirties Paris began to make a different, additional impact as fashion spread more widely and more quickly. In the 'twenties nearly all the leaders there had been French. Now, as though with some occult knowledge that fashion was to become more international, the Paris designers also become international, with arrivals from many countries coming into prominence. Molyneux had begun the cycle of change. Mainbocher was an American from the Mid West who had gravitated into fashion from fashion drawing for *Vogue*. Piguet was Swiss, Maggy

120 A Mainbocher evening dress of 1936, in chiffon and embroidered lace with the new turban

Rouff Belgian, Balenciaga Spanish, Schiaparelli Italian. It was Schiaparelli who made the most dramatic contribution to fashion, starting her career in 1928 but leaving an influence that has lasted till today, though she retired in 1954 and closed down her house.

Elsa Schiaparelli was at once a high fashion creator and a fashion catalyst. She gave fashion a new direction and also initiated a kind of splinter movement that was the genesis of all the fantastic, way-out fashions which have been weaving their way through the late 'sixties and the 'seventies. In her endlessly inventive activities she was almost the Mary Quant of her day – but she was also something quite different and quite contradictory, being a past-master of formal elegance. She was an aristocrat of fashion as well as a rebel leader.

By 1928 and the arrival of Schiaparelli people were beginning to tire of the naiveté and figure-obliterating lines of the 'boyish' look and Schiaparelli voiced a view that was in key with the times when she declared that she 'felt that clothes had to be architectural; that the body must never be forgotten and it must be used as a frame is used in building . . . the more the body is respected, the better the dress acquires vitality'. Harmony had to be maintained in the way that the Greeks conceived it. Shape had to be restored: 'Up with the shoulders! Bring back the bust into its own! . . . Raise the waist to its forgotten original place!' That was one side of Schiaparelli. The world was ready for just such a change and the fashions of the 'thirties did all that she had proclaimed.

She is generally credited as being the originator of the squared, padded shoulders, first shown in *Vogue* in 1933, which prevailed continuously from then until the arrival of Christian Dior's New Look in 1947 and were the outstanding feature of pre-war and wartime fashions. The trend was seen everywhere, but she was its chief promoter. Shoulder pads were not only built into tailored clothes, but were used on everything and were on sale at all stores, ready to be tacked into all kinds of dresses. Sleeves were gathered at the shoulders to create a leg-o'-mutton look and to accommodate the pads. Such shoulders had a virtue not previously perceived – they emphasised the slenderness of the waist and hips. They were also, and this was probably a practical point in their favour, a heaven-sent blessing to the growing ready-to-wear trade because they did much to solve the besetting problem of making clothes in stock sizes which fitted properly at the shoulders. The new artificial width and padding covered individual differences and at the same time offered the manufac-

121 *'Bring back the waist': a Schiaparelli evening gown and cape of 1938 in a fabric designed for her by Dali*

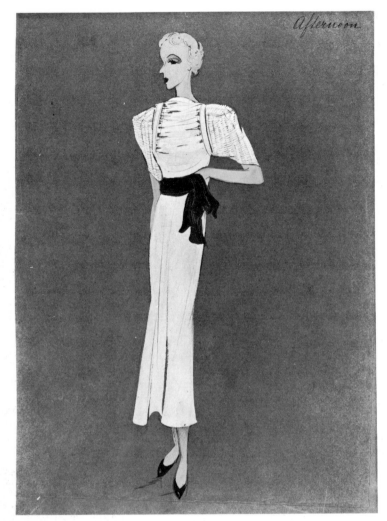

afternoon

*122   Built-up shoulderlines were gener-
ally attributed to Schiaparelli, but were
widely adopted. Worth, 1935*

turer a way of giving his clothes a tailored look that had something of the 'bespoke' in it.

Schiaparelli made formal clothes of great elegance, architec-
turally beautiful as she specified, and she made them for many
years with great success. But there was another quite different
side to her, and it was there that she started her business – literally
a one-woman one. She brought the exotic into fashion, when
she began designing hand-knitted jumpers which incorporated
motifs and patterns from negro, Cubist and Surrealist art. They
were knitted for her by immigrant Armenian women in Paris
(those inescapable, necessary immigrants who are the makers of
fashion!) and when she wore one at a smart luncheon party she
was spotted by a fashion buyer from an American store, who

ordered 40 on the spot, with matching skirts. This was daunting, as no facilities for skirt-making existed *chez* Schiaparelli, but she was undauntable and somehow the order was carried out and delivered. After that there was no going back or standing still and Schiaparelli moved on. From sweaters she branched out into tweed sports clothes and then to evening wear. She also launched culottes.

But what made her stand out from all other fashion-makers of the time was the immense range of her inventiveness. Collages made from newspaper cuttings were used as designs for fabrics for blouses, scarves and beachwear – an inspiration drawn from the newspaper hats worn by women workers she had seen in the fish markets of Copenhagen. Burnouses from North Africa, embroideries from Russia and Peru were the basis of fashions she created. Hessian was used for dresses and American cloth made dressing gowns. Tree bark, Cellophane, straw and glass were incorporated into fabrics used for clothes. Schiaparelli visited English and Scottish factories to study fabrics. She used tweeds woven in the island of Skye. She designed a range of materials for Viyella and designed clothes for that company. She made the bright pink, which she called Shocking, her hall mark.

With her, fantasy knew no bounds. In her own words, she 'set off cascades of fireworks'. Tweeds were used for evening clothes. Padlocks fastened belts. Buttons were animal masks, miniature guitars, paper-weights, feathers, lollipops, 'but not one', she said, 'looked like what a button was supposed to look like'. Fabrics were printed with elephants, clowns, horses. Brooches were phosphorescent. Handbags were shaped like balloons, or they lit up or played tunes when opened. One hat was in the shape of a shoe, with a Shocking pink heel – and fashion leader Mrs. Reginald Fellowes wore it. Another was a replica of a lamb cutlet, complete with frill, and this was Schiaparelli's own choice.

She worked with artists like Cocteau and Christian Bérard, who designed fabrics for her, as others before them had worked with Poiret. Salvador Dali created window effects for her, among them a fantastic bear with a stomach that was a chest of drawers. That was for the boutique she opened in 1935, which was the first of its kind and the model for what nearly all couturiers were to do in the future, as well as for a kind of independent shop that was to play a large part in fashion-making and fashion-selling about 25 years later. Lelong had opened a boutique in 1933, but it was different, created for selling his *'robes d'édition'* – a selection of less costly clothes which needed

123 *One of the sweaters with which Schiaparelli launched her fashion career in 1928. The knitted-in butterfly bow and fake scarf in white against black background were the precursors of many such* trompe l'oeil *devices*

124 *Schiaparelli hat in felt with lace brim. Jacket of pink silk brocade with circus horses, the buttons being leaping acrobats. Necklace of gilded pine cones attached with purple velvet bows to yellow grosgrain neckband. 1937–8*

only a limited amount of fitting. Schiaparelli's was for all her bright inventions.

Anita Loos, of *Gentlemen Prefer Blondes* fame, was her first private customer and in the 'thirties she dressed film stars galore, among them Marlene Dietrich, Claudette Colbert, Norma Shearer, Lauren Bacall, Gloria Swanson, Michèle Morgan, Constance Bennett and Simone Simon. When Mae West sent her a life-size plaster cast of herself in the pose of the Venus de Milo as a model for the dresses she had ordered for the Hollywood film *Sapphire Sal*, the figure inspired the shape of the bottle Schiaparelli used for her famous scent, *Shocking*. She went to America and worked in Hollywood, where top designer Adrian followed her lead with padded shoulders for the film star styles which everyone copied. That was how Greta Garbo and Joan Crawford became extreme embodiments of the built-up shoulder fashion, helping to spread it round the world. She went to London, and had a branch there until the outbreak of war in 1939. At that moment her latest success was the miniature 'doll's hat', which had a great vogue. In Paris, before the Fall of France, she caught the mood of the time with a 'cash and carry' collection, featuring enormous pockets to hold the shopping and day dresses adapted for evening, and also giving a special emphasis to Maginot Line blue and Foreign Legion red as colours. Starting with a lecture tour in America which had been arranged before the outbreak of war, she spent most of the war years in America.

One teasing fashion trend emerged briefly in 1939, to be engulfed by the war. After years of comparatively little change, of easy-fitting fashions, closely defined waists began to be seen in the Paris collections. Chanel showed a wasp-waisted full-skirted suit very unlike her prevailing style and Lelong also featured the tightly cinched waist and full skirt in dresses of the same season. Molyneux presented full dirndl skirts. *Vogue* rhapsodised on the beauty of a tiny waist and hinted, very gently, at the return of tight-lacing, declaring that 'The only thing you must have . . . is a tiny waist, held in if necessary by super-light-weight boned and laced corsets'. Events caught up with that fashion and it disappeared completely. What would have happened had war not broken out is mere speculation, but it is curious that in the New Look, the first post-war fashion to make a strong impact, a slim waist was featured. Had fashion just gone into cold storage during hostilities?

6 Developments in fashion manufacture between the wars, 1918–1939

I

The spread of ready-to-wear fashion between the wars was due to the facts that it had become easier to reproduce, that techniques were improving and that the stimulus thus given to the manufacturer coincided with the rise of a new, vastly increased demand for his products. More and more women were wage earners who did not want time-wasting fittings but had enough money to follow fashion and look beyond what was merely hard-wearing and 'safe' – never drastically out of fashion but never really in it. The status symbol aspect of fashion was losing its importance; class distinctions were becoming blurred in dress just as they were in the world at large. An era of inexpensive fashion had begun, in which change and variety were more valued than costly impressiveness. Stores and dress shops

125 *Inexpensive dresses were shown in store catalogues like this one of 1924. Many colours were available, but no mention is made of sizes*

responded to the need by introducing new, more varied ready-to-wear departments stocked with moderately priced clothes and by drawing attention to this in advertisements and catalogues. 'In the rush of modern life,' said one famous London store in the early 'twenties, 'many women of today have not the leisure to have their clothes made to order, as they have no time for fittings and other incidental details. . . . To meet the ever-increasing demand for fashionable up-to-date ready to wear coats, costumes and gowns, we have recently produced a number of models . . . all moderately priced, and at the same time embodying the style, cut and workmanship of a garment made to order.' Previously they had stressed their made-to-order facilities in great detail.

This was the top end of a trade which at this time was full of variations. Until the end of the 'twenties British ready-to-wear fashion was a conglomerate of good, bad and indifferent design and manufacture, without any clear lines of demarcation. The producers varied from substantial, fairly efficient manufacturers, usually individuals or private companies, and the still busy workrooms of big stores, to small workshops, again sometimes highly skilled and at others little more than botchers. Many small firms would make anything and everything, taking on all orders and switching, as one man who was in the trade in the early nineteen-twenties recalls, from footmen's uniforms to women's evening coats and dresses at the drop of a hat. On one occasion, he adds, he was even asked to make a woman's riding habit for a friend of the factory owner. He had scarcely seen such a thing before, but he was a craftsman and, with much toil and trouble, it was completed successfully.

The development of the manufacture of women's fashions in the first post-war decade was authoritatively surveyed in 1928 by S. P. Dobbs who, in *The Clothing Workers of Great Britain*, says: 'Women's garments are now for the first time being made in bulk by factory methods. Very soon it seems as if only the most exclusive men's and women's garments will be made by hand, so that dressmaking and tailoring will be purely luxury trades.' His investigations showed, however, that there was still a great lack of standards, with every imaginable kind of production and distribution of men's and women's apparel co-existing in factories carrying anything from 5 to 5000 employees. Increasing changes of fashion and the desire for individuality were inhibiting technical developments in the women's outerwear trade, because short production runs encouraged the continuation of handicraft methods and small workrooms.

Light dressmaking was pursuing its own rather easier course. 'A very large number of mantles and gowns, dresses, blouses and even underclothes are made in the workshops of department stores and drapers and fashionable modistes', where, on the whole, good working conditions prevailed. Of 50,000 dress workers in London, Mr. Dobbs says, about 25,000 were in wholesale production, the rest with retailers or private dressmakers.

Since 1914, he records, the status of the women's clothing industry had been greatly improved by fresh legislation, especially the setting up of new Trade Boards in 1918 and 1919. These laid down the 48-hour week, which remained for the next 25 years, and minimum rates of pay. The situation was further helped by better, though still imperfect union representation, and by improvements in techniques, including the use of more power-driven machinery. This constituted 'a minor industrial revolution, so that industry which before the war was disorganised . . . is now comparatively well organised, and usually carried on in a factory or large workshop'. Like many other students of the clothing trade before and after him, Mr. Dobbs permits himself a hopeful forecast: 'The time is perhaps not distant when clothing will take its place beside textiles, engineering, shipbuilding and the other staple trades of the country, in which nation-wide organisation accompanies a considerable degree of uniformity of methods and conditions. And yet, at the present moment, the variety we are faced with is sufficiently bewildering.' It has remained so ever since, and in some respects never more so than in the present 'seventies. Immense progress has, indeed, been made, but it co-exists to this day with the persistence of the bewildering variety which blurred the picture in 1928.

The growth and development of manufacturers, many to be powers in themselves in future years but most of them starting as small operators, is one of the biggest between-wars stories of fashion-making in Britain. Names and reputations were established, many of them bringing distinctive features and their owners 'signatures' to the clothes they designed and made. They developed better techniques. They acquired modern factories. A substantial number began to sell their fashions under their own branded names, many of which soon became well-known and some of which remain famous today. The earliest advertisements by named British manufacturers, dealing in 'wholesale and export only', appeared in *Vogue* in the early 'twenties, but it was not till towards the end of that decade that branded fashions

126   *Elegance in a ready to wear evening dress of 1928. Fuller skirt and dipping hemline*

began to be widely advertised for the retail market as 'obtainable from all the best houses in the country', 'obtainable at leading outfitters all over the world', often with lists of main stockists quoted.

This was the start of a new cycle of fashion-making and fashion-selling which was to become a main means of bringing fashion to millions of women. It was created in most cases by the enterprise of individuals who rose out of the existent conglomerate of manufacturers, transforming small workshops or modest family businesses into substantial companies. Some of the giants of today started to grow at this time. As in the case of the department stores, this phase of fashion is a series of individual success stories, the courses of which follow fairly similar lines, and exemplify what was happening to fashion manufacture over a wide area.

In the process of advancement America, though she had never claimed to have originated ready-to-wear fashion, developed it well ahead of Britain and the rest of the world. Immediately after World War I she moved rapidly to a point in efficient large-scale production which Britain took some ten more years to reach. She introduced technological improvements in production, including powered cutting machines, a decade before Britain. British manufacturers owed – and readily acknowledged – a great debt to America.

There were various reasons for America's lead. There too the new generation of working women had no time for custom-made fashion, but the rise of large-scale manufacture was further

stimulated by the existence of a vast market. Fashion could be thought of in terms of long production-runs because the clothes could be distributed over immense areas. America had, too, the great new asset of Hollywood as a pace-setter in popular-style fashion. The industry in America also benefitted from the fact that it made a later start, so that mass production in the contemporary style of other major industries was natural to it. It was not inhibited, as Britain was, by a long tradition of handicraft methods which clung to British production long after mechanisation could have replaced many of them. This tradition did, however, result in the British ready-to-wear trade having higher standards of manufacture than America – and it kept this quality while adopting American expertise.

Recalling the state of British wholesale fashion in the early 'thirties, Harry Yoxall, later chairman and managing director of British *Vogue,* said: 'It was half a generation behind the ready-to-wear trade that I have seen when working for American *Vogue.*' The American fashion-setters had installed themselves firmly in Seventh Avenue, New York, which became a synonym for ready-to-wear fashion in a way that contrasted with the scattered production areas in Britain. And, once installed there, the Americans forged ahead. American designers soon began to be known by name for clothes that had a new, slick look, one of the first of such designers being Jane Derby, whose main inspiration came from the classic simplicity of Chanel.

The time-lag between Britain and America applied to clothing in general and not only to fashion. Referring to America, Dr.

Margaret Wray, in *The Women's Outerwear Industry*, says that 'from the second half of the nineteenth century onwards there was developing a ready-made clothing industry that was far in advance, in size, in the use of machinery and in the quality of its products, of the men's clothing industry in this country, where, even as late as 1914, there was a tendency to regard ready-made men's clothing as rather cheap and nasty'. When it did start to develop on factory lines, British men's ready-made clothing took its lead from America, using machines for sewing, cutting and pressing which had been invented from 1850 onwards but which were not brought into use till much later in the men's trade, and still later in fashion-making – understandably, in the latter case, because there had to be great changes in the end product before such devices could be used profitably. That was not until after 1918, when the simpler styles of women's clothes made factory production effective, while the rapidly-growing retail market made it an attractive proposition for the enterprising maker-up. Dr. Wray sums up the developments which took place at this time: 'Between the wars, factory production of ready-made garments gradually replaced bespoke production as the main source of women's outerwear supplies. This placed the industry technically in advance of any other country except the United States. But, in comparison with many other industries, (even with other clothing industries) women's outerwear can be regarded as a very young industry in 1939.'

One man whose life in fashion from this time covered more varied ground than most was Julian Lee, later president of Britain's Apparel and Fashion Industry's Association, the main organisation which represented the lighter side of the fashion industry, and, for five years, until March 1971, AFIA's representative of manufacturers on the Clothing Economic Development Committee. His career was typical. He started work in 1921 in a family business that made blouses and dresses. It originally had only a sample workroom with a few machinists, a cutting room and some finishers, sending garments to out-workers to be made up and receiving them back for finishing and pressing. He recalled that in his early days he would cut out as many as 300 individually sized dresses and costumes per week, all in different styles, materials and colours, for special orders for stores and shops.

Soon he started developing, moving to bigger premises in Golden Lane, in the City, exchanging the treadle machines for power-operated ones and acquiring special machines for various processes, including hem-stitching, overlocking, button-sewing

Below, right: A dress in one of the new checked linen and cotton mixtures; it has a square yoke buttoned up on to the sleeves, and is worn with a silk scarf filling in the square neck line

Below: A good afternoon coat in linen and wool tweed. It is fitted to the waist, and, has raglan sleeves carried up to form a high collar, through which is slotted a fringed silk scarf

A tailored sun-dress in check linen, which is worn over a blouse and shorts, a combination which will be seen a great deal on beaches this summer

The shorts and blouse, shown separately, are severely tailored in pastel linen, with a black patent leather belt, and black pocket-tab and buttons

Right: A classic tailored dress for one of the new repp linens; it has sleeves in one with the yoke, deep pleats back and front, and a patent leather belt

Centre: A more "dressy" linen frock which the older woman will find becoming; it is in pale blue linen piped with navy, and has cornet pleats on each side of the bodice

Above: A formal afternoon outfit in linen; the dress is white, the jacket navy with white flower buttons. It has the new fronts not meeting, but fastened with a tab

and felling. He soon built up a large business with wholesalers, whose salesmen took out his sample garments and passed on orders to him as they received them from shops. They had their own labels for the garments Mr. Lee made, and they provided their own boxes for dispatching the clothes to the retailers. At the same time Mr. Lee branched out into mail order business, for a leading firm in this activity. By the late 'twenties he was manufacturing clothes which carried his firm's name and was building up an export business. In 1928 he started a pioneer venture for the women's ready-made trade of the time by making stock outsize garments with a range of from 42-inch to 60-inch hips – at this time three sizes were the usual maximum and none of them catered for the larger figure. Technically he was also on the move, and in this year he was already experiment-

130 Joan Crawford in a 1930's dress with the exaggerated built-up sleeves which she helped to promote

ing with new Bellow cutters, constructed rather like secateurs, which he had imported from America, and was developing on bulk production lines.

In 1933 he established the name Marley Gowns for an inexpensive-to-medium range of fashions, and by 1939 the capacity of his company was 10,000 garments a week. These were made by the combination of an indoor staff of about 70 and the use of sub-contractors, most of them with factories of their own geared up to large-scale manufacture. He was an early pioneer of popular-priced beaded dresses, with a table of about 12 beaders to carry out the hand beading that was fashionable in the late 'twenties and early 'thirties for the dance frocks then in enormous demand. Popular fashion, he recalls, was still one season behind couture, as public taste still moved at a fairly slow pace. He was designer as well as general administrator. In the 'thirties a new fashion influence reached its peak – that of Hollywood. Mr. Lee produced what were known to the trade and public as the Joan Crawford dress (with a long white roll collar caught up at one side above the waist) and the Ginger Rogers coat (with a caracul collar and three caracul buttons). Both sold in thousands.

A different picture of fashion in the 'thirties comes from the late Mr. S. Cope, till 1980 managing director of Eastex, part of the great Ellis and Goldstein group. At this time he was in the family retail business of Copé, which had high-class fashion shops in Harrogate and Glasgow. Paris was still the lure in that sphere, and he recalls not only buying models in Paris as the basis of the business but also bringing over French fitters to join the staff of the shops and serve the needs of the exclusive clientèle which was still Paris orientated.

'Before World War I there was no such thing as organised fashion production in Britain and the impetus which brought it into existence between the wars and led to the growth of large-scale manufacture came from America. Making up there was years ahead of Britain, especially in dresses, which were more and more ousting the skirt and blouse which had been the "uniform" of the ordinary woman in pre-1914 days.' That is the view of Max Radin, who has lived through the change and taken a substantial part in bringing it about. He started as a contractor in 1932 with four sewing machines bought on hire purchase and a small makeshift factory which had been a stock house. He developed rapidly in the inexpensive dress trade, in the 'thirties, introducing Rhona Roy dresses, and in 1946 formed his present company, Ramar, of which he is managing director. In addition to his own range, he also manufactures extensively for Marks and Spencer.

The inexpensive dress, he recalls, started its life mainly in the home workshop, which was responsible for a large amount of fashion, and it was at first made in one size only. Specialist dress shops were increasing, especially after the 1914–1918 war, and alterations were an accepted part of their existence. Skilled labour for this was still obtainable – and cheap. This did not alter the fact that sizing – or the lack of it – was the great defect of British manufacturing, because it meant that a considerable number of women could not wear ready-made dresses at all, so far away were they from the 'standard' measurements, which, incidentally, varied greatly from one maker to another. When different sizes were attempted, the old principle of adding or subtracting an inch all round one pattern was still flourishing – and was still failing to work, because women are not made that way.

Sizing is the most important factor in ready-to-wear fashion, but British manufacturers were slow to realise it. It was not tackled until the early 'thirties, when certain enlightened British fashion men brought over a little band of American experts who introduced systematic and detailed sizing on the lines that had given America its lead in fashion manufacture. The first arrival was Sam Krohnberg, who came over about 1933 to join the company which had been set up to make Peggy Page dresses, a range that is still flourishing and comes top in the current profitability tables. He introduced American sizing and also set new standards of manufacture and planned production.

His brother, Lou Krohnberg, followed him soon afterwards and also helped British sizing at this time, working for Ellis and Goldstein. Another American, Joe Luchs, started making dresses in Britain under the name of the De Luxe Company and contributed substantially to the improvements in current sizing, styling and manufacture. Hollywood dresses was another range started in Britain under American direction.

Another American who was to have a great influence on the development of British ready-to-wear was Jack Liss, who came to Britain from the U.S.A. about 1935, operating at first as an importer of cheap but fashionable American dresses, which he sold to the stores at 5s. each. He was, however, an expert technician and he started business on his own by forming the Jack Liss Dress Company to manufacture better quality dresses on American lines under the name Princess Dresses. He was also connected with the making of Laura Lee Dresses, started by

131   Inexpensive fashion spreads. A corded crepe evening gown selling at £2 and a lace evening ensemble costing £3 at a London store in 1933

another American, and from this stemmed today's Wendy Dresses. In addition to great expertise in styling, he was adept at pattern-making and grading of a standard unknown in Britain until his arrival. He also had an outstanding feeling for fashion.

Under this American stimulus a great vogue for pretty but inexpensive ready-to-wear dresses spread and led to the arrival of many new dress houses in the inter-war years and to bringing factory methods and better quality production into the popular area of fashion. The Americans were specialists in operating within a specified price group and in gearing their production to a fixed level, and this was of great benefit to British manufacturers. Under their lead well-defined ranges now began to appear in Britain. There was Kitty Copeland, started by John Cope, and Rhona Roy, already mentioned as the creation of Max Radin. The various lines with feminine names became known in the trade as 'the chorus girls'. A basic idea behind many of the ranges now appearing was to produce dresses in a range of reliable sizes which could be sold wholesale for 15s. and retailed at a guinea. The immense chains of Guinea Gown Shops all over the country in the 'thirties were something new to British fashion and were welcomed rapturously, especially by the young of that time, in much the same way as the popular boutiques were to be acclaimed by the next generation. Historically the interest of the Guinea Gown Shops was that they marked a step forward in the production of popular fashion on a large-scale manufacturing basis and with a range of sizes which, if not perfect (and where sizing is concerned perfection is still being sought), were a considerable advance on what had previously been available.

In the 'thirties, too, imports of U.S. dresses were immense. Complete lines would be bought by stores, one large group buying 100,000 at a time. Immense quantities of American materials, chiefly cotton, were also bought for making up in Britain. This lasted until 1939, when most of the Americans went home, and in the post-war world fashion developed on new and different lines.

2

It was natural that, with improving techniques, ready-to-wear fashion should go up in the world. This was also encouraged by changing social conditions. The heavy unemployment in Britain in the 'thirties and ever-rising taxation helped to put a curb on extravagant dressing, just as America's economic troubles were doing, and even those who could still afford it usually realised that it was out of keeping with the times. Fashion was on the move out of the couture level to something less expensive. The demand was increasing for good quality ready-to-wear fashion which would appeal to the big stores and speciality shops by attracting the clientèle of the previous bespoke trade. This meant good manufacture, sizing and finishing.

To meet this need there rose in Britain what became known as wholesale couture. If this seems something of a contradiction in terms, it none the less describes fairly aptly a kind of fashion that linked the two worlds. Paris was accepted as the leader, the inspiration, and her seasonal 'line' was followed, but it was adapted to the needs of manufacturing techniques and to the everyday lives of fashion-conscious women among the great middle classes. This area of fashion, which was to develop considerably independence of design, soon became an important one and has remained so until today.

Its rise is personified in the career of one of its pioneers and leading spirits, Lou Ritter. A man whom his associates in the fashion world describe as standing head and shoulders above all others, he has had more than 50 years' practical experience in fashion. He had a link with the early days of fashion manufacture, because his father was an outworker who started by making clothes for wholesalers who supplied shops and stores. In 1919, at the age of 15, Lou Ritter began work in the small factory which his father had by then established. He recalls going through all sections of the factory, and declares that the chief thing that struck him was how primitive sizing was at that time, with every size being cut from a single pattern. When he was 19, in 1923, he went into the retail trade, opening three dress shops, where he sold garments made by his father. He disliked it intensely, chiefly because 'the sizes were all wrong'. Nine out of ten garments had to be altered, which for him meant working all through Saturdays and Sundays to make them fit the customer. In 1927 he started manufacturing on his own, concentrating on sizing and selling direct to shops, with two representatives to cover the country and London as his own 'territory'. The business grew from small beginnings, and he was among the first to adopt American sizings for the high quality fashions he was now making. Leading stores began to buy from him and in 1936 he started his still-famous brand, Dereta, and took his first full page advertisement in British *Vogue*. He did business with Harrods from 1929, working closely with their buyers in adapting Paris couture lines to ready-to-wear and also observing

132   Copy of a Paris model of 1929. Printed crepe de Chine dress with self coloured silk coat lined with printed fabric

133   A three piece of 1935 by Dorville

fashion trends in Germany, where the ready-to-wear firms were, he recalls, much quicker on the draw than Britain so far as Paris was concerned. Dereta has remained a top name in fashion ever since those days.

A notable part in the development of high quality ready-to-wear fashion was taken by Olive O'Neill, for quarter of a century the designer, and latterly also managing director, of Dorville. Her main achievement was to give her own authority to the adaptation of Paris couture to the needs of her sector of the ready-to-wear market. She left art school in her native Southport under a cloud because she insisted on mixing colours like royal blue and turquoise, rose pink and orange in her fashion designs. In this she was, as often again, ahead of the general fashion, but it was the only time she failed to be accepted. After designing fashions on a small scale for a Southport shop she came to London and joined Rose and Blairman, who had come early to the 'brand' market by adopting the name Dorville for the imported knitwear which was their first area of fashion soon after World War I. In the late 'twenties she started supplementing the knitwear with the classic clothes that became her hall-mark. They were clothes with a casual elegance which was to be an important part of Britain's contribution to the fashion scene from that time.

When she began designing Olive O'Neill set up a factory to make the clothes under her own supervision, starting with five machinists but expanding until she had 500. She too was profoundly dissatisfied with the current British standards of manufacture and, above all, with current sizing. She met and was greatly impressed with Jack Liss and as a result, under his influence, she adopted American methods of sizing, grading and manufacture. She went to New York and brought back an American-trained factory manager, Vasso Amergo, who ran the factory for many years. She studied American sizing on the spot by going over to New York again and bringing back a pattern-maker who became the first to apply the American sizing system in full to British-made fashion. Also from America came two machinists to teach her British factory workers how to use the considerable number of American 'gadgets' which were the next things to arrive at the factory. Each year, both before and after World War II, she went to America to see what was happening in the production field, and when she found something that was suitable for her needs she would go off hotfoot to its source to get it for her factory.

Another innovation which was to snowball in later years was her close association with fabric manufacturers. She worked personally with Stevensons of Dungannon, co-operating with their technicians in the production of special materials and colours for her use. She worked similarly with Heathcoats and later on, in the 'fifties, was responsible for her company being entrusted with a large-scale pilot scheme to launch Courtelle with a million pound advertising and promotion campaign to put it across to the fashion world – which was done with resounding success. This kind of tie-up between fabric or fibre manufacture and fashion house has now become an important part of fashion promotion.

Fashion in our time owes much to Frederick Starke, not only as a manufacturer but also as a leader in creating a structure that would make the fashion industry effective at home and overseas. Appropriately, he was born into fashion. The name had been known there since the beginning of this century, when his grandfather established his company, A. Starke and Co. in Great Portland Street, thus becoming one of the first fashion manufacturers to operate in the area which has become the great West End centre of the fashion trade. The firm next became Madame Starke, being taken over by Frederick Starke's mother before 1914, when she ran it and was also its designer. Frederick Starke himself was a late starter in the trade into which he was born. It was three years after he left University College, where he read commerce and modern languages, that it suddenly came to him that fashion should be his business. That was in the late 1920's. Soon afterwards his mother retired and he set up a company under his own name – the first wholesaler to use his name as the brand one. After war service in the R.A.F., when he also managed to keep the firm together, he was, in 1945, the first manufacturer to show a wholesale collection in the couture way – with set presentations to buyers at specified times and with a team of top model girls wearing fully accessorised clothes. This innovation spread through the trade rapidly and flourished for many years, becoming a major event in the world of fashion manufacture and selling.

Case histories like these are representative of the 'top end' of the fashion trade's growth during the significant 'thirties. The fashion business at this level was then largely in the hands of private companies or partnerships, most of which were to go public or to disappear in the post-war years, when fashion became big business. In the 'thirties they usually had small factories and they were in many cases also served by the increasing number of small workshops, sub-contractors and home workers. It was quite usual for fashion houses to have their own

135 (centre) *Cardigan suit of 1930 in tweed-knit wool, worn with fashionable beret*

136 (right) *The popular dress and coatee of 1930, in lace*

134 (left) *Fashion in the significant 'thirties, when ready to wear made great advances. Great variety was achieved. A tea gown of 1930 in georgette, with the natural waistline, tucks on fitted hip-line and longer skirt with uneven hem*

designers, to do their own cloth-buying and to make up their prototype models in a model or sample room, but to use outside sources of labour for the actual manufacture. This procedure is still being used extensively in both Britain and America. It is particularly favoured by the more creative and avant-garde folk in the fashion business, who do not wish to see their clothes mass-produced or to have the onus of managing and financing a factory laid upon their shoulders.

The use of sub-contractors and outworkers was given a further stimulus in the 'thirties by the new influx of refugees from Europe, especially from Germany and Austria as the Hitler régime gained force and Jewish persecutions reached a new ferocity. Many of these immigrants were, as in the past, skilled tailors and dressmakers and they were readily absorbed into the industry, fortunately under much better working conditions and with better rates of pay than in the old days of sweated labour, but with much improvement in working conditions still needed. Many of them were expert in women's fashion-making, especially in Continental styling.

A considerable number of the new arrivals operated in small workshops and factories, often based on family units or with racial links. Dr. Margaret Wray records that in London alone such small manufacturing units increased from 250 to 750 between 1930 and 1939. They were well adapted to the versatility and variety of fashion, and were able to specialise in certain kinds of manufacture which would be difficult for the large factory to undertake, as they would involve training of an uneconomic kind, with limited uses.

Another incentive to the production of fashion was given by the imposition in 1931 of import duties on all cloth and wearing apparel. A considerable amount of women's fashions had been imported from Germany and America, and as these now became more costly British manufacturers were given an impetus to expand their production and to facilitate this by making fuller use of the technical developments which stemmed from the U.S.A. The import duties also encouraged the production in Britain of light-weight fabrics for fashion wear, many of which had previously been imported from the Continent, mainly from France and Italy.

The result of all these factors was that the British ready-to-wear fashion trade made substantial progress. In January 1932 *Vogue* carried an announcement about the 'London Fashions

137   More variety from 1938 ready to wear. Elegant day fashions worn with the fashionable fox furs

138   Many types of manufacturer contributed to the increasing variety of fashion. Here a trio of knitwear designs for spring 1937, made in a London store's own factory

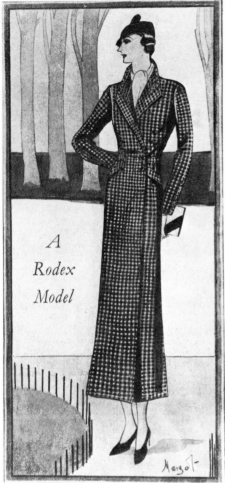

139 (and facing page) Rodex coats were established in fashion in the 'thirties. As country classics they were depicted in the very elongated style of fashion drawing which prevailed. Early 1930's

Group, composed of members of the leading wholesale fashion houses in London' and having as its purpose 'to establish London as a definite fashion centre and consolidate the reputation of London fashions throughout the world'.

By the mid-thirties top fashion houses promoting their own brands also included Vivian Porter and Matita (both very early on the scene in the 'twenties), Stefney, Koupy, Mary Black, Brenner Sports, and Mercia. During these and the following pre-war years there appeared a considerable number of other names that were to become famous for the large-scale manufacture of medium priced fashions. They included Thomas Marshall (Marlbeck) of Leeds, an early arrival in the 'twenties; Tootals of Bolton, with Chesro dresses, in 1930; Windsmoor, in the early 'thirties and Berkertex, in 1936. Other companies, already established, branched out at this time with brand names. Among them were Steinbergs which, founded in 1904, had become a substantial fashion producer and in 1929 decided to market their fashions under the name Alexon. Later they introduced a further range, Dellbury, to cover high class coats and suits. By 1939 Alexon was an established name not only in Britain but also abroad.

During the 'twenties and 'thirties the men's clothing trade was being developed very actively by companies which made the garments and also sold them to the public through their own shops – Montagu Burton, Hepworths and others did this. Women's fashions were not, on the whole, dealt with in this way, but were usually sold in the early days to wholesalers and later to store and shop buyers, who either called at the manufacturer's showroom or were visited by his representatives. There were, however, some notable exceptions to this procedure. These were nearly all companies which had long been concerned with the manufacture of men's as well as women's clothes and they extended their methods of direct selling to the public to include the latter, in which many of them became increasingly involved. Burberrys had been making women's clothes of many kinds, both made-to-measure and, latterly, also ready-made, since the turn of the century. Aquascutum, which had started in men's wear before the mid-nineteenth century, had similarly begun making women's coats and costumes in 1909. Both sold direct from their own shops as well as building up their own wholesale businesses for selling to other stores and shops.

In the late 'twenties Jaeger rather suddenly developed on similar lines and became a significant force in fashion. This company had been started right outside fashion, being founded in 1883 by a City business man, Lewis Tomalin, in pursuit of a health crusade to convert the public to the use of fabrics made only from animal fibres, as advocated by Dr. Gustav Jaeger, of Stuttgart. At first the garments were imported from Germany and sold in a London shop opened by Mr. Tomalin, who had acquired the rights in Jaeger for Britain and the U.S.A. After about five years manufacture began in Britain. Jaeger clothing, both outerwear and underwear, was popularised by leading intellectuals as a result of the enthusiastic advocacy of George Bernard Shaw, and it was made fashionable by being taken up by Oscar Wilde and his circle. Business grew, further Jaeger shops were opened and a wholesale side was started in the 1890's. There was a mild injection of fashion into women's Jaeger outerwear at the beginning of this century when H. F. Tomalin, son of the founder and an enthusiast for *art nouveau*, introduced designs inspired by this trend, but, of course, in pure wool. Emphasis in the Jaeger business was still strongly on the original health principles.

Traditional Jaeger garments had a regular faithful following, but times were changing and in the general slump of the late 'twenties it was felt that a completely different presentation was needed. Maurice Gilbert, a young man who had had a meteoric career in Selfridges, was engaged to run the Jaeger shops and was given *carte blanche* to formulate and carry out a policy for them. He went all out for fashion development. Forming the conclusion that Jaeger fabrics were wonderful but the styling appalling, he brought in a former colleague from Selfridges, Anne Terrill, as designer and proceeded to launch Jaeger into fashion with a Chanel-type suit as the first *tour de force*. The spearhead of his activities was the Jaeger shop, then in Oxford Street, which acquired a spectacular new look, emerging from the era of shop mahogany into a brave new world of chromium and glass, designed by Frederick Etchells. Massive advertising started and if the Jaeger die-hards were appalled by it all, the Duchess of York (now Queen Elizabeth the Queen Mother) said 'I do like your advertising; it's so amusing', and the then Prince of Wales (the late Duke of Windsor) declared about this time that 'British industry has to adopt, adapt and improve' – at which Jaeger took new heart. The production of elegant, fashionable clothes at moderate prices developed, the company claiming that 'Thanks to Jaeger you can no longer tell a shop girl from a Duchess'. They made quality clothes of outstanding style, with a character of their own. They made for the new young market which was growing rapidly. They were pioneers in the co-ordination of

140 *Jaeger fashions about 1931*

colours, which is still a feature of their fashions today. 'We don't sell clothes, we dress women,' said Mr. Gilbert, explaining the importance of this matching policy. From this time onwards it would have been difficult to find at Jaeger anything which Dr. Gustav Jaeger would recognise as of his inspiration, but *requiescat in pace* – small quantities of the original porridge-coloured underwear is still made for export and is much sought after in, of all places, Hong Kong!

Another early source of direct selling to the public was the Co-operative movement, although clothing was, of course, only a comparatively small part of its activities. At the turn of the century it had 1,717,000 members and a yearly turn-over of £50 millions. By 1914 membership had risen to 3,153,000 and the turnover to £88 millions. The Co-operatives rose along with the prosperity of the working classes and were favoured by regular wage earners and small salaried people. Their link with fashion, at any rate in the earlier part of this century, was more significant as opening the way to the later great spread of multiple stores as a popular source of fashion than in the degree of its influence on the fashion industry.

Between the wars multiple stores were increasing rapidly and catching up with the department stores, which had mostly attained their peak, but the area of activity of the multiples was at first mainly concerned with the increasingly large and prosperous working classes. The growth of mass media of communication – the cinema, radio, the press and all forms of advertising – was, however, bringing in uniformity of standards of taste among the populace, and this led to a further spread of fashion and therefore to countrywide chains of shops that could satisfy the immense new needs. In *St. Michael. A History of Marks and Spencer* Goronwy Rees records that there were 300 variety chain stores throughout Britain in 1924 and 1302 in 1939. The total number of multiple shops was 24,713 in 1920 and 44,487 in 1939. They were not, of course, all selling fashions.

It was, in fact, not till the 1920's that what Michael Marks had started in the 1880's as a penny bazaar became concerned with fashion. Although it had been established as a chain store in 1894, the between-the-wars price limit of 5s. greatly restricted its fashion activities. The years between 1918 and 1926 were described by Lord Marks as 'the formative period' of the Company, when policies were shaped, largely as a result of frequent visits to America made by him from 1924 for the purpose of studying administration, business and stock control methods there. The policy of Marks and Spencer from then onwards was 'adopted very largely as a result of the lessons which the chairman had learned in America'. The move towards concentration on women's fashions as one main area of merchandise began, largely as part of this policy, in the 'thirties, when manufacturing methods had advanced sufficiently for it to be possible to contemplate producing popular fashions within the 5s. ceiling price. The working girl and the woman of limited means now wanted 'clothes that were inexpensive, light, comfortable and attractive, as befitted her new status in society'. This demand was an important development in social history. 'One might perhaps say,' comments Goronwy Rees, 'that the discarding of the steel or whalebone corset, the flannel petticoat, in favour of a webbed elastic girdle and cotton or artificial silk underclothing, did more for women's emancipation than the

141   Inexpensive ready to wear fashions in 1934

Summer in Town

Left: Two afternoon outfits, the first in a pale beige crêpe de chine with darker beige spots, the coat trimmed with blue fox. The second in black crêpe with white spots and green with white spots; white hat and collar

Three versions of the useful straw boater hat, showing the variations in the sizes of the crown

Right: Suit of heavy printed silk with pleated skirt and tight-waisted jacket with frills; muslin blouse

vote.' That process of discarding was not brought to the mass of women until Marks and Spencer and other multiple stores took up their cause in the 'twenties and 'thirties. To do so they had to work closely with manufacturers and potential manufacturers, because it was not their policy to set up their own factories. Specialisation in textiles and food as their main activities was established by Marks and Spencer in the 'thirties, when those two commodities accounted for 90% of their business. In 1936 two-thirds of their turnover came from textiles. Between 1929 and 1939 the number of stores increased from 126 to 234, some of them rebuilt, and the floor area increased from 365,000 square feet to 2,206,000 square feet. Although real development in fashion was to be a post-war story, the structure it was to follow was laid down in the 'thirties, when close collaboration with manufacturers, open display, self-selection and fixed prices were already established.

7 Fashion by decree during and after World War II, 1939–1947

I

The Second World War changed every aspect of civilian life in Britain, regimenting it for everyone in large things and small by legislation which was needed because of the dislocation of everyday existence. Air raids meant that everyone was liable to be in the battle line and evacuation reshaped whole communities. From December 1941 the conscription of women was authorised and young women without the responsibility of children could be – and were – directed into war work. Great numbers of them joined the women's services. For civilians there was a scarcity of almost every commodity. Fashion which, in the 1914–1918 war had been left to make its own adjustments to a much less abnormal situation on the home front, was now subjected not only to the pressure of events but also to a large degree of control by government decrees. What you wore, how it was made, what it cost and what you bought – all that had ceased to be solely your personal concern. Nothing like this had ever happened before. In ancient Rome and in some parts of Europe in the Middle Ages people below a certain rank had been forbidden by sumptuary laws to wear certain types of garments, but what happened now was different because it applied to the whole community, regardless of wealth or rank.

The effect was drastic. Paris, the fountainhead of fashion, disappeared in the summer of 1940 so far as Britain, America and the rest of the 'free world' were concerned, and it did not emerge again until the Liberation of France in 1944, when the autumn collections were announced as 'the first free demonstration of the couture since 1940'. After the fall of France some of the Paris houses had resumed work in 1940 under the German occupation, with Lucien Lelong leading the Chambre Syndicale de la Couture Parisienne. In so doing they inevitably had to

143   Women at war. Ambulance drivers awaiting an emergency at a Chelsea garage are trouser-clad but have neat hair-styles or turbans. 1940

144   Everyone was liable to be in the battle line. Nurses and air raid wardens on duty in the London blitz. 1941

145   For the A.T.S. a military-style uniform based on that worn by men in the army. 1939–45

146   Land girls pause to watch fighters returning in July

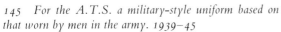

accept German clients throughout the hated Occupation, but they also contrived to maintain Paris as a fashion centre and to frustrate the German plan to move the whole of French couture, lock, stock and barrel, to Berlin and Vienna. This was a constant threat, outmanoeuvred by the efforts and the ingenuity of Lelong and his fellow designers. Other couturiers operated in the unoccupied zone. Others went out of France for the duration of the European war. Schiaparelli went to America, as did Mainbocher, who has been established there ever since then, giving considerable lustre to the development of American fashion. Molyneux went home to London and Angèle Delanghe also set up business there; others went out of business for the duration and Chanel disappeared for 15 years.

In Britain the dual problems of shortages of labour and of materials for clothing the civilian population led to action being started early in the war by Ernest Bevin, who, in Churchill's coalition government, began to shape the Utility scheme which was introduced in May 1941, with rationing of clothes following in June. From then on, clothes could be bought only by the surrender of fixed numbers of the very limited quota of coupons given to everyone biannually. The Utility scheme involved at first 50% and later 85% of all cloth manufactured, controlling its quality and price. In 1942 a series of Making of Clothes (Restrictions) Orders was introduced, covering nearly all clothing. The use of trimmings was curtailed, the maximum width and length of skirts were specified and the number of pleats was restricted, as was the amount of cloth used in each garment. Clothing manufacturers were limited in the number of styles they could make within a given period. Minimum standards of making-up were established.

By traditional definition this looked like the total suspension of fashion and some experts, writing soon after the war, considered that this had been the case. Dr. Willett Cunnington described the clothes of the war years as 'domestic battle dress' and denied them the description of fashion, because fashion implies freedom of choice and this is non-existent when 'costume becomes nationalised and purely functional in character. It is adopted for use and ceases to reflect the wearer's taste and personality.' From June 1941, he continued, there was 'a phase that might be called dictated costume'.

To the creative designer this would, in normal times, have been a desperate kind of frustration, but the restrictions were very much in tune with the mood of the time, and to that extent had some affinity with prevailing attitudes to fashion. The Board

147 Prototype Utility suit designed in 1941 by Hardy Amies shows enterprising use of checks. Blouse, also Utility, by Capt. Molyneux

148 *A wartime fashion show, aimed at demonstrating the most economical ways to use materials, 1943*

of Trade also adopted certain measures to maintain the link between Utility clothes and recognised fashion sources. A number of leading designers worked with the Board to produce models of the kind of fashions that were permissible within the Utility scheme. The group which undertook this work included couturiers Michael, Bianca Mosca, Molyneux and Hardy Amies and representatives of the wholesale trade, including Olive O'Neill. Prototype dresses, suits and coats, designed in accordance with this plan and now on view at the Bethnal Green and Victoria and Albert Museums, show a considerable sense of style and fashion and stand comparison with other preceding and following ready-to-wear fashions. The restrictions meant discipline but not death. The problem of sizing was also helped at this time by the co-operation of the light clothing trade with the British Standards Institution in specifying in detail the minimum measurements for different sizes.

Another loophole of some importance existed by which fashion could keep a few of its muscles flexed. Although manufacturers had to devote 85% of their output to Utility clothes, made from allocations of cloth based on their pre-war records of purchases in various categories, after that they were allowed to buy the remaining 15% of materials in a 'free' market – that is from non-Utility materials. These were in short supply at the mills, but it was permissible to weave limited amounts after Utility requirements had been met. From these materials manufacturers added to their ranges a small number of what were known as 'general' garments. These were free from Utility restrictions and therefore gave more scope to designers and manufacturers. They were of better quality and finish and though they did not enjoy the freedom from purchase tax enjoyed by Utility and were not sold at controlled prices, they were in great demand. They were usually 'rationed' by the manufacturer to the store or shop concerned in proportion to the number of Utility clothes the buyer had ordered. By this means fashion was given some scope and ready-to-wear kept its medals. It is, perhaps, significant that these 'free' clothes followed the lines of the Utility ones, with the same squared-up shoulders, narrow hips and short skirts.

A further control was exercised over fashion during the war by the concentration scheme which was announced in May 1941, but not brought into operation until July 1942. It meant that, in order to release factory space for the storage of munitions and other wartime equipment and also to economise in materials and release manpower – and womanpower – for war work, a limited number of factories was designated for clothing manufacture. As a result manufacturers were in many cases required to combine with each other in order to stay in business. Their employees became classified under Essential Works orders, which meant that they could not be dismissed or leave their jobs, that they were paid guaranteed wages and that conditions of work were laid down. Newcomers could not set up in business as clothing manufacturers.

All this was obviously putting shackles on fashion and in so far as its immediate creativeness and normal cycles of change were concerned this proved to be so. There was a slow-down. The square-shouldered suit with the regulation straight or frugally pleated skirt, reaching just over the knees, the plain jacket or coat, with its severe lines and even the buttons rationed, so that you could not have them at the wrists, the plain shirt blouse – these were none of them capable of very enterprising treatment,

149   Non-utility styles of 1943

150   A wartime Utility-suit—but fashion goes to the head with a coupon-free floral hat and veil. 1942

151 *Head scarves were seen everywhere.*
From a 1944 store catalogue

but there was no compulsion in the Utility scheme to adhere to the strict letter of what was produced. Shoulders, for instance, could have been rounded, the whole line softened. Coupons did, however, reduce purchasing power drastically so far as variety in the wardrobe was concerned and they applied to nearly everything, including underwear, stockings, shoes and gloves. Bare legs appeared in city streets, but at times they were coloured with sun-tan creams or lotions to improve their appearance. A straight dark line was even drawn down the back of the legs to simulate the back seam which was usual in stockings at that time.

Head scarves were seen everywhere, on all occasions, and as hats were not rationed the wearing of these scarves was a matter of choice, not compulsion, and therefore could rate as fashion. It proved to be a lasting vogue, for head squares have been in fashion ever since then, on royal and aristocratic as well as plebeian heads, and are often rich and elegant and printed with beautiful original designs. Until the war such headgear had been nothing more than part of traditional peasant costume in many parts of the world.

Slacks were much more generally worn than before and were almost a necessity in the 'blitz' and for some of the war work done by women – and that was almost everything. Wooden-soled shoes were introduced as leather became scarce and they had the great advantage of a lower coupon value than leather. Wedge heels, of wood or cork, also became popular towards the end of the war and continued to be in fashion for several years.

Somehow, in spite of all these upheavals, fashion did not die. The top manufacturers stayed in business and their Utility clothes, avidly sought after by the fashion-conscious, kept something of the individual 'signature' which most of them had by then established. They also made the most of the scope afforded by the 'general' styles. In 1943 *Vogue* advertisements announced that 'Susan Small is *still* obtainable from all good shops' – and others were in the same vein. The same fashion magazine chose Utility styles for its 'Choice of the Month', and in features like 'A Portfolio of Wartime Economies' it gave several pages of pictured suggestions for the 'one and only' dress, coat, suit and so forth that coupons would stretch to for the coming season. These suggestions offered a quite considerable variety of choice and were by no means merely drab body coverings or 'civilian battledress'.

Various other devices and contrivances were found by which fashion could be given a degree of variety and raised from its wartime rut. Furnishing and curtain fabrics were unrationed and

152 *One escape from Utility restrictions was do it yourself home dressmaking.* Picture Post *offered patterns for these dresses, with pleats and full skirts, in 1941*

153 *The Utility scheme went on till 1952, but fashion continued to show variety. Here a suit of 1946 is made in sungold box cloth and is crisply tailored*

though the choice was limited they were a tonic to the clothes-starved and could make a very successful appearance as coats, suits and dresses. Even unrationed black-out materials turned up in this guise. This was, of course, outside the ready-to-wear area; you had to make them up yourself or find the 'little dressmaker' – if she could be found anywhere at this late date.

Although fashion was slowed down by restrictions and was resorting to subterfuges, it nevertheless emerged from this period with a structure which, so far as manufacturing was concerned, was better than in pre-war days. It was given a strong forward impetus which became apparent when restrictions and controls were at long last eased – which was not for some time, because clothes coupons lasted until 1949 and the Utility scheme until 1952. There were many reasons for this paradox of light coming from darkness and for the improvements in fashion production which resulted from the Second World War. 'The geniuses who invented the Utility scheme had a great say in the development of the fashion industry,' says Frederick Starke, whose fashion house was a leader in high quality ready-to-wear from pre-war days on through the 'fifties and 'sixties. By controlling quantities and prices, the Utility scheme, he points out, compelled manufacturers to choose their cloths carefully, often for the first time. Their standards of manufacture were also controlled, not only by Government regulations but also unofficially by the exigent requirements of a buying public which had to surrender coupons for every purchase, and therefore demanded long-wearing, well-made clothes. Before the war, says Herbert Goodier, secretary of the Apparel and Fashion Industry's Association, costing was in most cases done by little more than rule of thumb or guesswork. Very few fashion firms had a clear costing practice and their methods often harked back to private dressmaking days, when little more than buttons and thread had to be accounted for. Time was valued much too low and the cost of designs, prototypes, duplicates and so forth was very rarely properly assessed. Profitable and unprofitable styles were hopefully expected to balance each other, on a kind of roundabouts and swings calculation.

This aspect of fashion manufacture came to be taken seriously largely as a result of wartime necessity to adhere to the profit margins laid down by the Utility scheme. In 1945 Mr. Goodier, a chartered accountant turned fashion man, was urged to write a book on the subject and did so. 'The laying down of Government specifications for cloth,' he says, 'meant that this subject had to be given close attention by manufacturers who, being limited to a fixed allocation, had to make themselves knowledgeable about it and buy judiciously. In addition, the concentration scheme, by preventing the mushrooming of new companies, which were often speculative, fly-by-night operators, led to a stability and efficiency which had previously been lacking in the fashion business. Those who were in it now had the responsibility of organising themselves to get on with the job, maintaining set standards and making the best use of labour and materials, both of which were hard to find.'

Experience in the mass production of uniforms with the maximum speed and the best use of labour also led to more scientific and better mechanised methods of large-scale production in the clothing trade as a whole. So did the fact that labour, of which there had always been a surplus in the years between the wars, was in short supply during the war and continued to be so in the post-war years of full employment.

It is also arguable that the restrictions on trimmings and the paring down of ornamentation and fussy detail on styling not only simplified production but also had a beneficial effect on much of fashion which, especially in the cheaper sector, had been addicted to covering up poor design and manufacture with bits of trimming intended to catch the eye and conceal deficiencies.

All in all, these factors combined to produce a stability and prosperity which had previously been rare in the fashion industry. This proved to be a springboard for further developments not only in the techniques of manufacturing but also in the promoting and marketing of fashion. 'A revolution has taken place behind the smokescreen of wartime conditions,' declared the Apparel and Fashion Industry's Association in 1950. The manufacturer came to be an efficient business man who was either something of a technician himself or who accepted the need for technical men to head his production. All the main features of present day large-scale production date from after World War II – the big modern factory, the planning of production, the breakdown of manufacturing processes, the introduction of trained management and technicians.

The year 1939 was therefore a line of demarcation in the making of fashion. Dr. Wray, taking a long view of the course of manufacture, said in 1954: 'Women's outerwear production is both one of the oldest and one of the newest industries in this country. The manufacture of women's clothing dates from the beginning of known history but, in its present form as a factory industry using power-driven machines for most of its production operations, it is of surprisingly recent origin; even as late as 1939 the industry retained many traces of handicraft methods.' Today the factories are bigger than ever and more highly mechanised than in 1954, but the handicraft methods are still also in the picture – in some ways more than in the recent past.

Fashion restrictions were imposed in America as well as in Britain during World War II, but for a much shorter time and with a much quicker recovery. Price controls on clothing were not imposed until 1943, when the maximum selling price was frozen at that year's estimate. The manufacturer was compelled to produce a certain number of cheaper lines, in order to counteract the wartime tendency to concentrate on the higher price brackets as clothes became scarce. Style restrictions and specified measurements were also imposed. The War Production Board in America restricted the use of materials used in clothing so as to achieve a 15% saving in yardage. Under the L 85 scheme there was a ban on such fabric-wasting items as turn-up cuffs, double yokes, sashes, patch pockets and attached hoods on coats.

Loss of contact with Paris meant that for the first time the

154   Trim tailored lines in Utility fashions of 1945

155 *Wartime restrictions were imposed in America too. A suit of 1945*

United States became its own centre of fashion. This was more of a revolution there than in Britain, because the great American ready-to-wear industry had followed Paris more closely than had Britain. But now native talent acquired a new confidence and developed a self-reliance which were to give America a special kind of leadership in fashion that had nothing to do with Paris. Dorothy Shaver, later president of Lord and Taylor, was particularly active in the encouragement of young designers in the direction of sports and casual clothes in which America was to be an important creative force as the demand for 'play clothes' spread. During the war American expertise in design and manufacture also gained world-wide prestige from the uniforms of the American women's services, which were greatly admired. Philip Magnone helped to create the uniforms of the women of the U.S. army, while Mainbocher was responsible for those of the women attached to the Navy.

2

In addition to the development of the structure and standards of fashion during and after the Second World War, several events during the war showed fashion for the first time trying to organise itself for more effective functioning as an industry with a stake in the British economy.

British *couture* fashion, rather surprisingly, took a step forward in this direction at a time when it might have been expected to reach a standstill. The new blood injected into it in the 'twenties and 'thirties had brought in talents of a higher quality than those of the previous Court dressmakers. The newcomers worked on a small scale compared with leading Paris houses, but they had creative ability, outstanding taste and considerable business acumen, as time was to show. Exports had begun before the war but Hardy Amies, surveying the development of London couture, said in 1954: 'The whole idea of an established and organised *haute couture* in London is very new. Its biggest impetus to organise itself came with the encouragement of export during the last war; and, in my opinion, the serious exporting of *couture* models from London only began in the year of the Coronation of George VI in 1937.'

The biggest single step towards putting British couture on the map had been taken by Norman Hartnell in 1937, when, on the occasion of the State visit of the King and Queen to Paris while the Court was still in mourning for the late King George V, he designed for the Queen an all-white wardrobe which was a sensation in the French capital. Hartnell was, of course, already well-known in Paris, but this was his biggest impact. From this time British couture began to take on a better image abroad.

Norman Hartnell has described how in 1942 he approached first Colonel Fay, managing director of Worth, and then his fellow designers, urging a common front to the Board of Trade in face of wartime restrictions. This effort, aimed at developing top fashion exports as an aid to the national economy, was consolidated by the business head of Harry Yoxall, then managing director of *Vogue*. He knew that certain French couturiers had come to London after the fall of France and that, in addition, two British fashion exiles, Charles Creed and Edward Molyneux, were back in London. He arranged a meeting of these fashion leaders with top London-based couturiers and, as a result, the Incoporated Society of London Fashion Designers was born in 1942. The constitution was drawn up with the aid of Margaret Havinden, of Crawfords Advertising, who became the first chairman, and the Hon. Mrs. Reginald Fellowes was the first of a number of distinguished presidents, being followed by, among others, Lady Clark, Lady Rothermere and Lady Hartwell.

Early members were Norman Hartnell, Peter Russell, Worth, Angèle Delanghe, Digby Morton, Victor Stiebel, Hardy Amies, Molyneux, Creed and Michael Sherard – the 'Top Ten' as they became known. At various times Mattli, Bianca Mosca, Lachasse, John Cavanagh, Michael, Ronald Paterson, Rhavis and Clive were elected. The total changed frequently, mainly owing to members either going out of business or opting out of couture, usually into ready-to-wear or boutiques. Fabric manufacturers also supported the Society and Harry Yoxall records that, at the start, 'a certain cohesion' was created by its formation, with fabric manufacturers lending their support in the shape of money and materials and the Government giving facilities which encouraged the development of much-needed wartime fashion exports. The 'Inc Soc' was a considerable force in the 'fifties and 'sixties, and from the start it set high standards, produced some brilliant fashion makers and presented British fashion impressively at home and abroad, mainly in the U.S.A. It set the practice, which lasted for many years, of co-ordinated showings of members' collections each season on a few successive days, so that British couture was presented effectively within its own framework and as part of the whole fashion picture, and also so that overseas buyers could visit all the houses within their necessarily limited visits to Europe. The week before the Paris showings was chosen for these shows, so as to rebut any sugges-

156   Norman Hartnell's afternoon dress of 1945, when couture fashion was promoting exports

157   *Designs for 1946, Frederick Starke*

tions that London was looking over the shoulders of the parent fashion creators of the French capital. The Society's main story was a post-war one, but its start during the war was opportune and its drive for exports was to develop effectively in the post-war era of expansion.

Also indicative of a new and better integrated fashion industry, with more effective management and more constructive policies, was the banding together of high quality ready-to-wear manufacturers by the formation in 1947 of the London Model House Group. This was the brain-child of Frederick Starke and the Group was instituted at a meeting of leading fashion manufacturers called together with a view to setting up a means whereby they could present a united front in their dealings with buyers and suppliers and in the co-ordinated presentation of their collections. Post-war improvements in production had, by then, been achieved, but, Mr. Starke recalls, there remained large areas of confusion. Confusion over dealings with suppliers and retailers. Confusion over dates when collections were shown, which meant that visiting provincial and, even more important, overseas buyers could easily miss some of the straggling presentations. The group originally consisted of Brenner Sports, Dorville, Frederick Starke, W. & O. Marcus, Rima, Silhouette de Luxe and Spectator Sports. Soon there were added the Jersey Company, Koupy Models and Simon Massey. The first joint announcement of their forthcoming synchronised shows on the week starting June 9, 1947, saw the group set on its course. Export was a prime aim; it was a part of national trade policy and British ready-to-wear fashion was being encouraged to make every effort to achieve a substantial contribution, of which it was believed to be capable. From the start, the Model House Group, under the chairmanship of Leslie Carr Jones, did much to enhance the prestige of British ready-to-wear fashion at home and abroad. It established and maintained standards for the top end of the fashion industry which gave it something of the prestige long enjoyed all over the world by British men's tailoring. It was a further mark of the success of the Model House Group that it provided the blue-print for a larger and more ambitious group, the Fashion House Group of London, into which it evolved in 1958.

In other ways too fashion was on the move in the immediate post-war years. In 1947 the Apparel and Fashion Industry's Association was established by the amalgamation of the Apparel Manufacturers Association and the British Fashion Trades Association. It was the first-ever national organisation of British manufacturers in the women's dressmaking industry – the lighter side of the trade. The heavier side was represented by the archaically named but still very active British Mantle Manufacturers' Association. These bodies spoke for their sections of the fashion industry in negotiations with Government departments, Trade Unions and other bodies.

Efforts to make the industry more attractive to those working in it were also started in the years after the war. Wages and conditions of work were a matter of dissatisfaction in many quarters and many clothing factories were still old, gloomy, ill-ventilated, badly laid out and lacking in health and welfare services. The National Tailors' and Garment Workers' Union campaigned for a national board composed of employers, Trade Union and Government representatives to organise the industry and it put forward an eight-point programme defining the functions of such a board. At the 1945 Trade Union Congress a resolution was carried demanding for clothing workers a shorter week, the abolition of overtime, two weeks' paid holiday, equal pay, a guaranteed week and adequate welfare and working conditions. With the advent of the Labour Government in 1945, Sir Stafford Cripps, as President of the Board of Trade, initiated

158　Television was to be a new force in spreading fashion. Here, in an early 1946 show, a delphinium blue afternoon dress in patterned crepe was featured

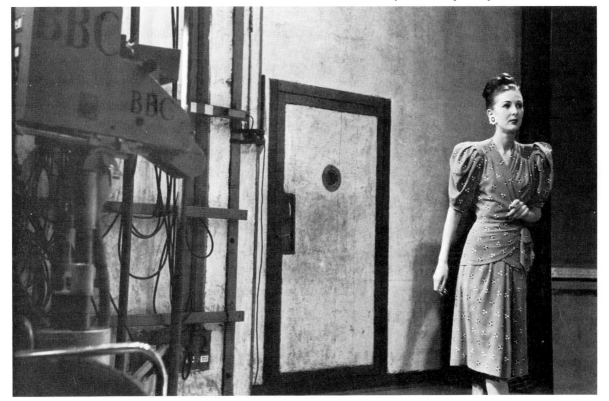

a policy of establishing working parties to guide every major industry in the consumer field on the path of prosperity. A working party for the heavy clothing industry was set up in 1946 and issued its report in 1947, proposing a central body of representatives of employers and employees and independent members, to deal with all aspects of the industry. A similar procedure was followed for the light clothing sector of the industry and for the rubber garment section. With the Conservative Government of 1950 there was, however, a reversion to a *laissez faire* attitude and relations between employers and workers remained unsatisfactory for some years. In 1956 the General Secretary of the Tailors' and Garment Workers' Union repeated the old reproach, saying: 'The black blot of a sweated industry is still with us.' There was at the time a very low minimum wage of £6 19s. 4d. for men and £4 11s. 8d. for women. It was not till 1960 that the garment workers 'established the only comprehensive national organisation in the clothing industry and spoke with one voice for its members', said the authors of *The Needle is Threaded*.

The state of the fashion industry at the start of its post-war development was examined in 1950 in a report, *The Present Position of the Apparel Industry*, produced by AFIA and described as a model for all other industries to follow. It stressed that 'our industry is based on fashion and has, therefore, to be flexible and elastic and prepared for change'. Although the fashion element was strongest at the top, 'Utility had not been a dividing line between fashion and non-fashion because fashion affects all clothing'. It noted that 'both in the U.S.A. and Britain there is a movement towards large production units, with progressively improving production techniques'. Redistribution of working areas was an important new factor, combined with which there were teething troubles and a persistent shortage of trained labour and of new labour. Independent contractors were relied upon by many manufacturers and they comprised much of the surviving craftsmanship and were therefore very valuable. Full employment was also encouraging the use of home-worker organisations as an additional production force.

The report also dealt with the retail market and especially the position of the multiples in it, pointing out that after a pre-war phase of growth they had gone through a recession but since the end of the war they had regained or nearly regained their place. They controlled more shops and were themselves more numerous. For the year ended January 31, 1950, sales of women's fashions had increased by 10% in department stores, 13.3% in the co-operatives and 27·4% in the multiples. In the U.S.A. clothing had reached the supermarket. Trade union membership unfortunately, remained low in Britain, with just under 30% of the workers belonging to the National Union of Tailors and Garment Workers – 134,000 out of about 500,000.

Summing up, the report concluded that: 'The industry is peculiarly a product of the present century. During the past twenty or thirty years it has made immense progress. Though it is still growing up, it still bears the imprint of its origins and present-day problems can only be fully understood in the light of its historical development.'

A comparable record of American manufacture in the immediate post-war years exists as the result of a detailed study of the subject made by Margaret Disher, a British expert on clothing technology, whose book, *American Factory Production of Women's Clothing*, published in 1947, was the result of a visit to the U.S.A. to investigate women's clothing manufacture for the benefit of the trade in her own country. She found that 'before the war the United States Clothing Industry was in a constant state of instability. Rapid style changes formed an evil which was not the consumer's fault. It was the industry's own making through its eagerness to create new business and it took a heavy toll of bankruptcy to prove that an endless variety of styles does not necessarily increase total purchases. But the war-time demand for quality rather than variety gave the industry its chance to develop and become prosperous.' As in Britain, the war had brought steady employment, freedom from slack periods – and now, in 1947, the industry was trying to find out how to maintain this stability in normal conditions.

In America, as in Britain, there was a fanning-out of production, in this case from its main centre in Seventh Avenue, largely for reasons of shortages of labour. But, unlike Britain, American expansion, in addition to being geographical, also involved the production of certain types of fashion in certain areas. Thus Dallas became a big centre for sportswear. California, especially Los Angeles, became notable for sports and beachwear. In the new centres, as in Britain, sectional work prevailed. The out-of-town American factories were located in areas where, in other industries, industrial engineering was the accepted practice, so it was taken for granted that this method should be used when labour was trained for fashion manufacture. In older centres, as in Britain, continental immigrant labour, with its traditional handicraft methods and its hereditary tradition of craftsmanship, strongly resisted modernisation. One trouble was that in

the post-war years the average age of the craftsman or crafts-
woman was between 55 and 60. And with the growing prosperity of society they no longer wanted their families to stay in
the trade, but to move out into the professions or some other
more progressive occupation. The same thing was happening in
Britain.

As in Britain, there were also Union problems. The International Ladies' Garment Makers' Union had the difficult task
of representing the disparate elements involved in fashion – the
craftswomen from the immigrant population and the new army
of less skilled factory workers trained in a limited number of
processes for the purpose of forming links in a chain of engineered production. By 1947, however, the Union was well
established and collective bargaining was the accepted method
of dealing with wage disputes. Educationally the Union was
progressive, with study classes organised under local educational
directors in subjects ranging from social science, economics and
public speaking to industrial problems.

In 1947 sizing was still receiving great attention in America,
which remained ahead of Britain in this respect. The National
Bureau of Standards in Washington was giving the world the
lead in standardised sizing.

All in all, post-war expansion saw the American fashion
industry standing more on its own feet than ever before, with
less reliance on French originals, and industrial production taking
over more and more from the custom-made sector – just as was
happening in Britain.

8 New looks for all from 1947

I

In February, 1947 Christian Dior launched his famous New Look in his first Paris collection, having established himself as a couturier on November 15, 1946. The years-old wartime line, with its square shoulders, narrow, short skirt and flat-hipped, severe jacket was demolished at a stroke, evoking extremes of delight and fury. The new shape had unpadded, rounded shoulders, a shapely bust-line, a closely defined waist, slightly padded hips and full, billowing skirts that reached well below the calves and were often accompanied by wide, flounced petticoats.

To fashion-conscious women frustrated by the monotony of prevailing fashion which had changed little for years this came with the force of a new, personal liberation. Dior meant it to be something like that, to be an escape from 'a poverty-stricken, parsimonious era, obsessed with ration books and clothing coupons'. With this purpose, he said: 'I designed clothes for flower-like women, with rounded shoulders, full, feminine busts, and hand-span waists above enormous spreading skirts.' To create clothes of this kind he used elaborate workmanship and great expertise: 'I wanted them,' he said, 'to be constructed like buildings.' They were all lined with cambric or taffeta, beautiful to inspect in detail, created by methods which were in part new, in part a return to old techniques long forgotten. This meticulous craftsmanship brought joy to the hearts of discriminating manufacturers and wholesalers who were present at the unveiling of the New Look – even though some of the perfection must be lost in the adaptations which it was their business to evolve from these masterpieces. Dior aimed at the established, mature clientèle, but youth was attracted to this fashion revolution: 'Thus the New Look,' he commented, 'became symbolic of youth and the future.'

159 *Dior's New Look of February 1947 in a cocktail dress*

160 *Dereta's version of the New Look, Spring 1947*

British and American manufacturers in the forefront of fashion saw their designers coming back from Paris and the Dior show walking on air, feeling that a new dimension had been added to the dull world in which they had been working for so long. Manufacturers plunged into the production of New Look clothes and the public demand was instantaneous. Dereta, which produced a grey flannel New Look suit with startling speed, saw 700 of them vanish from the rails of one West End store within two weeks. The only limits were those imposed by the fact that, because of the amount of material it needed, the New Look could appear only in non-Utility clothes, of which production was still restricted.

To other manufacturers who had stocked themselves up with clothes in the current wartime style the New Look was, on the contrary, a disaster. One of those whose large and well-established firm was caught badly by the change, recalls the dire collapse of the retail market for the old-square-shouldered styles and the selling of a whole season's output at throwaway prices in order to clear the production lines for the innovation.

As the Utility scheme was still in existence, officialdom raged. Harold Wilson, President of the Board of Trade, denounced the New Look. So did Sir Stafford Cripps. Dame Anne Loughlin declared that 'It seems to be utterly stupid and irresponsible that time, labour, materials and money should be wasted upon these imbecilities'. Similar comments poured forth from various other quarters, but in the enclaves of fashion-setters Dior's claim: 'I brought back the neglected art of pleasing' silenced criticism.

In America Dior was acclaimed even more loudly than in Britain, but while Britain was having her first post-war change of fashion in the New Look, America had been quick off the mark to adopt the first fashions Paris had shown after the Liberation, and was already familiar with full skirts and balloon sleeves. Their adoption had, however, created a storm of protest there in 1944. American soldiers were still fighting and dying in France and France herself was appealing to America to send her clothes for urgent civilian needs – and at the same time using twice as much material as was necessary for Paris couture clothes. In America the L 85 restrictions were still in force in 1944 and a ban was imposed on the manufacture of copies of Paris models shown in the fashion magazines of the time. The War Production Board protested against the 'unhealthy condition in the women's apparel trade', and even proposed a press censorship to prevent the showing of pictures or descriptions of 'Paris

161 The art of pleasing as interpreted by Worth in 1948, with rounded shoulders and long, full skirt

162 Green velour coat by Hardy Amies, shown at a parade held by the Incorporated Society of London Fashion Designers in November 1948 and attended by Queen Elizabeth the Queen Mother

163 Utility fashions also reflected the change. A dress of 1947–8 in tartan wool

164 The New Look was generally established by 1948: a full-skirted coat by Victor Stiebel in beige tweed with strapped fastenings

fashions which are in flagrant violation of our imposed wartime silhouette'.

Comments on the New Look at the time of its arrival and afterwards continued to be controversial. In 1953 Dr. Willett Cunnington described it as 'illusory, for it recalled the least appropriate of styles, the draped dowdiness of the 'eighties', and claimed that it did not greatly affect the home market in Britain, not being much to the taste of British women. In 1971 Madge Garland expressed the opinion that the New Look was not new, but praised it as 'the afterglow of the sunset of French taste which had led the civilised world for 400 years, the last coquettish womanly clothes before baby dolls, mods and minis took over'. James Laver saw it as nostalgic, an expression of the longing of women to return to the good old days of a sheltered life in which they were cherished and protected from the hard realities of post-war existence – to a never-never land for which Edwardian male fashion was at the same time being revived. He recorded that 'within a year it had won acceptance almost everywhere'. In 1950 Schiaparelli described the New Look witheringly as something which, 'cleverly planned and magnificently financed, achieved to the greatest din of publicity ever known the shortest life of any fashion in history'. The latter statement was manifestly untrue. The effect of the New Look in ridding fashion of the squared-up military shoulders to which it had clung for years (incidentally, Schiaparelli's own square shoulders) was immense. The way was opened for elegance and though the extreme New Look was, like other fashions, modified for general wear, it sparked off a whole post-war cycle of fashion. Rounded, gentle lines, a feminine look, a delight in elegance all came back.

But Dior, who introduced it all, did so with the kind of big business backing which had never been known in couture before then. From the start his entry into couture was different. He intended to enter the diplomatic service but when, in 1929, family finances suffered in the general crisis, he left the School of Political Science to go into business as an art dealer with two friends. He left this because of ill-health and emerged about a year later, in 1938, as a designer with Piguet. In 1942 he went to Lelong and, in addition to designing, learned the techniques of dressmaking in great detail. Through a friend he met Marcel Boussac, the textile king, who launched him as a couturier. He started on a bigger scale than any house had previously enjoyed, with a staff of 60, including some key people from Lelong, and with the immense resources of the Boussac empire providing administrative organisation of unprecedented size and quality. Boussac experts looked after the commercial side of the house, and by 1956 Boussac employees engaged in the rebuilt seven-storey Dior building numbered 1200. They were responsible for budgeting, costing, statistical analysis and finance in general. Couture had become big business on a modern scale.

The instant success of the spring 1947 collection brought Dior an Oscar in the summer of that year from Neiman Marcus, the first ever awarded to a French couturier, and an invitation to go to Dallas. This he did, to present 'a crazy collection of immensely wide and extremely long skirts, the New Look pushed to extremes', in an atmosphere of such enthusiasm that, he continues, 'the Golden Age seemed to have come again'. Christian Dior New York was established in 1948 because of the prohibitive customs duties imposed by America on imports, and a combination of French and American staff ran it as a separate house with its own collections. Christian Dior London was set up in 1954 on similar lines, after earlier special showings of the Paris Dior collections in Britain at the Savoy and the French Embassy and private viewings for Queen Elizabeth the Queen

165 *Elegance as seen by Worth in 1948 and 1949*

Mother, Princess Margaret and other members of the Royal
family. In the single decade of his reign the Dior empire grew
by leaps and bounds, until it covered nearly every country in the
Western world and nearly every area of fashion and fashion
accessories, including furs, stockings, jewellery, scent and
scarves, plus men's ties. Within six years of the start there were
six Dior companies and 16 associated companies all over the
world. More than 1000 people worked in the 28 workrooms in
the Paris headquarters.

Dior did not rest on the laurels of his first success but went on
to present collection after collection to the acclaim of the fashion
world. The New Look was followed by many different looks,
distinguished and flattering and widely copied by leading manufacturers, who faithfully took their lead from him. In the 'fifties
he created a series of themes to which he gave names that hit the
headlines – the H. line of autumn 1954, the Y line of 1955, and
the A or trapeze line and the F line of 1956. The growth of the
house and its name continued after Dior's sudden death in 1957,
and as a vast fashion complex it still has companies operating all
over the world. Dior was succeeded as designer by Yves St.
Laurent for a brief time. Then Marc Bohan, who previously had
his own small couture house, was established in this rôle, which
he still holds, creating Dior clothes.

An influence which was probably as strong as that of Dior,
which continued for much longer but was based entirely
on personal leadership, was that of the enigmatic Spaniard,
Cristobal Balenciaga, the unapproachable arbiter of fashion who
retired in 1968 with a name and reputation that had been magic
for 30 years. He left his native Spain during the Civil war and
with the aid of a friend established himself in Paris in 1937, after
going to London in search of a job and failing to find one. What,
one wonders, would have happened to British fashion if he had
set up his house in London instead of Paris? He worked in
extreme isolation, even from his own staff, never gave inter-
views and in later years refused to take part in the organised rota
of showings to buyers and press, in protest against the com-
mercialisation of high fashion and the exploitation as 'news' of
extreme and untypical elements in it. This caused great inconvenience, but so significant was his contribution to fashion that
he could not be overlooked and special visits to Paris were made
to see his collections. With his retirement his house closed – and
from then the collapse of couture began to look more and more
imminent. He died in 1972.

Among Paris couturiers of the post-war days Pierre Balmain

166   Dior 1966 with a different look

167   A Balenciaga evening dress of 1961

168   Balenciaga's evening skirt and blouse, 1962

was outstanding in several respects. Born in 1914 near Aix les Bains, where his mother had managed a dress shop and his father had a wholesale drapery business, he first studied architecture, but was attracted to fashion as a career and in 1934 started with Molyneux, 'this tall, aloof Englishman, who held the fashion world in the palm of his hand during the nineteen-thirties', as he described his first fashion mentor. Five years later he moved to Lelong, working there as a designer side by side with Dior, until he left to form his own house in 1945. He visited London, where his collection was acclaimed, and after the 1947 launching of the New Look he set out on a world tour which included America and Australia. He met Magnin who in San Francisco had exclusive Californian rights in Balmain designs. He went to Dallas, where he already had a tie-up with Neiman Marcus. Two years later, when he had acquired three American model girls to show his clothes more effectively to American customers, he again toured America and lectured there on fashion. He opened a ready-to-wear shop in New York and showed his collection at Havana and Caracas, and also in the Argentine and in Chile. He dressed film stars of the new generation, among them Sophia Loren, Brigitte Bardot and Melina Mercouri, as well as the ageless Dietrich.

From the start his approach to fashion was practical. 'The basic life of a couturier,' he said, 'is to dress women for ordinary living.' But his main concern is the wardrobes of his private customers and the keynote of his designing is the '*jolie madame*', elegant, graceful, poised, well-bred and totally aloof from fashion 'gimmicks'. He believes, his notable directrice Ginette Spanier explains, 'that there is a natural evolution of line'. But he predicts sadly that if a future student of civilisation analyses our era, 'he will see a world in full evolution in which the traditional effort of creation, and the creation itself, are in course of becoming anachronisms'. Meantime, he continues to be a perfectionist, an arbiter of elegance in a confused world. He employs 600 people in his workrooms, shows his collections to between 100 and 300 people a day and runs his house on businesslike lines – 'every dress is costed', says Ginette Spanier, 'as carefully, item by item, as the most mundane object sold in a supermarket'.

The post-war years saw the emergence of a new group of Paris couturiers whose influence on world fashion was to be important in the following years, keeping Paris in its prime position as a kind of Castalian spring to which all fashion seekers would return. These new Paris figures were, unlike their predecessors of the 'thirties, mostly French and they were nearly all men. Chanel returned in 1954, but only one new woman came to the fore, Nina Ricci, an Italian among the French. Grès remained prominent and notable for her continued eclectic elegance. Yves St. Laurent soon established his name on setting up his own house. Jacques Fath attained great eminence before his early death in 1954. Marcel Rochas also died young and, like Fath, contributed greatly to the social gaiety of the fashion world as well as to its more practical brilliance. Other newcomers were Jacques Griffe, Guy Laroche and Hubert de Givenchy. In 1948 Fath designed a special collection which was manufactured on a large scale in America and just before his death he was engaged in arrangements for designing further similar collections and also for manufacturing ready-to-wear fashions in Paris by American methods. He had already engaged U.S. staff to launch this venture, among them a pattern maker, cutter and forewoman trained in American techniques.

Other forward-looking designers, also mainly French, included Pierre Cardin and Courrèges. Many of this generation of designers achieved great success while still in their 'twenties – which was something new for Paris couture and a significant indication of the way fashion was moving. Significant too was the fact that they did not all start in the grand manner; Givenchy's first collection was all made in gingham, for economy's sake. It was a triumph.

An important development in the post-war dissemination of fashion was the setting up of direct channels from couture to the stores of the world. Instead of selling models or *toiles* to manufacturers or stores for copying, couturiers began to make comprehensive arrangements with stores, giving them exclusive rights to their designs in the country concerned. Thus over a number of years, Harrods 'bought' Courrèges, Fortnum and Mason acquired Ungaro, Selfridges got Philippe Venet and Debenham and Freebody scooped up a group of French and Italian names. Christian Dior, on the other hand, set up its own retail outlets and was followed later in this procedure by Yves St. Laurent. In 1955 the French couture, which had lagged behind America and Britain in the ready-to-wear business, sent a committee to America to study production methods. The members were greatly impressed by the freedom from standardisation which existed there, and also by the up-to-dateness of the fashions being produced. Subsequently French fashion began to develop substantially in the ready-to-wear sector, which proceeded to absorb much of existing couture.

In Britain in the 'forties couture, which until then had held its elegant skirts well away from the ready-to-wear market, moved towards a course of running in double harness. The start came from the top when, in 1942, Norman Hartnell began designing ready-to-wear dresses for Berkertex, the company which had been established in 1936 by Leslie Berker and which was to develop into one of the biggest in the manufacturing field. Hartnell was associated with it for some years, and then took a further step into large-scale fashion by becoming fashion consultant to Great Universal Stores. In this activity he began to design fashions for the mail order business which was part of their activities. This, however, did not affect his position as the top figure in British couture and a Royal dressmaker. Michael, another of the outstanding couturiers, became design consultant for Marks and Spencer in 1961 and, after combining this with his successful and prestigious couture house, he closed the latter in 1971. Mattli also combined couture and ready-to-wear and Ronald Paterson did so until he closed in 1970.

169   Suit by Norman Hartnell in light grey tweed, 1948

Hardy Amies, who during the war had been concerned in exporting collections of his fashions to the United States and other parts of America, continued this activity after the war and received big orders from American stores, among them Marshall Field. Establishing himself in Savile Row in 1946, he found his couture business also expanding, but he too began to look more widely at the world of fashion and observed: 'During all my visits to the United States, I could not but notice how few and small were the businesses that dealt in hand-made clothes. Any that kept going with any sort of renown had tacked on to them or connected in some way, an important ready-to-wear business, either wholesale or retail or both'. As an example he noted Hattie Carnegie, with half of her best models from Paris, half her own making, and concluded that 'an expansion which modestly imitated the powerful Hattie Carnegie organisation might be well worth envisaging'. To do this he would, he considered, need the help of the wholesale manufacturing industry, because of the difference between the techniques of couture and ready-to-wear. He also noted how Paris boutiques were bridging the gap between the two. It was not long before action had been taken by him in both these directions, with a boutique attached to the Savile Row premises and a flourishing ready-to-wear section of his business being operated as one of the many fashion interests of the great house of Selincourt.

A different course from couture to ready-to-wear was pursued by Charles Creed, of the sixth generation of that couture family. He had started his fashion career on the retail side in New York, going there with the purpose of studying the clothing trade after leaving school in 1928. He went at the invitation of Andrew Goodman, son of 'Eddie' Goodman of Bergdorf Goodman, and became an apprentice at that famous store. He worked as a floor walker to start with, but soon asked if he could design some fashions and was introduced to one of the oldest established manufacturers on Seventh Avenue, A. Beller. After gaining some experience in designing there, he went to Philip Magnone, one of the leaders of American top manufacture, remaining there for three years before going to Paris to join his father in the family couture house.

At this time Patou was very much in the public eye in America, and had been showing his Paris collections on American models to attract American buyers and private customers. Charles Creed had the idea of following up his American experience by taking over to America small collections specially designed for that market. This was successful and many leading

stores bought his clothes. Visits to America became a regular
event. Creed also went to Hollywood before 1939 and dressed
film stars there. After four years in the British army, he returned
to America and secured a contract to design for Philip Magnone,
but to have the Creed label on every garment. He next started
his own London house and continued to combine couture with
ready-to-wear collections for both Britain and America until his
early death in 1966.

2

What was fashion like for the ordinary British woman in the
immediate post-war years? While clothes rationing remained in
force, which was until March 1949, she still had to buy sparingly
and, even with the impetus of the New Look, change could not
be complete or sudden. She bought new additions to her wardrobe in a practical mood, following orthodox lines and trying to
maintain suitable clothes for the various occasions in which she
was involed. Shortages and rationing did not lead to a breakdown of fashion traditions; on the contrary they upheld them
and when the last traces of post-war privations went in the early
'fifties there was no exuberant fashion explosion but rather a
move to maintain the *status quo* in dress. The fashionable day

*170 (above)   An elegant 'little black dress' in
crepe, net-trimmed, with draped back, by
Frederick Starke. 1948*

*171 (left)   Hat, gloves and rolled umbrella
complete a middy suit in grey flannel by
Dorville, 1952*

*172 (right)   Brand names became better
known. A slim suit of 1955 by Frederick
Starke*

dress, suit and coat were classics, trim, well-made and carefully accessorised. 'What to wear with what' was a favourite theme of *Vogue* and other fashion magazines and it meant a studied choice of hats, gloves, handbags, scarves and other items. For evenings there was a considerable vogue for the strapless dress, with boned bodice and usually a full, bouffant skirt. Other evening dresses were sleeveless, with shoulder straps and low necklines, and were all clearly defined as being solely for after dark wear. Careful attention was given to hats until the mid-fifties, when it began to be permissible to go hatless and still be well-dressed. New upswept hair styles which would be ruined by a hat helped to bring in the change. People dressed with care and some formality for town, whether for work or on pleasure bent. Gloves were worn not only with such outfits but with almost everything, down to cotton summer dresses which, on all but the most casual occasions, were accompanied by little white cotton 'shortie' gloves reaching just to the wrists.

Good post-war clothes were not cheap – a suit costing 20, 30, or even 40 guineas was quite usual at the better end of ready-to-wear fashion, which indicates that clothes have not risen in cost so much as most things in recent years. But in the 'fifties cheap clothes were much cheaper. Many makers and stores which started in the cheaper sector have gradually up-priced themselves, notably C & A, which now has high fashion departments with prices up to about £100 for a garment.

In the sellers' market of wartime well-known names had become better known, especially when they were brand names, mainly because they were an assurance of a certain quality, and this trend continued. The *Branded Merchandise and Trade Marks Directory*, Dr. Wray notes, shows that branded names increased threefold in every main category of women's outerwear between 1939 and the early 'fifties. Named fashions were extending from high quality to the middle and even the cheap areas. The manufacturer hoped to build up brand loyalty in the customer, who knew what size, styling and quality to expect from him. Stores benefited from the considerable advertising the makers undertook and from the display matter they provided for windows and departments, but some of them regretted – and resented – the move, feeling their own identity being eclipsed.

In 1951, the year of the Festival of Britain, which was a tremendous gesture of hope for the future, *Vogue* proudly produced a special Britannica number, devoted to the presentation of British achievements. It included an eight-page feature on *The Rise of the Ready to Wear*, the theme of which was that

173   *Elegance in the 'fifties. A suit of 1958*

174 *Summer fashions, 1951*

175 *The mood of the 'fifties, flattering, well-designed and wearable fashions. 1953*

'the most fastidious and fashion-conscious woman can dress immediately for any occasion in ready-to-wear clothes'. Illustrations included fashions from Jaeger, Dereta, Brenner, Marcus, Rima, Mary Black and Susan Small, all of them showing elegant, clean-cut clothes, worn by model girls with a well-groomed, upstanding look, all of course, carefully hatted and gloved and with not a hair out of place on their neat heads.

That was the need of the 'fifties. To get back to normal, which meant to order and stability, was the general longing and fashion voiced this conservative mood in a series of smooth, well-balanced lines, embodied in clothes of notable elegance, carefully designed, well-made and flattering. Dolman sleeves, swing-back coats, standaway collars, a choice of narrow or full skirts rang the changes within a concept that catered for all. For most of the decade skirts were fairly long – to at least mid-calf. Fashion derived to some degree from Paris but from a Paris freely adapted by the skilful designers of the ready-to-wear manufacturers. Although the status-symbol aspect of fashion was on the way out, there was still a tidy, conventional agreement on what was to be worn where and when, a sharp distinction between various social occasions. As late as 1959 *Vogue* could run a feature

176   Slim skirts were pegged to make them still slimmer for fashion photography. Ronald Paterson called this design Crozier in 1957, because it followed the line of a bishop's staff

on *Clothes for the Occasion*, defining what the smart woman would wear for a lunch date, a lunch party, racing, a committee meeting, a garden party, cocktails, dinner, the theatre, a dance and a wedding. Every one of them was different. It couldn't happen today.

American influence on fashion gained strength at this time. In the early 'fifties America, having developed her designing and manufacturing skills during the war, depended less on Paris. She was taking her own line in producing casual clothes of a kind which belonged to the way of life then prevailing, and to the future, and which had few links with traditional fashion. They drew their strength from America's prime aptitude for good, large-scale manufacture. Separates and co-ordinates were the main developments and these were to spread over the rest of the fashion world as life became more informal and leisure increased. In this kind of fashion California, where it was the natural way of dressing, became the main source. The extreme of the casual trend was the wearing of jeans. These derived from the levis invented by Levi Strauss, who went to California in 1850 as a gold prospector and made work pants of indigo blue denim, reinforced with copper rivets. They made his fortune more successfully than, in all probability, gold would have done, and they were rediscovered and elevated into a new fashion for young people of the 'fifties of the next century – and for the not so young too.

The 'fifties also brought many other fashions which were in no way derivatives of couture, as had been usual in the past. Dior had brought back bosoms, but it was a far cry from his elegant curves to the 'sweater girl' bra, which came into fashion about 1953 and lasted for some years, in spite of Dior's attempt to 'abolish' the bosom in 1954. This style, with its two projecting cones, usually stiffened and with whorls of stitching, was as remote from nature as the 'flattener' bra of the 'twenties. It was the last distortion of the female figure to be imposed by fashion, but it did not interfere with nature as tight lacing and even the flat bra of the 'twenties had done. It merely superimposed something, without discomfort and – it seems today – without grace or attractiveness. At its literal peak, in the mid 'fifties, it was also Hollywood's last fling before people stopped looking to films for fashion – because they stopped going so often to the cinema. (Attendances in Britain dropped from 1,395·8 millions in 1950 to 500·8 millions in 1970, while the number of cinemas fell from 4584 in 1950 to 3034 ten years later and to 1529 in 1970.) The sweater girl's chief embodiment was Jane Russell and one top-selling style of bra was called the Hollywood Maxwell. Girls and women everywhere encompassed their bosoms with the formidable garment that exaggerated their shape beyond all probability. If they felt that nature had been niggardly they wore a padded version. It was also often wired underneath the bust to add to the effect and it was hitched up tightly by the shoulder straps to add to the desired 'uplift'. Film stars of the time were even said to have been 'made' by being heavily endowed with this vital statistic rather than by their acting talent.

Other fashions which met the growing needs of the mass market and did not identify with couture were numerous in the 'fifties. The dirndl dress had a certain correspondence with Dior's New Look, but the young adopted a new version of it, sleeveless or with small puff sleeves. It billowed out over a profusion of petticoats. These rivalled their Edwardian predecessors, but were in substance usually very different, being made

178   The dirndl dress of the fifties was much favoured by the young. c. 1954

SHIRLEY POPPY
In pink and grey or blue and grey.   **8½ gns.**

DAISY CHAIN
A black and white print on grounds of sugar pink, clover green, marine navy, grey, or grapefruit.   **6½ gns.**
In other styles from 98/6.

177   Jane Russell, film star embodiment of the exaggerated bust admired in the fifties. Here a three dimensional advertisement for her film 'The French Line' shows America's 'queen of pulchritude' many times larger than life size. Below, the 'sweater girl' bra

179   A sophisticated version of the full-skirted dress in Paisley patterned cotton with eight yard skirt finely pleated. By Frederick Starke, Spring 1956

180   The return of the short evening dress after nearly thirty years. This version in pure silk organza, scattered with embroidered appliqued bows. By Roter, 1959

of nylon, frilled or lace-edged but drip-dry and non-iron. Sometimes they were of stiffened nylon net, but occasionally nostalgic lace-edged cotton was used, starched and ironed as devotedly as half a century before. The shirt-waister, of American fame, also appeared in a full skirted version, both in America and in Britain, and was very popular. American-inspired also was the ballet-length evening dress, which was fashionable and widely worn for a number of years during the 'fifties. It took various guises, full-skirted or slim. Until then, short or long as a distinction between day and evening dress had been unvarying since the late nineteen-twenties.

Hair styles became extreme in the 'fifties, and most of them were young fashions. The most conspicuous was the 'beehive', with the hair, shoulder-long or more, drawn up to the top of the head, back-combed zealously to give it bulk and height, then turned in with pins or surmounted with a chignon, real or artificial, and finally lacquered into stiffness. The height of this vogue came in the late 'fifties, but it flourished for some years previously and also in the following years. Popular, too, was the quite opposite style, the scraped-back pony-tail, still worn today by the young. In less extreme styles the hair was usually swept up rather high in front and at the ears, in loose waves, but it was generally fairly short, reaching only to the nape of the neck.

The American casual look was given fashion reinforcement on an international scale by the arrival of Italy on the main fashion scene from the 'fifties. The first big Italian show, held in 1950, set a quite different picture from that of Paris. It was centred upon leisure clothes and casual wear, with Pucci taking the lead in a dazzle of colourful prints which were to captivate people everywhere from then until today. Here too was Simonetta, then the most successful of the Italians; her husband Fabiani; Fontana, oldest established of the group, and the young Venetian Capucci. The Italian shows quickly took their place in the fashion tours of American as well as of European buyers and each season during the 'fifties and afterwards new names appeared, the most outstanding being Irene Galitzene, Patrick de Barentzen, Milo Schoen and Valentino. Store buyers were quick to give their attention to the Italians, whose shows brought a new bolder colour and also a new inventiveness and way-out elegance and a kind of 'brio', to fashion. Italy has never exercised the authority exerted by Paris in former days, but this was perhaps part of her strength – the days of authority were past and variety and novelty, *panache* and even eccentricity were more sought after and admired.

*181   The casual look for evening from Italy in wool jersey
skirt, jacket and blouse. 1961*

*182   An Italian print for casuals by Cole of
California in 1964: shoulder-buttoning shifts,
one with matching bikini*

A particularly strong influence exerted by Italy on fashion
from the 'fifties onwards was the introduction – or rather
revival – of the chunky sweater, reminiscent of previous hand-
knitted efforts and even of Chanel's First World War seaman's
jerseys, but now transformed by its styling and colour. Huge
polo or turtle necks, attached hoods, wide armholes and spectacular colours, including bold stripes, made these sweaters
dashing and exciting as well as very practical. From about 1954
the 'Italian' sweater was a much-followed fashion – and, with
endless variations, it still is. Designers and manufacturers all over
the world have copied it. In Britain the 'sloppy Joe' has become
a home-manufactured article, with Scottish mills taking a lead
in ringing the changes on it. Sweater dresses have been widely
worn for some years. In America Mainbocher introduced a

quite different variation on the sweater theme with his elegant evening sweaters of the 'fifties, gay with embroidery, beads and sequins. They are the only one of his American-based fashions to have achieved world acclaim and imitation, and they have become increasingly popular with the growth in recent years of easy, relaxed leisure clothes for stay-at-home TV evenings or today's informal entertaining.

Another fashion feature of the 'fifties which derived from Italy and was taken up by the masses as well as the classes was the stiletto-heeled shoe, with its pointed winkle-picker toe. For many years Italy took the lead in shoe fashions. Top shoemakers were featuring fantastically high, narrow heels by 1951, but the great vogue was in the later 'fifties and it continued into the 'sixties. For years hordes of the young – and not so young – teetered about their business on four-inch heels that narrowed almost to a point. Innumerable floors and carpets – not to mention feet – were ruined by them. In some famous buildings special overshoes with substantial heels were supplied and had to be worn before admission was granted. Airlines complained about the damage done to the floors of their planes.

Boots, worn by nearly all women in recent years for most of the winter and sometimes in summer too, have footprints that

183   Chunky woollen sweater, worn with the tapered slacks which were fashionable for many years in the 1950's and 1960's

184 (right)   The chunky sweater was popularised by the Italians and has remained in fashion since the 1950's. Here it is seen with dramatic collar edged with stripes and bobbles in 1962

185 (far right)   Sweater dress by John Carr Doughty in pure lambswool yarn in an elegant late-day style. 1964

go back through fashion history. In this century smart little button-up versions, with cloth tops, were an Edwardian fashion. There was a short-lived 'Russian boot' in the winter of 1925–1926, but in those days footwear which revealed that you hadn't a car or didn't travel by taxi in wet weather was contrary to the spirit of fashion. As a fashion which seems to have come to stay, boots date in their more modern guise from about 1940, when sheepskin or wool-lined versions, usually short-legged and zipped, and with some resemblance to those worn by R.A.F. men, were bought as defences against cold and wet. They were in short supply, but were brought home from Ireland in the immediate post-war years by British holidaymakers in that near-at-hand land of peace and plenty – for the Irish Free State had not been at war and had had no rationing.

To start with, the younger generation took little interest in boots as a fashion item, choosing instead to brave the elements in 'winkle-picker' shoes with stiletto heels. But with shorter skirts and smarter styles of boots the young sought them eagerly. From stout leather and tough sheepskin they began to be made in patent leather, coloured suède and shiny plastic. They were given a high fashion accolade when Courrèges showed them in his 'space-age' collection in 1964, in shiny white PVC styles reaching well up the calf. With the mini-skirt in the following year boots even became thigh-high, like those worn by guardsmen.

In the face of all this diversity and popularising of fashion, Paris in the 'fifties lost some of her previous exclusiveness and prestige as a source of fashion beyond compare. But still she remained powerful. When Hubert de Givenchy, trained by Schiaparelli and 'finished' by Balenciaga, opened his own house in 1957, he introduced what became known as the 'sack'. He seemed to have dealt a blow to fashion's respect for line, but although the sack ran into early troubles and became shapeless and unbecoming, it was a landmark, leading to the chemise dress and the shift, which have been worn fashionably ever since. Since it came into the picture tight waists have never dominated fashion and designers say that its influence on them has been immense.

3

While the great era of store development had ended by 1939 and subsequent changes have been in the nature of diversification and updating rather than in reconstruction or growth, other fashion outlets have changed greatly between the post-war years and today. With the expansion of the fashion market on popular lines the multiples came into the picture. With their country-wide distribution they were well placed to take advantage of the new demand and they became increasingly concerned with fashion. Many of them had started many years back; Fleming Reid, the pioneers, opened their first Scotch Wool Shop in 1881 and had more than 200 branches by 1900. But they were not concerned with fashion until the 'fifties. Dorothy Perkins and Etam both started with stockings and underwear, but although they grew to having between 50 and 100 branches each in the years between the wars, fashion came into their area only after World War II, and their rise to being a major outlet is recent. Other many-branched retailers which became important in fashion from now were Swears and Wells, Morrisons, Willsons, Barnett Hutton, Richard Shops and C. & A.

All these placed their emphasis on up-to-date fashions at budget prices, aimed at the woman of modest means who wanted to be in fashion. Their window displays and general presentations were gay and colourful and the prices tempting. Slick, novel, lively display was their aim, rather than the leisured dignity of the old-established stores. They were attuned to the new quick-buying market and they aimed at giving value for money by all the means they could. With this purpose most of them extended their activities to include some concern with manufacturing. They would have special lines made exclusively for them. Sometimes they also supplied designs and materials.

The variety chain stores, stemming originally from Wool-worths, which made an unsuccessful start in America in 1874, were also a post-war development so far as big-scale fashion was concerned. They had little connection with clothing of any kind in the 1920's, but came into this market during the 'thirties, when Marks and Spencer took the lead but still had no real fashion

status. Immediately before World War II these stores, with
Littlewoods and British Home Stores also prominent among
them, went ahead of the multiples in their volume sales of
stockings and underwear, but during the war they lost ground
because coupons meant that what was cheap and attractive but
not long-wearing gave way to more enduring, if more expensive
products. Expansion began again soon after the war and it
became rapid and extensive from 1949. The first big opportunity
given them was the end of rationing, as this was coupled with the
continued Utility scheme by which price-controlled, good-
value, tax-free clothing was available till 1952, when the
Utility scheme ended. The variety chain stores, with their self-
selection, prominent pricing of everything and the attractive
prices made possible by the cutting down of customer services
to the minimum, began to make inroads into the fashion market,
which was spreading among all classes. As big groups, with
special buying techniques and low distribution costs, they were
able to give exceptionally good value for money and they began
to acquire considerable fashion know-how.

Marks and Spencer gave the lead to this type of fashion selling.
As their merchandise development department had been established in 1937 they were right on the touch line when post-war
expansion became possible. The system they set up brought
a new approach to fashion making in that they controlled their
products all along the line to an extent never before attempted.
Thus they would buy cloth in the grey from the weaver and
have it finished to their own specifications by merchant con-
verters who were put under contract. In 1938 they were testing
such cloths at their own research headquarters. At the same time
they started a system by which manufacturers were placed under
contract to produce goods for them. This system, set up when
their pre-war 5s. price limit was still in force, had as its immediate
purpose the control of costs. Consultation with manufacturers
was necessary to maintain the ceiling price throughout an
increasing number of goods. It was developed on a large scale
after the war and under it women's outerwear became a major
activity of the company from 1949 and moved increasingly into
fashion.

A large design department created the styles and the chosen
manufacturer was supplied with fully graded patterns and the
most explicit and detailed making-up specifications, from the
kind of machines to be used to the number of stitches required
for each operation and even the precise ways in which button-
holes were to be made. After the liberation of styling in 1952,

when the Utility scheme ended, fashions at Marks and Spencers began to be up-graded and sizing was increased to include the short, the tall, the outsize women and the teenager. The high standards they set in every area of production were reflected throughout the fashion trade. The 'fifties, says Goronwy Rees, 'transformed Marks and Spencer from one among many retailing organisations, into something which one might reasonably call a national institution, which played a vital and indispensable part in the life of the British people.'

In the process of development, Marks and Spencer extended their association with their manufacturers to giving expert advice on everything from factory buildings to all-over organisation, the training of workers and their wages. Their own laboratories tested materials, thread, seams, pockets, and pre-production was carried to its ultimate point by them before manufacture began. As a result Marks and Spencer took over a significant part of the fashion market and became an important producer of clothing of nearly all kinds. 'Between 1950 and 1968 Marks and Spencer more than doubled their share of the clothing market, and today their textile sales account for over 10% of the total consumer spending on clothing,' said Goronwy Rees in 1971.

This is, of course, made up of men's, women's and children's wear, but the chief emphasis is on women's wear. A recent breakdown of figures shows that Marks and Spencer account for the sales of a third of all slips, bras, sweater dresses and ladies' underwear in the United Kingdom, for a quarter of all knitwear, girdles and nightdresses, a fifth of all skirts and pyjamas, a tenth of ladies' dresses (more if jersey is included) and of hosiery.

The more they develop the more emphatic do Marks and Spencer become on quality. Since 1961 they have had Michael, for many years, until late 1971, a leading couturier, as consultant designer, working with their own team of designers. Today there are more than 240 stores throughout the country. 'Before the war it would have been unthinkable that such stores were designed to be used by everybody, whatever their class or income,' says their historian. Today it would be unthinkable for them not to be. Royalty shops at Marks and Spencers, foreign tourists of all kinds and degrees flock to them as compulsively as the wealthier groups used to be drawn to the Paris couture houses, and Marks and Spencer have carried their challenge abroad with increasing exports to many countries, including France.

9 The young explosion splits fashion from the late 1950's

I

In 1948 London's Royal College of Art established its School of Fashion. It got off to a good start with, as its first professor, Madge Garland, former fashion editor of *Vogue*, later a fashion consultant and an outstanding writer on fashion. She was succeeded by the late Janey Ironside, a fashion expert with a special flair for guiding the young, and then by Joanna Brogden. The School was a long overdue acknowledgment of the need for a fashion designer of a new kind, not only gifted with an intuitive sense of where fashion is going but also equipped with practical knowledge of how it is produced for today's large market. The school's curriculum was comprehensive – as it needed to be in the post-war climate of expanding fashion and increasing wages and costs in which it rose. Fashion design now had to be geared more closely to sizing and grading; it had to take into account the amount of material needed and the amount of work involved in manufacture, because most manufacturers produced within a specified price range and profits could be jeopardised by even such small things as an extra button or an intricate pocket.

Schools of fashion with very comprehensive courses covering all such needs in both theory and practice soon flourished in colleges of art all over the country and became a main recruitment source for the designers and design teams behind large-scale fashion production. These schools hold end-of-session fashion shows of students' work, often presented with professional skill and considerable bravura. They are attended regularly by talent spotters among both manufacturers and couturiers, many of whom have established prizes and travelling scholarships for outstanding students.

But this acknowledgment of the need for trained designers also had a spin-off in the opposite direction. It gave an immense impetus to the movement for fashions for the young which dates from this time. This was something new, because although the fashions of the mid and late 'twenties had been very youthful, they had not been exclusively for the young. They were The Fashion, and it was a question of take it or leave it, whether you were 17 or 70. At fashion's call you cropped your hair and your skirts or you were out of the picture. Now, in the 'fifties, there was an explicit breakaway movement into fashions which effervesced out of the ideas of youth; narcissus fashions which had a great vogue among the young but alongside which other, more traditional fashions continued to flourish and to meet the needs of most women over 25.

These new fashions for the young had little to do with the Paris Establishment or, indeed with any other Establishment. Nearly all their leaders and creators were young; most of them recently art-school trained and uninhibited by what fashion had been or was doing outside their own young world. Whether these fashions would have succeeded as they did without the fashion schools and their technical training, know-how and guidance is a moot point. What is certain is that the schools produced many of the trend setters and successful innovators among the designers of the new young fashions, which were so different from anything that had been seen before.

America, it has been said, discovered the teenager, but this new candidate for the focus of fashion, who had, of course, always existed in fact but not in fashion, now began to be important on both sides of the Atlantic. The initiative in dressing her was, to a large extent, seized by Britain. Teenage fashions and young fashions in general began to be a special category of fashion there from the 'fifties, but they did not reach their full development until the 'sixties brought the 'youth explosion' in the shape of the generation born in the post-war bulge in the birth-rate, brought up in the violently changing society that emerged from the war and now vociferous in proclaiming and claiming what they wanted from life. They wanted fashions that expressed their particular attitude and mood and both within their ranks and outside there was a scurry to meet their needs, for the very practical reason that market research showed that the young, living in a world of plenty, were earning their share of that plenty and that clothes were the biggest item in their expenditure. It was good business to see that they got what they wanted.

The lead in bringing this about was given by Mary Quant, herself, when she began, not much older than those she was to

187 Fashions that expressed their particular attitudes

dress. Paradoxically and against all the rules, as is the way of
fashion, she was not a product of the fashion schools. She went
to a school of art, Goldsmiths College, part of the University of
London, but her entry into fashion was made after she had
studied for, but failed to obtain, the art teacher's diploma
towards which she was prudently steered by her Welsh-born
parents, themselves teachers. In 1955 she started her fashion
career in the workrooms of Erik, the milliner, but the real
beginning came soon afterwards with Bazaar, the Chelsea shop
which was the joint venture of herself and her future husband,
Alexander Plunket Greene. To start with they bought their
merchandise from manufacturers, but she soon found that she
was not getting the kind of fashions she wanted, and decided
to produce them herself. 'I had,' she said, 'always wanted the
young to have fashions of their own . . . absolutely twentieth-
century fashions . . . but I knew nothing about the fashion
business.'

188   Designs by Mary Quant in the late
'fifties

She proceeded to learn the hard way, thinking out the kind
of clothes she wanted, then learning how they could be made.
She started by buying Butterick patterns and altering them and
by going to 'a few frantic evening classes in cutting'. She bought
materials over the counter at Harrods because she didn't even
know that they could be obtained wholesale. She had to sell one
day's output of dresses, made in her bedsitter by a few sewing
women with a few hastily-acquired machines (against the
regulations, but that was another thing she didn't know), before
she could buy the next day's materials.

But it paid off handsomely. 'We were,' she says, 'at the beginning of a tremendous revolution in fashion. It was not
happening because of us. It was simply that, as things turned out,
we were a part of it.' She was credited with creating the 'Chelsea
Girl', symbol of the new fashion movement, but disclaimed it,
because 'no one designer is ever responsible for such a revolution.
All a designer can do is to anticipate a need before people realise
that they are bored with what they have already got.' Her
anticipation was so accurate that by 1962 Mary Quant and
Alexander Plunket Greene were 'ultra front room people'
pictured in *Vogue*, with Bazaar designs by Mary shown alongside. It was an odd coincidence that on the next page came 'Mrs.
Exeter', *Vogue*'s famous and elegant not-so-young fashion
model who had been riding high since the mid 'fifties but who
was soon to dwindle to an occasional diary feature and then
disappear altogether in 1964 under the young invasion. At this
moment the rising and the setting sun met.

Mary Quant enjoyed spectacular successes in America, but in spite of the teenage discovery there, her kind of clothes, she explains, were London-inspired, because 'London led the way to changing the focus of fashion from the Establishment to the young. As a country we were aware of the great potential of these clothes long before the Americans or the French.' It was her great achievement to develop this potential to a degree that left everyone else, including America, behind. The 'London Look' is history now, but it swept the world in the early 'sixties and did great things for British fashion. It meant chiefly the new young look – crisp, lively clothes, endless and often startling inventiveness, a disregard for conventional categories of day and evening, formal and casual clothes – and shorter and shorter skirts. It was only a stage further to 'Swinging London' and the creation of an image that was poles apart from the discreet tailor-made as the symbol of British fashion. 'Mary Quant,' said *Vogue* in 1965, 'blazed a trail, weathered the storm for the young designers. Fine now and the temperature's rising.'

189   Skirt above the knee in a Hardy Amies suit for Spring, 1970 in yellow gabardine, from the boutique collection

190   Military style maxi in boldly checked tweed by Alexon Youngset 1969

The high spot of all this was the mini-skirt which dates from 1965 – the thigh-high style which had never been seen before, except perhaps in the tunics of Greek girl athletes, as shown in classical sculpture and frescoes, and in medieval men's tunics. It had nothing in common with past fashion motivation. It was the ultimate in youthful assertion and bravado. It defied fashion's natural changes and became almost a way of life for its faithful followers. It sent all other fashionable skirts up to the knees from 1966 to the end of the decade. It had an offshoot in the tunic worn over the trousers by women of all ages and later sold as a dual purpose garment. In spite of high fashion's endeavours to lengthen skirts, in spite of the sporadic appearances of the 'midi' and the 'maxi', mid-calf and ankle-length skirts, in the late 'sixties and early 'seventies, many skirts remained around knee-length or higher.

Having launched a new cycle of fashion, Mary Quant next set about studying the problems of mass production, because 'the whole point of fashion is to make fashionable clothes available to everyone' and 'fashion must be created from the start for mass production with full knowledge of mass production methods'. She knew that to work on this scale would be impossible without the support of a strong, established manufacturer, and she found her answer in Leon Rapkin of Steinbergs. They launched the range called the Ginger Group and produced it for some years. She also realised that costing and finance were becoming important as her activities grew, and a business man, Archie McNair, became a third partner in the Quant organisation.

Thus in her own personal progress Mary Quant reproduced in miniature the whole story of the fashion industry, from the small workroom and its out-workers to big business. Growth was speedy. The first big overseas success came in America in 1965 when, in a whirlwind tour, she showed 30 outfits in 12 cities in 14 days, to the accompaniment of 'pop' music and in a high-speed dance routine of her own devising. She extended her American commitments. She showed with other British manufacturers at the Crillon in Paris in 1967 and sold 30,000 dresses to France as a result. Soon she had a business worth over £1,000,000 and was selling to 150 shops in Britain, to 320 outlets throughout the United States and also to nearly every other country in the Western world. She was committed to designing 28 collections a year. In 1966 she received the O.B.E. for her services to fashion exports – and went to Buckingham Palace in a mini-skirt.

What *Vogue* in 1968 called 'Quant country' flourished and its

191 *The thigh-high style, alone and paired with bell bottom pants. Mary Quant Ginger Group, 1969*

ruler's 'talent for revolutionary fashion attitudes' seemed unquenchable. If it did not startle so much, that was because its success has been so great that it was generally accepted.

Among the fashion changes of recent years brought about by the young fashions the one that spread most widely was the change-over from stockings to tights. The stocking, entrenched in centuries of unquestioned acceptance, at once necessary and ornamental, met its Waterloo in the mini-skirt. Tights began to be worn by more and more people. Their invention, however, cannot be attributed to the new designers, because they first appeared in 1960, made by Morley, though they were intended for warmth and not for fashion. At that time they were usually made of wool; they were fairly thick and often came in bright colours. They were meant for sportswear and did not become a fashion until the mini-skirt rose to a level which made a gap between the stocking and the skirt almost inevitable. Visible suspenders and bare thighs had been alluring in the can-can girls of the 'eighties and 'nineties, but not even the most venturesome teenager found them desirable in her daily life in the 'sixties. It did, however, take quite some time for tights to push stockings off the main counters and relegate them to a back place in the shops. Advertisements for stockings appeared regularly in fashion magazines until 1969, when there came a prominent announcement that 'Annabella isn't wearing panties. She's wearing something much better. Charnos Hold-me-Tights.' In that year tights accounted for 160·9 million pairs out of a total of over 470 million pairs of stockings and tights. Soon they completely dominated the market. Most noteworthy of other changes in the hosiery market was the drop in sales of fully-fashioned stockings, once essential to the well-dressed woman, from 72·7% of the market in 1964 to a mere 5% in 1971. Women had also taken to tights regardless of the length of their skirts or their age, finding them more comfortable and much neater. The girdle and corselette gave way to a large extent to the pantie-girdle or pantie corselette. Mary Quant, always on the right wave-length, had been designing tights since the vogue got under way, making them in various patterns, with lace effects and open-mesh designs, as well as in metallic silver and gold.

Bazaar, the shop that started everything in the young sector of fashion, closed after a few years its purpose completed, but not before it had grown three branches and triggered off a whole new way of selling the kind of fashion it had introduced. Its highly individual, gimmicky fashions created a kind of happy conspiracy between the shop and its customers. Bazaar, Mary Quant recalls, 'became a kind of permanently running cocktail party'. Shopping for clothes became fun. Clothes were fun. The boutiques, starting in Chelsea, spread over the whole country and became, in the 'sixties, as clearly defined an area of fashion selling as the long-established department stores, chains and multiples. They rose because the young wanted them – which means that the young were not being catered for by the stores and other retail outlets in the way they wanted. The formality of established shops was intimidating; the staid approach which might be flattering to the mature woman was frightening to the young. So was the mute reproach that would often follow failure to buy. In the boutique you could riffle through the rails at will and at ease. The staff would be young, like yourself. There would often be music, a coffee bar in the background. More important, from the practical point of view, was the fact that the

boutiques set up a rapid feed-back of fashion trends from the customer to the owner. He could keep pace with the movement of the very volatile, quickly changing youth market in a way that was impossible in the big store, but which was demanded by a generation which wanted everything new as tomorrow.

The idea and the name of the boutique were not, however, wholly new. Lucien Lelong started it all in Paris when, in 1933, he opened a boutique in his couture house, selling in it his '*éditions*', less expensive versions of his model clothes which needed only one fitting or none at all. His venture roused protests in the couture world, but before long his lead was being followed by many other couturiers, notably Schiaparelli, whose endlessly inventive accessories found their outlet there from the mid 'thirties. London couturiers also opened boutiques at various times in the 'sixties and some of them became more important than the parent house. John Cavanagh switched entirely to boutique business and the Hardy Amies boutique has for many years had an increasing part of his collection channelled into it.

192 (opposite) Young fashions shown in 1965 at the débutante charity dress show at which the year's 'debs' acted as models

193 Dior ready to wear. Shorts shown in London in 1968

All these, however, were rightly and properly called boutiques, as they were shops within couture houses. The new boutiques were different, being independent ventures, but perhaps they were justified in the name they took because they were shops with a difference – or differences, because they had infinite variety. They ranged from amateurish ventures, here today and gone tomorrow, to sophisticated enterprises, offering some of the most elegant fashions of the day. They could be cheap, gay and gimmicky, the chosen haunts of the young and trendy, with daylong 'pop' music blaring out from coffee bars doing good business in the rear and frenetic clothes spotlit on crowded rails. They could be expensive and exotic or expensive and austere. They were the great way of being different. Some had many branches. One, Biba, started by fashion artist Barbara Hulanicki as a mail-order boutique in 1964, became a direct-selling boutique and then, in 1969, a new-style store in Kensington. Boutiques spread everywhere, not only to the big towns but also to nearly every village. In 1971 the *Daily Mail* estimated that there were 15,000 of them, doing £300 million worth of business a year, mostly with the age group 15–24 years. Their prevalent note is youthful, their life blood is novelty. 'Boutique country,' said *Harper's Bazaar* in 1966, 'is run for fashion independents by fashion individualists; young designers with their own ideas, gifted buyers who skim chic from round the world. Boutique country exists to give you fun with clothes.'

The essence of boutiques is variety – and quick-change variety. They are constantly looking for new ideas. For them a design has only a few weeks to get from the drawing board to the rails . . . and off them. Perpetual motion is their aim. This, when it began, was a revolution in selling and it meant a revolution in making. From time immemorial fashion had been geared to the seasons, with manufacturers producing their collections twice a year, for spring and autumn, or, at most, four times, with additional, usually smaller, summer and winter ranges. The buying public obediently burst into fresh bloom with the spring trees and wrapped itself in new protective coverings when the earth turned bare in autumn. Not any more, said the boutiques, knowing their market. They aimed to be shops for all seasons.

The big manufacturers, whose production is aligned to seasonal collections, with long runs of a succession of styles and programmed delivery dates, could not adapt to the new anarchy of the boutiques. Nor would they want to. It was not their market. The kind of high speed production of small quantities of endless designs which the boutiques needed was, on the other hand, a 'natural' for those faithful age-long servitors of fashion, the outworkers and small contractors, ready with their special skills and hard-working ways to tackle the wildest extravagances that the boutiques could dream up for tomorrow's selling. To them the boutiques brought new scope and opportunities.

The boutiques, with their special kinds of young fashions and new ways of selling them, also had a considerable effect on other areas of fashion selling. The department stores reacted by

194 Young fashions across the Atlantic. Anne Fogarty's belted culotte dress in melon coloured wool. 1967–8

re Silk Crepe-de-
ine Jumper Suit
ious. White/Black
rk/Black, Blue &
ask Grey/Black
25½ guineas

Guipure lace dress
over Taffeta slip.
Colours. White Black
Ecru, Pale Blue
28½ guineas

Part Silk Shantung Organza
Dress. Colours. Navy Grey
Pale Blue   25½ guineas

SPECIALITY MODELS

195   Easy flattering well made clothes. 1953

opening special sections planned on boutique lines and quite different in every respect from the rest of the store. They bought from different sources, put everything on display in the crowded boutique way, engaged young and trendy salesgirls dressing them in boutique-style clothes. They often had background 'pop' music. Harrods had Way In, murkily navy blue with 'pop' music and 'in' clothes for 'in' people – young men, incidentally as well as young women. Selfridges turned over a substantial section of the ground floor of the Oxford Street store to the Miss Selfridge shop, an outsize in boutiques which has proliferated into a series of separate Miss Selfridges both in and outside London. Harvey Nichols had its 31 Shop, Peter Robinson had a basement under Oxford Circus full of way-out fashions. It was the same all over the country.

Many manufacturers have also latched on to the new trend to the extent of introducing new ranges to meet the needs of the young. These usually consist of younger and less expensive versions of their own kind of clothes – a revival of the original Paris boutique theme. They are made by the same methods, are sold successfully by the orthodox system.

The compulsion to climb on the young bandwagon was strong. In 1967, when the youth movement in fashion was probably at its peak, the age group 15–19 bought 48% of all coats, 60% of all dresses, 42% of knitwear and 48% of skirts, with corresponding proportions of other fashion lines. Between 1968 and 1979 the total number of young women between 15 and 19 increased by 12.4% and of those between 20 and 29 by 4.4%. It is too good a market to dismiss lightly, but at the same time people are living longer and remaining fit and active for longer. The older woman, the chief customer of the couturier a generation ago, is still interested in fashion, though probably she does not look to the couture today. This group, and all the other over-twenty-fives, who make up the remaining 50% or more of the market, are keenly interested in fashion and susceptible to its changes, but they do not necessarily want the fashions of the young, though they may be influenced by these fashions. They usually want easy, flattering, well-made clothes. They are the main market of the big, good quality manufacturers, the giants and others who have grown in size along with the growth of the young fashions. Thus Berkertex, who make a million dresses a year, define their aim as a line that is 'immensely wearable with an accent on the age group 20–50. In fact, grown-up beautiful clothes at moderate prices – a sure fire commercial success. The size range is from 34–46 inch hipline.'

Frederick Starke thought in the 1960s that 'fashion will have
to exist on two levels. Everyone is trying to climb on the
bandwagon of the young trendy fashions, but they are going on
a different course from the mainstream of the fashion industry.'
The boutique policy of dribbling in constant little handfuls of
new designs, each bringing in new variations, appealed, he
believed, to only one section of the public and was suited to only
one kind of making-up technique. There were others, and they
were flourishing. The need for lively, wearable clothes which
are flattering and in good taste and available in a full range of
sizes at acceptable prices is great. The success of the giants of the
trade shows the truth of this. Boutique clothes usually come
only in small sizes, stopping at size 14. They present great variations in the quality of their workmanship; in 1971 the managers
of the Miss Selfridge shops held a meeting with 16 of its clothes
suppliers to try to improve the quality of their goods, because
'retail opinion considered that up-to-the-minute clothing should
be better than it was'. Some improvement was subsequently
recorded, but the criticism is one frequently made in regard to
boutique fashions, mostly, however, by those not generally
attracted to them. Durability is not, on the whole, what the
boutique clientèle puts high on its list of fashion requirements.

2

While the young revolutionary fashions were proceeding apace
in the late 'fifties and the 'sixties, the British fashion Establishment was enjoying what hindsight now shows to have been a
sunset of considerable activity and enterprise. Exports in
particular engaged the attention not only of individual fashion
houses and manufacturers but also of organised fashion groups,
supported by the Board of Trade. Efforts started at the top and
in the early 'sixties the Incorporated Society of London Fashion
Designers, after seeming to languish, launched out into a series
of ambitious ventures which had a substantial effect in putting
Britain's fashions on the world's map and especially on the
American area of it. The start was made in 1960, when British
couturiers presented a combined collection in Paris right in the
middle of the showings of the French houses and roused sufficient
interest for 23 top American buyers to accept an invitation to
fly over to London on Sunday (their only free day) for a high

speed closer look at London Fashions. Substantial orders were placed as a result.

The Society next linked itself more closely with the general world of fashion by adding to its ranks a strong group of associate members, consisting of representatives of the chief auxiliary fashion trades, including furs, hats, stockings, cosmetics, jewellery, foundationwear, knitwear and shoes. Along with these it presented an annual series of combined fashion shows for overseas buyers, staging them in spectacular settings, including St. James's Palace, Lancaster House, Osterley Park House and the Crush Bar of the Royal Opera House, Covent Garden. These shows were given special prestige by the presence of Queen Elizabeth the Queen Mother.

Members of the Society also set out in person to tackle the American market. In 1964 a number of couturiers, energetically led by the Society's chairman, Edward Rayne, and its administrator, Lady Joubert, and accompanied by a team of model girls, took a selection of top British fashions to a ten-day fashion festival at Las Vegas, where Britain was a winner in a 23 nation fashion contest. In the following year another couture team, under the same leadership, again took a fashion collection across the Atlantic and held shows in New York, Washington, Houston, San Francisco and Los Angeles. The New York show

196   Fashion parade in the Crush Bar at Covent Garden Opera House. 1962

When the singing had to stop

Alfredo Bouret

From left to right:
Lady Macbeth—black satin and paillettes by Ronald Paterson.
Carmen—fringed orange crêpe by Norman Hartnell.
La Traviata—fringed white satin by Hardy Amies.
La Tosca—red velvet by Creed and suede Russian boots by Rayne.
Le Coq d'Or—gold lamé by John Cavanagh.

sketches by FAITH PEARCE

*197 British couture fashion in 1960.
A Hardy Amies coat of distinctive
design, in diagonal tweed in black and
white*

*198 Eau de nil satin makes this
evening dress and stole by Norman
Hartnell, with opalescent sequin embroidery. The model was bought by film
star Elizabeth Taylor. 1958*

*199 A dramatic ball gown in shocking
pink brocade by John Cavanagh 1958*

was staged at Magnins. In San Francisco it was part of a British
week being held there and was attended by Princess Margaret
and Lord Snowdon, who were also present at Los Angeles. The
publicity was immense and it rubbed off on British fashion as a
whole, setting a standard which the flourishing ready-to-wear
trade was able to support.

Meanwhile British wholesale fashion manufacturers had also
been on the move. By the late 'fifties the production of good
quality fashion had developed greatly in the hands of large, well-
established manufacturers and it became evident to the members
of the London Model House Group that, for exports to make
the impact of which they were now capable, combined action
should no longer be confined to a small group of top companies.
In 1958 32 manufacturers were invited by the Group to a meeting
at which the Fashion House Group of London was launched.
Twenty-eight manufacturers joined. The basis of selection was

200 *British wholesale fashions were being shown abroad. Part of a Frederick Starke collection in Norway*

that the Group should be made up of those who were the best in their field. Leading fabric and fibre manufacturers gave their support, among them Courtaulds and I.C.I. The group was led initially by Mr. Leslie Carr Jones, chairman of Susan Small and until then chairman of the Model House Group, all of whose members joined the new organisation.

The first big step towards stepping up exports was to institute a twice-yearly London Fashion Week, the first of which was held in May, 1959. During it all members showed their collections to overseas buyers in their own showrooms, but the new high-spot was a combined fashion show with a difference. The 'Fashion Spectaculars', devised by Michael Whittaker, showed skilfully-grouped fashions representing the best of British ready-to-wear in a series of 'scenes' which came somewhere between song-and-dance acts and ballet. This was an innovation in fashion presentation and had a long run of increasing success in the spacious setting of Celanese House. It struck exactly the right note at the time, when something dramatic and new was needed to boost British fashion in the prevailing intense competitiveness. The first show was attended by 73 overseas buyers, but the numbers rose impressively to a total of 1300 from 35 countries. Resultant exports, which at the start of the Group's life had amounted to only £300,000 a year, rose ultimately to more than £5,000,000 – about a third of Britain's total fashion exports at the time.

By 1962 selling drives ranged from Germany and other European countries to America and Australia, collections being shown in San Francisco, Los Angeles, Melbourne and Sydney.

201 *Finale of a Fashion House Group Spectacular in the early 1960's*

202 *Young designers were encouraged by being given associate membership of the Fashion Group. L to R John Bates, of Jean Varon, Roger Nelson and Bob Schultz, with the designs which won them this recognition in 1965*

203 *A group of model girls who took part in the first big combined show held in Paris in 1963 by the Fashion House Group*

An ambitious venture was the first showing of British ready-to-wear in strength in Paris in April 1963, when a very successful presentation was attended by the late Duke and the Duchess of Windsor and the British Ambassador, Sir Piers Dixon, and Lady Dixon. Two hundred and fifty garments were shown in a little over an hour at the Pré Catalan. A second impressive combined show took place in Paris in the following year at the Royal Monçeau.

The Group's biggest venture was its American visit in October, 1965, when, with the co-operation of the Government and of Cunard, a large representative collection was taken to New York on board the Queen Elizabeth. The plan, master-minded by Frederick Starke, then chairman of the Group, was to present a complete 'Fashion Spectacular' in the ballroom of the liner while she was berthed at New York. For this biggest-ever live fashion export drive the personnel included 20 manufacturers, 18 British model girls, production and administration teams and 12 members of the British fashion press. Four shows were given, starting with a V.I.P. evening, one hostessed by Lady (Sylvia) Harlech, wife of the British Ambassador. The visit was an instant success, with immense T.V. and press coverage all over America and general acclaim. The clothes were seen by 1000 American buyers. It took the new mini skirt to New York in a big way and girls wearing it were photographed in Times Square and stopped the traffic on Broadway. Back in London, the *Daily Mail* re-staged the show for a crowded assembly of its readers in the Royal Garden Hotel.

Later overseas fashion tours went to European countries, including Switzerland, Denmark, Sweden, Germany, Italy, France and Belgium. In 1968 the Group folded. Why? Moss Murray, who handled its promotion, says: 'It was too successful. It quadrupled exports and in some cases increased them tenfold. But some firms began to feel that they were doing so well that they did not need the joint activities – and costs – of the Group and also that benefits were rubbing off too much on non-members.'

By 1969 only four members of the Incorporated Society's previous Top Ten and First Eleven were showing their collections on the agreed pre-Paris seasonal dates. In the next year only one appeared. The rest had either closed down or opted out into ready-to-wear or boutique business to such a degree that they showed at dates chosen to meet these needs. Likewise the end of the Fashion House Group, whether it was due to a surfeit of success or to other causes, indicated a major change in the structure of fashion. The independent top manufacturers who had joined forces as the Model House Group and who had led the expansion into the Fashion House Group were in most cases either going out of business under the pressure of changing conditions or were being absorbed in large manufacturing groups. The need for corporate solidarity had largely passed away. The intimacy which had bound the Model House Group together no longer existed and the new big organisations could to a large degree promote their own interests without help. It was, too, the day of the hard sell, not of the fancy spectacle.

Two years after the Fashion House Group disbanded the Clothing Export Council was established. Its basis is much broader in that it deals with all clothing and that membership is open to all manufacturers and wholesalers. Financed by members' subscriptions and supported by British fibre and fabric manufacturers, it is controlled by an elected committee. It is recognised by the Department of Trade and Industry as the voice of the whole clothing industry for export marketing and therefore has an over-all authority never before achieved. It organises twice-yearly Fashion Seasons for overseas buyers, undertakes export missions and joint ventures. Its members have the benefit of Government facilities. It negotiates with the appropriate Government departments regarding financial assistance towards promotional activities at home and abroad. It advises and helps visiting buyers on export opportunities. What it lacks, apart from not being a special outlet for the fashion industry is what might be regarded as an asset – it does not pre-select British fashions for export promotion. He who pays the piper calls the tune.

But the idea of fashion-makers getting together to further a shared outlook has been continued to a limited degree by the Associated Fashion Designers of London. This group was formed in 1964 by a number of young manufacturers who, because the Fashion House Group restricted its membership to a total of 30, could not be admitted to its already full ranks. They decided to go it alone, in their own way – and it is a way that has paid off. Instead of establishing a permanent group of members and therefore a closed shop, they have a committee of six as their only continuous entity, and within it an executive committee of three does the planning from season to season. Manufacturers are invited to take part in the shows, which still take the form of 'spectaculars'. On one occasion 20 companies took part in the fashion event, at the next 40 were involved. A nucleus of about a dozen, mostly in the young sector, has become more or less permanent, giving stability to the group. Export remains the main target and accounts for about 90% of the sales that result from the shows. These are attended by 2000 to 3000 people, about 70% of them from overseas or representing overseas companies. The A.F.D. also takes shows to various European countries and is associated with the Clothing Export Council in its activities. Under this new régime British clothing exports rose spectacularly, from about £30,000,000 annually in the 'fifties and early 'sixties to £91,000,000 in 1968, £100,000,000 in 1969 and over £123,000,000 in 1970, of which it is realistic to assign more than half to women's fashions.

With the Incorporated Society and the Fashion House Group languishing in London from the mid-'sixties, Paris couture also began to wilt as a leading force. After the first flush of post-war

204 *Paris with a difference. Cardin's 1966 dress and visor hat with spaceman look*

205 *Courrèges 1968 with dress in white wool gabardine and knee length socks*

206 *Patou in 1967 shows young bolero-topped suits in wool fleece*

activity and Dior's shot in the arm there were some uneasy comings and goings and a series of major movements into the ready-to-wear by, among others, Nina Ricci, Yves St. Laurent, Cardin and Lanvin. The exclusiveness and the authority of Paris were in retreat. It had, for instance, long been part of the Paris *mystique* to place an embargo of a month on the use of photographs by the press and sketching at Paris shows had been rigidly forbidden. Givenchy allowed sketching in 1957, when his famous 'sack' appeared instantly in the powerful American *Women's Wear Daily*. In 1958 the ramparts fell and most of the couturiers allowed sketching and immediate publication. Dior capitulated two years later. When Balenciaga, the last of the 'pure' couturiers, retired in 1968, it was the sunset of couture. In the January, 1971 collections Paris lowered the ban on the publication of photographs and the London *Times* noted this as 'breaking the traditional mould of the fashion industry which

207   Yves St. Laurent's 1971 blazer and pleated skirt in wool gabardine and flannel was a trend setter

may never be mended' and as 'surely the final admission that trends are not set by any one level of fashion house any more or by any one city'. Yves St. Laurent said that clothes were a form of protest, thereby turning the tables completely on established couture which had always aimed at bringing elegance and pleasure, grace and beauty to the world of fashion over which it ruled. By 1971 one leading fashion writer's report on the Courrèges and Givenchy collections was headed succinctly: 'Quel Bore!'

When did traditional law and order depart from the fashion scene? To go down Memory Lane in the back numbers of the fashion magazines is to find the general picture of fashion moving on the accepted lines until about the mid-'sixties. Well established names prospered. Most top manufacturers had their own factories. In 1964 the knowledgeable authors of *The Needle is Threaded* could say: 'The vast majority of the clothes we wear, whether specially tailored suits, or ready-made underwear, raincoats, shirts, skirts and the rest, are factory-produced in an industry serving almost the whole population.' There were

209 (opposite)   Paris when it swings—with Cardin in 1971

210 Transparent plastic coat and linen dress in a 1966 outfit

clothes for the time of day and the occasion. There was no doubt about what went with what and it was all carefully accessorised. Then there is a break. 'Get moving,' commands *Harper's Bazaar*, ushering in a feature on 'Paris when it Sparks. Paris when it Swings. Paris when it Whirls, Charms, Scores, Dazzles, Shines.' Then 'London moves into Swing.' In 1966 British Nylon Spinners were saying in a glossy magazine advertisement that:

> *Breakaway girls like porridge with lumps*
> *Breakaway girls like roses in dumps*
> *Breakaway girls often let down their hair*
> *Breakaway girls wear clothes with flair.*

The caftan arrived in 1967 and it became possible to go around in the kind of loose, Biblical robes that had not been seen for centuries. 1969 was a see-through summer, with transparent clothes worn with nothing or next to nothing under them. Courrèges's diaphanous dresses were fortified with sequins at strategic points. Ungaro made clothes from metal or plastics discs, linked together with rings. Cardin 'cuts his mini skirts as mini as they'll go', said one fashion magazine, and, following his lead, 'London cuts it short'.

The glossy magazines went overboard with the new fashion mood. Fantasy clothes – draped robes, Turkish trousers, Oriental tunics, pinafores, dresses that were all floating scarves and winged sleeves – were photographed in fantasy settings, their wearers skimming over the countryside, brooding in ivory towers, leaping on beaches. It was a Celtic summer for one magazine, with everything photographed in wildest Wales. By summer 1970 *Vogue* declared firmly: 'Clothes. They are purely for decoration and they have more to do with you in particular than anything in general.'

Paris too became younger. There was quite a stir in 1970 when designers introduced 'les knickers' – a kind of plus fours or pantaloons which had a very brief life. More success attended Paris's 'new knitted clothes for running, jumping and living on the top of the world', because they were wearable even if you preferred your feet to be on terra firma. There was a craze for 'what is beautiful and sexy and zany enough'. Blue rouge and golden ears were shown in a beauty article with the defiant caption: 'Why not?' There were clothes for the New Druids, in wool, suède and leather, tied with thongs and worn with grass hats – 'Not so much clothes as robes, heroic dressing' – and they were photographed, of course, at Stonehenge. It began almost to mean that you could wear anything anywhere. No one would stare for more than a moment if you walked along Knightsbridge wearing a djellaba or a Sherpa coat or turned up at a party dressed like a Red Indian or a cowboy or in the shortest mini or the longest maxi. There was a drooping 'thirties look and even a return to the squared-up shoulders of the 'forties. There were high-waisted Empire dresses and in the summer of 1971 there were hot pants. 'Doing your own thing in fashion,' commented the *Times*, 'is a time-consuming activity and it needs a lot of confidence. In 1970 it was the fashion.'

New names rode on the crest of this new kind of fashion. They were legion and of all kinds. Sometimes they worked on a small scale for only a few retail outlets. Sometimes they developed largely and importantly. Outstanding was Jean Muir, who started as a salesgirl in Liberty's, went to Jaeger as a designer for six years, and in 1962 was backed by Courtaulds when she went to

211 Spring, 1971, when 'hot pants' were worn even in offices

Jane and Jane, from which she emerged to work independently under her own name. From the start she sold throughout Britain and also to Henry Bendel of New York. Soon she was selling all over the United States, Canada, Australia and Europe. Her clothes are expensive, elegant, distinctive and mannered. Ossie Clark came to the fore, for a time, with highly individualistic fashion. Thea Porter, also in the high price bracket and selling to top shops, was a painter who started designing clothes in 1964. Zandra Rhodes, a product of the Royal College of Art Fashion School, began by designing and printing highly individualistic textiles and went on to turn her fabrics into fashions in 1969, when she was 'discovered' by American *Vogue*. Bill Gibb, ex-St. Martin's and the Royal College of Art, designed for Baccarat for some years, then started on his own in 1972 with a complete team, including designers, cutter and business manager to support him.

For the most part fashion leaders rely upon contractors and outworkers to produce their clothes. The explanation they give is that under today's conditions factory overheads and labour costs are prohibitive for the independent fashion operator. That is why, in contrast to the hundreds of employees at the factories of the giants of the fashion trade, the fleets of buses that transport them from nearby villages to work and the pantechnicons that ply from factory to showroom every day, you will at any hour of the day see men running up the staircases of showrooms in the Great Titchfield and Margaret Street area of the wholesale dress trade, eagerly delivering armfuls of dresses, then running down again with a roll of cloth over one shoulder. They are the contractors who make up for the small – and not so small – new fashion firms.

John Williams, secretary of the Association of Clothing Manufacturers, which was formed in 1961 by the amalgamation of two existing contractors' associations, estimated that more than half of all fashions are made up by contractors. These are of all kinds, from a single worker or a family group to units employing up to 200 people. The average size consists of between 40 and 50 working together. They make more coats and suits than dresses – which are simpler to make and therefore tend to be produced in factories. As costs rise more and more firms, even large ones, are contracting out. The increasing variety of fashions is also causing many big manufacturers to use contractors, because to produce everything in their factories would lead to confusion on the production lines. A great many contractors work on boutique fashions, where rapid changes of

212   An early Jean Muir dress, designed while she was with Jane and Jane. 1964

213   *Doing your own thing.*
See-through pants dress
designed by Ossie Clark. 1969

style and short runs of a great number of designs are unsuited to
modern factory organisation. The bigger contractors often have
their own outworkers, and send a van round daily, complete
with a supervisor, to collect and deliver work, and to examine
finished work so as to ensure that quality is maintained. The
outworker system has great advantages for married women and
the outworker, being self-employed, is economically a good
proposition for the contractor, who need not pay insurance, or
employ her all the time. But sweated labour persists in the
clothing industry, still being widespread in the 1980's.

10 Growth and prosperity of the top manufacturers, 1960's and early 1970's

I

In contrast to the splinter movement of fashion, activated by the young sector of the market and proving a law unto itself, the remaining half or more of the British fashion world was dominated from the late 'fifties by a group of giant manufacturing companies which had been growing steadily for some years and which in most cases became public companies in the 'fifties and 'sixties.

After the war many manufacturers had found their premises too small for their expanding business and often old-fashioned and ill-equipped to deal with the needs of the brave new world of fashion. In the booming economy of the 'fifties and early 'sixties there was also, for the first time in history, apart from the years of the two World Wars, a shortage of workers in the established fashion manufacturing centres, London, Manchester and Leeds. The fashion industry began to spread out to other parts of the country, in many of which heavy industries absorbed male labour but few opportunities existed for women and girls. Fashion manufacture opened up in a great number of new and scattered areas, among the chief ones being South Wales, the North East of England, Plymouth, Portsmouth and the West of Scotland. The factories there were usually purpose-built and, as 'green' labour was being widely employed, a new impetus was given to training schemes in up-to-date factory methods of production which drew upon the experience gained in large-scale wartime production, especially of uniforms for the services. American expertise was also drawn upon once more; links with U.S.A. production continued and grew. Aquascutum, who since 1949 have manufactured in Canada as well as in Britain, maintained a close liaison with their trans-Atlantic operation which in the 1950's and 1960's was American-orientated. 'We have always received from the U.S.A. the greatest practical help as regards improving manufacturing processes', they said. They were particularly impressed with the high degree of attention devoted by American manufacturers to the finishing of fabrics before manufacturing began.

This advance in production methods was by far the greater change because, while the young trend involved the use of old methods of manufacture and revived the use of widely scattered outworkers and small contractors, the big fashion makers developed new methods of making up. A wealth of new technology was introduced. Administration was streamlined. Production was controlled by technicians and was planned to ensure a smooth flow from start to finish of the manufacturing process. This was a compulsion placed on the big manufacturers by their expansionist policies and because of the rising cost and scarcity of labour, of which they had to make the best possible use. Their success depended upon uniformity of quality and regularity of production through the long runs required for large markets working to a regular calendar of orders, deliveries and retailing.

The razz-ma-tazz of boutique fashion was not everyone's choice and it produced a reaction to more classic clothes, together with the requirement that they should be available all over the country and in all sizes. This the big groups could achieve; their financial and administrative resources could ensure steady output, uniform standards of styling, sizing and manufacture and effective distribution. What they could not do – and they readily admitted it – was to rush hot-foot into evey new trend or to set trends. Working on a large scale, they were involved in heavy capital investment in their fashions and they dared not gamble on the success of an untried novelty. Nor, as they knew, did their customers want them to. Flattering clothes that reflected accepted trends but subdued them with an element of tradition were what they aimed to supply.

The chief casualties in this new alignment of fashion were the independent top ready-to-wear fashion houses, many of them still private companies and family businesses with limited capital. They had had a long run of succcess, in most cases since the 'thirties, but they had now become vulnerable in face of rising costs, shortages of labour, increasing competition from above and below and the growing vagaries of fashion which they tried to follow closely. Heads began to roll and in some cases the drop of a hem or the raising of a waistline could change one season's profits into the next season's disastrous losses. But

many of these houses, with their well-known names and high reputations, were attractive to the new big operators already concerned in fashion, anxious to upgrade their image and possessed of the capital, administration and production facilities which could bring stability to an area which still had great potential. Certain of the independents welcomed the chance of coming under this new umbrella. In a number of cases they remained personally actively concerned with the future of their companies. When, in 1956, Lou Ritter, who owned $92\frac{1}{2}$% of the shares of his company, Deréta, and also a substantial part of Rembrandt, was approached by Ellis and Goldstein, he accepted their offer to go into their group, but remained for the next 15 years as managing director of Deréta as well as a director of the parent company. Susan Small was acquired by Courtaulds, but retained its entity and personnel, and when Frank Usher became part of the Selincourt group it too continued to have its own

214　Frank Usher continued on its course after becoming part of the Selincourt Group. An elegant trouser suit in black silky jersey with cropped jacket, white tie, gold cuff links and red carnation. Winter 1972

215　Silk chiffon hand painted in a stunning design for Frank Usher's 1972 evening dress

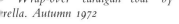
Wrap-over 'cardigan coat' by ~~rella~~. Autumn 1972

217 Jerkin and trousers by Harella in contrast wool jersey. Autumn 1972

218 Linda Leigh trouser suit in Trevira for the 'not so slim'. Autumn 1972

designers, showrooms and production organisation.

Although these and other well-known names remained before the public, the big groups which controlled them were, to the women who wore the fashions for which they were ultimately responsible, often as anonymous as the often un-known outworkers and sewing women who have been the mainstay of fashion through most of its history. The giant of them all is Selincourt, with 1972 assets of £12,000,000, 3400 employees, exports of more than £2,000,000 a year and a trading profit of £1,408,000 for 1971–1972. Selincourts sell nothing under their own name. They consisted then of 22 companies, nine of them big producers in different areas of fashion and including Frank Usher, Harella, Linda Leigh, Garlaine and Skirtex. When they bought Linda Leigh in 1959 they took over its head, Louis Mintz, who became managing director and deputy chairman of the whole group. They ran all their fashion companies separately. They produced 50,000 garments a week in their factories in various parts of the country,

219 Alexon dress and jacket in soft blended diagonal wool tweed with braided jacket. Autumn 1972

220 Flared skirt, short jacket and white piqué collar and cuffs on Alexon's cotton piqué suit for spring 1972

including Romford, Ilford and Brighton. This accounted for about 95% of their output, their use of sub-contractors being only marginal. Their other interests included fabrics for both fashions and furnishing, laces and nets, quilts and fasteners. They also manufacture substantially for Marks and Spencer. It was a long way from the 1857 Sélincourt, which sold early ready-to-wear cloaks and mantles under its own name.

They had a direct link with the early development of women's clothing manufacture in Louis Mintz. He started his career in 1913, working in a clothing workshop run by his father in a converted public house in the East End of London. It was a family affair, with Louis and his sisters all lending a hand. When orders were received they were written up on the wall and disaster came when the workroom was re-papered and they lost their order book! Louis Mintz developed the business until it became a very substantial one, with Linda Leigh, founded by him in 1951, as its main range. When he sold it to Selincourt he was the main shareholder – a case of the tail wagging the dog!

Steinbergs, starting as the one-man enterprise of the young Alexander Steinberg, was founded by him in 1904 and the first stage of its growth culminated in the introduction of the big Alexon range in 1929 and its rapid expansion in the following years. It had developed so far by 1935 that the company moved their production unit out of London in order to keep pace with rising labour requirements which could not be met in the crowded capital. They set up a modern production unit in South Wales, on the Treforest Industrial Estate near Cardiff, and within a few weeks a hundred local operatives were being trained in conformity with the company's established methods and standards of production. The move proved to be, before long, very much in the national interest, because throughout the war the entire factory was switched to the production of a million uniforms for the armed forces.

In common with other segments of the fashion industry Steinbergs found the experience gained in this way beneficial to themselves, and after the war their expansion took on an increased momentum. In 1947 they became a public company, Steinberg and Sons (South Wales) Ltd. The foundation stone of a new, bigger, factory at Hawthorn, near Pontypridd, was laid in 1949 and in 1950 the factory was opened there. In the 1960's, with a number of extensions added to it, it employed between 600 and 800 people, producing 4000 lined garments (coats and jackets) and 6000 unlined ones (casual wear) per week.

Two other factories were later set up by Steinbergs in South

Wales, one at Port Talbot and the other at Mountain Ash. In 1961 the West Auckland Clothing Company was acquired, after being an associated company since 1956, and this gave Steinbergs an additional large operational factory for their growing production requirements. In addition to Alexon, Steinbergs manufactured Dellbury, Horrockses Fashions and Youngset and they shared Butte-Knit with Jonathan Logan of America. In the year 1971–1972 they had gross assets of £5,000,000 and made a profit of £540,774. They had 2149 employees and exports amounted to just on £1,000,000. In addition to their fashion activities, which accounted for 74% of their turnover, they had also a handbag division – Pexella, Chanelle and Essell – and Texifused inter-linings.

The Eastex factory at Luton, the largest and most modern fashion factory in Bedfordshire, was one of the chief production units of Ellis and Goldstein (Holdings) Limited, which was founded in East London in 1910 but whose development was largely a post-war story. In the 1970's they had assets of nearly £6,000,000, profits of £827,000 and employed 3776 people. Their exports were nearly £1,250,000. In addition to Eastex and Deréta, they also manufactured several other well-known brands, including Laura Lee. They moved to Luton in 1939–

221   An Eastex fashion parade in the mid 1950's

222   Eastex fashions 1972

1940 as part of the Government's plan to disperse London's industry and with the immediate purpose of making clothes for the Services. As soon as the war was over expansion in the production of Eastex clothes began. It was the first range to be made specifically for the shorter figure which market research had shown to be the predominant one. Very appropriately, they launched their brand for the five-foot-two figure in 1952. Extensions to the factory were soon called for, including building on an empty site next door and, in 1967, adding a new floor. The factory size was doubled, and by 1970, with 80,000 square feet of factory space at Luton, they employed 800 people, about 120 production workers on each of the six floors. Each floor produced 1000 garments a week and, with a seasonal range of 200 styles, this meant a very speedy change-over from one style to another.

They were almost fanatical, they said, about quality, and reverted to a considerable degree to craftsman methods, even to the extent of garments being largely made entirely by one operator, highly skilled in sewing techniques. In pursuit of this excellence they operated very detailed training schemes, ranging from internal ones employing the Soundwell method for machinists, to further earn-as-you-learn courses run in association with the local technical college and with the City and Guilds Institute of London and the Clothing Institute. Such training at many levels was given prominence among the big manufacturers, with appropriate career opportunities awaiting the successful student. At Ellis and Goldstein it is the cornerstone of their activities. Their search for craftsmen and craftswomen was so intense that they rejected 51% of applicants for jobs, admitting through selecton tests.

Newest of the giants in the fashion industry was Raybeck, which acquired Berkertex in 1968 and became the second largest consortium in fashion, with 1970 assets of £7,916,000, profits of £1,830,000 and 4108 employees working in its aggregate of more than 20 companies. It began soon after World War II by making inexpensive coats in a small factory in the City of London. Their policy, said director Jerrald Victor, who became managing director of Berkertex and went over to them when they acquired Berkertex, was to diversify right through from manufacturing to retailing. In addition to their dress houses they also owned three groups of shops. Their first purchase, Pegg Page, had for some years been the top profitability house in the women's outerwear trade. In 1969–1970 its ratio of profits to assets was 63.7%, 29% above its nearest rival, Tricoville. Peggy

Page, incidentally was a triumphant veteran of the fashion
business. It started its life in the 'thirties when, under Harry
Massey, it was one of the first British companies to move ahead
of the crowd by manufacturing to the sizing and making-up
standards set up by the Americans who put the British ready-to-
wear trade on its path to success. Raybeck's main growth came
in the 'sixties, and it acquired Carnegie, Mary Harnes,
Alexander Green and the May Fox Company as well as the
Werff, Bradmore and Bobby Cousins shops and the Lord John
shops in the men's sector. It had large mail order interests and
sold on a substantial scale to multiples, including Richard Shops.
All the companies operated as self-contained units, but group
chairman Ben Raven was in constant touch with them all. At
Raybeck they regarded their links with the retail trade as all-
important. They had confidence in their merchandise and felt
that they must be in a position to present it themselves and not be
dependent on other people buying it for the retail market.

Their biggest problem was labour. They could double their
market and greatly increase their export figure of £888,000 if
they could obtain labour to make up their fashions, but they said
in the 1960's and 1970's, the Government would not permit
them to bring over the large number of Cypriot girls who could
meet their needs. They regarded the labour problem as urgent in
relation to the Common Market. 'England is far and away
supreme compared with the rest of Europe in price, styling and
production,' they said. 'We could be the greatest fashion
industry in Europe, but we are being handcuffed by the
Government's restrictions on imported workers.' They spread
their factories round the country. They resorted to home
workers to make up part of their garments, with finishing
carried out at their factories. But still they were short of their
requirements.

In its developments fashion persisted in the diversity which is
part of its nature. Windsmoor, which was founded in 1933 and
advanced sufficiently in that year to place its first advertisement
in the *Radio Times*, achieved its main development after the
1939–1945 war, when output rose rapidly from 2000 garments a
week to 11,000–12,000. The company was unique in that it was
the only one of the day's big names and big producers in top
fashion to use its name in retailing, to remain privately-owned –
and to be determined to stay that way. It was owned and
managed by three brothers, Cecil, Lionel and Maurice Green,
who were in charge of production, sales and cloth-buying
respectively. They were born into the business, as their father,

Charles Green, was manufacturing women's coats and costumes on a considerable scale from 1910, but they set up their own business in the early 'thirties, with the purpose of manufacturing high quality women's coats, dresses and suits. They had their own factory in London and by the 1970's had another at Macclesfield. About a third of their output was made in these factories. They had their own design team, made all their own models and all Windsmoor clothes were cut under their own roof by their own staff, but two-thirds of their output were made up by contractors, who worked exclusively for them. They regarded this method of production as advantageous because it enabled the company to secure trained specialist operators for the increasingly varied output which, in accordance with fashion trends, they undertook. The largest of their contractors turned out 1200 garments a week for them.

Continuity with the past was carried into widening development for the present and the future by Aquascutum. The chairman, Gerald Abrahams, C.B.E., surveying the company's progress in 1971, said: 'Our record has shown over the years a steady advance with a broadened range of merchandise to ensure the leadership in fashionable fine quality clothing for men and women.' Queen's awards in 1966 and 1971 were evidence of their success – between the two awards they increased their exports by £1,000,000. Behind this success lies a policy of consistently producing their fashions (and other clothing) in their own factories. They even create their own cloth constructions, designs and colourings, by arrangements with British mills. Their technicians have developed many new methods of treating and finishing materials to achieve results that range from smooth handle to extra wearability. Their Aqua 5, introduced in the 1960's, reached new standards of water repellancy for the clothing industry.

By 1970 their factories for women's fashions, at Colchester, Leighton Buzzard, St. Albans and Bletchley, employed 600 workpeople. 'We have considered from time to time factoring out part of our production in order to keep up with sales demand,' said C. Reese, then one of their directors. 'For 20 years sales have been pushing production, but our conclusion is that the only way to maintain quality is to make your clothes under your own direction. Otherwise samples can be right, trial orders can be right, but when bulk production starts quality goes down.'

Labour was their besetting problem in 1970 – not only expert labour but also labour of any kind. Mr. Reese recalled that a

224 *Swing-back coat by Aquascutum in boldly checked tweed for Autumn 1972*

223 *Aquascutum's raincoat in permanently proofed cotton, with high waistline and sumptuous racoon collar and cuffs. Autumn 1972*

member of staff, who recently visited a high quality American women's clothing factory, commented on his return that nearly all the workers were elderly. Skill was hard to obtain. To keep up standards it was therefore necessary to make increasing use of expert technical direction of labour. People with professional training were being used increasingly, but even they had to be 'pushed right through the organisation. It takes a man five years to become Aquascutum-orientated and capable of taking major decisions on everything from fabrics to actual production,' said Mr. Reese.

Mechanisation also had to be pursued unremittingly. 'The trend will be,' he said, 'to do more and more without people. New attachments to machines must be found and used, such as simulated hand-stitching devices.' Cutting was being developed by the use of the Lanner spray marker, which sprayed yellow paint all round the pattern set on the material, outlining it like a stencil. America was already talking of doing bulk cutting with the Laser beam – the electronic device which, by burning through the material, achieves tremendous speed – perhaps a speed which would far outpace the rate at which material could be prepared for it.

Burberry's are also traditionalists who have moved with the times. In 1970, as part of Great Universal Stores, they were using new fabrics, including washable Terylene and cotton, and were increasingly diversifying their output, with women's separates, trouser suits and sportswear running parallel to their men's ranges and forming their newest development. They had also been organising much more bulk production of high quality fashion in their own group of factories, where all their production was carried out by a work force of 1500 people. Production was split up, each factory having its own special functions. The oldest, at Reading, specialised in samples and the basic work on cotton raincoats, which were later put into production at other factories. It also made up speciality merchandise which involved short runs with a high work content, the most difficult area of factory manufacture. At Castleford, near Leeds, they opened one of the most modern factories in Britain, geared up to the bulk production of raincoats, jackets and sports coats. It covered an area of 108,000 square feet and had £150,000 worth of completely new equipment. The factory at Littleport, near Ely, concentrated on commuter coats and in developing the less expensive side of both men's and women's ranges. At Treorchy, in Wales, bulk production of trench coats was the main activity.

Post-war dispersal of factories mainly affected large-scale manufacturers. The small workshops still tended to cluster round the accustomed parts of London and to be centred upon the East End and Soho, where immigrant workers had for so long been settled. There was, however, a certain amount of fanning out to the periphery of London, where many new factories were set up and were providing home workers with a considerable overspill of work. Post-war waves of immigrants also brought a large influx of new workers experienced in the clothing trade and they continued to make a substantial contribution to the making of women's fashions. The fresh arrivals came from various parts of Europe, but Cypriots, Greeks and Pakistanis predominated. They continued to be an important source of labour for all sections of fashion and have become increasingly so.

These new immigrants, like their predecessors, tended to work in small units, often family-orientated, rather than in the new big factories. Their numbers and the exact extent of their contribution to the making of fashion have always been elusive. They were particularly strong in light clothing and soon after the 1939–1945 war there was sufficient solidarity among them for them to form the Light Clothing Contractors' Association to protect their interests. For many years this co-existed with the older-established Master Ladies' Tailors Association of Clothing Contractors. The contractor and the outworker were both working for big manufacturers and their status required an effective organisation to represent them and safeguard their interests.

The contractor and outworker enjoyed a very different lot from that of the earlier generation. He was – and is – in great demand, and can usually command good payment for his skill.

225 *Burberry's classic trenchcoat in Terylene and cotton gabardine for 1972*

2

It was inevitable that the big manufacturers would want to ensure the availability of their fashions to the public by more positive means than simply relying on the orders placed at the beginning of each season by the store buyers who saw their collections. A successful style could, according to this process, sell out rapidly and repeat orders be delayed or even not placed at all because of the exigencies of factory production or merchandise control-systems operated by stores. Raybeck's acquisition of its own chains of shops was one solution. Another, provided by many manufacturers, was the shop within a shop, maintained, staffed and stocked by the manufacturer concerned, and devoted exclusively to the sale of his named brands. Burberry had pioneered this idea in 1932 and Jaeger opened a shop within a shop in Selfridges in 1936, following this up with others in the post-war years, but these were not completely developed in the later form of self-contained entities controlled entirely by the manufacturer. From 1950 Jaeger changed to having Jaeger sections, controlled by the main shop concerned.

The first of what were to become hundreds of shops within shops was set up by Berkertex at Spooners of Plymouth about 1949. Berkertex had been founded in 1936 by Leslie Berker, who came into fashion from engineering, and the simple, button-through dresses which were his first main fashion line were well suited to the mechanised production which attracted him as a means of achieving large-scale growth. After the war production was divided between a number of factories in London and a very large number of outdoor workers, ranging in location from Oakham in Auckland to Glasgow. Eric Crabtree, who had joined the board of Berkertex after the war, was entrusted with the task of rationalising manufacture and his approach to the problem was to establish at Plymouth what was at that time the

226   The Berkertex factory at Plymouth

biggest single dressmaking unit in the world, and also, it was claimed, the first fully mechanised dress factory in Britain. In the blitzed city a single-storey open-plan building, covering nearly ten acres, with 84,000 square feet of floor space, was acquired from the Government and was opened on June 6, 1948. In it a hard core of skilled technicians from London set about training Plymouth girls, who knew nothing of the needle trade, to be dress machinists. Within a very few years 1000 people were employed and 9000 dresses a week were being turned out to a very high standard of production. By 1970 output ran at about a million dresses a year and Berkertex continually kept up with the application of new developments in mechanical production methods.

In order to digest this great leap in output Berkertex proceeded to set up their own retail outlets within existing shops. At Spooners the innovation of a direct link between manufacturer and public proved an instant success. Berkertex business rocketed overnight after a spectacular opening at which Sir Norman Hartnell, who was then designing for the firm, showed his couture collection with his own model girls. When the next Berkertex shop opened in Southampton 20,000 people,

227 (left)   A lively look for Spring in Berkertex dress and jacket in plain and spotted Trevira/rayon. 1973

228 (right)   A different mood in Berkertex's sheer pleated shirtwaister. Spring, 1973

229 *A Cresta shop-within-a-shop*

Mr. Crabtree recalls, arrived to attend it and massive police reinforcements had to be called in to control the crowds.

In subsequent years, with Leslie Berker as chairman and Jerrald Victor as managing director, the Berkertex range became greatly diversified, to include dresses and jackets, light-weight dresses and coats, cocktail and evening wear, all of very varied types, aimed at the 25 and upwards age groups and in a middle price range that sold then from £8 to £30 – what they called 'grown-up beautiful clothes at moderate prices'. They had 2000 retail outlets, apart from the shops within shops, and in addition to their large showrooms in Oxford Street they also had showrooms in Manchester, Birmingham, Leeds, Cardiff, Belfast and Dublin. At the London Fashion Centre, which they maintained at their headquarters, they sold to the public not only their own fashions but also those of many other leading manufacturers. They also specialised in bridal fashions here, had 35 bridal boutiques in other shops, and another 'London Fashion Centre' at Huddersfield.

Eric Crabtree later moved on to create yet another retail

variant in the shape of the Cresta Shops, a 'multiple' version of the high quality 'madam' shop, and this group, numbering 71 shops, was the largest high-class fashion chain in the world, manufacturing a third of its own goods and buying or contracting out the rest.

The shop within a shop soon proliferated and was adopted by most of the top big manufacturers. Berkertex had 120 shops of this kind. Eastex were represented in about 160 Elangol shops, where all the Ellis and Goldstein ranges were sold. Windsmoor moved into the field in 1963, with their first shop at Swan and Edgars. They had 174 shops by 1970. They say that such shops accounted for 60% of their total business. Steinbergs had 60 Alexon shops, selling their Dellbury range as well as Alexon.

The shop within a shop, staffed, managed and stocked by the manufacturer, has the immense advantage that its rails can be refilled from the factories all the year round and special sizes and colours can speedily be obtained direct from the factory or from another shop within a shop in response to the customer's requirements. Brand loyalty is greatly encouraged. The shops also provide an invaluable feed-back from customer to the manufacturer both on general fashion trends and on local requirements. Area supervisors and the management of the manufacturers concerned keep in close touch with their shops.

Parallel with the development of large-scale fashion manufacturer has been the establishment and growth of organisations formed by the producers of the fibres and fabrics, which are the raw materials of fashion. Courtaulds was the only fibre giant which, with its subsidiaries, was involved in every stage of fashion making from the initial production of the fibres concerned right through to the manufacture of the finished garment in nearly every category. They acquired eight fashion manufacturers. It started in the 'twenties in order to show, by actual manufacture, how the new rayons could be made up. Such an operation was an innovation and it progressed. As man-made fibres and fabrics developed into major parts of fashion, Courtaulds' activities spread from technical, advisory and research advice to the marketing and promotion of fashions made in their fabrics. Tricel, Courtelle, Dicel, Celon, Vincel, Spanzelle all became familiar names used in fashion at every level. Courtaulds, who were amalgamated with Celanese in 1957, were at the service of the whole fashion industry, from chains and mail order groups to fashion creators and young designers.

The International Wool Secretariat was founded in 1937,

230 *The 'twenties look in an early advertisement for 'Celanese'*

231   *Mix and Match dress in Tricel brushed jersey by Shubette, worn with a jerkin in Courtelle Neospun. 1972*

232   *Long shirt in pen and ink print in trilobal polyester jersey, by Brettles, 1972*

233   *Edge to edge coat by Venet in printed wool crepe, 1970*

when the wool growers of Australia, New Zealand and South Africa felt the need to get together to stimulate the demand for wool in face of coming competition from man-made fabrics and, in pursuit of this purpose, to encourage the production of high quality wool merchandise. It started in a modest way, financed, as it still is, by a levy paid by wool growers in all the countries concerned, but it developed continuously, as will be shown.

Fashion-wise the I.W.S. aims to be actively involved from the spinning stage right through to the retailer. It guides the fashion industry, offering advance news of fashion lines, fabrics and colours. It shows films and slides and holds fashion shows. It features designs by young creators. It has been giving increasing attention to the ready-to-wear market, both French and U.S., in recent fashion reports.

The Cotton Board, set up during World War II in order to

234 *Bonnie Cashin's 'Nob Suit' with a style all her own, in a mohair and wool tweed fabric woven to her own specification, plaided in deep colours and suède-belted. Autumn, 1972*

235 *Another very individual Bonnie Cashin design. A coat she described as 'easy wrapping, happy on the wing thing'. In black, peat and dove mixture tweed, banded, and belted in musk coloured suède*

develop the export potential of the Manchester cotton industry, was a pioneer in follow-through promotional activities from the loom to the wearer. James Cleveland Belle, a fashion man who had previously been with the Bon Marché, Liverpool, was released from the Royal Corps of Signals to establish the Board, which was financed by a levy on raw cotton and was answerable to the Board of Trade. The Cotton Board, with Sir Raymond Street as chairman and helped by Sir Kenneth Clark (later Lord Clark), created a revolution in cotton fashions by engaging top artists, among them Graham Sutherland, Henry Moore, John Piper, Duncan Grant and Vanessa Bell, to design fabrics. Even more startlingly, they persuaded Lancashire printers and manu-facturers to produce cotton materials of a design and quality suited to high fashion. Top couturiers were commissioned to design cotton models and showed them in their collections. In the retail market Horrockses cottons established a vogue for sophisticated town and country cottons which reached a peak during the 'fifties. In America, previously supreme in this area of fashion, imports from Britain outdid the earlier exports of

236   Easy care trouser suit in Dacron polyester fibre, 1972

237   Border print in a cocktail dress of Qiana polyamide, 1971

U.S.A. models to Britain and Horrockses fashions were the first British clothes to dominate the windows of Altmans in New York every spring.

A couture look came to cotton, with spectacular prints and outstanding styling. When Molyneux closed down in London his designer, John Tullis, went to Horrockses to work with their designers. There were cotton evening clothes, cotton playclothes and even winter cottons. Royalty bought these cottons, and designs frequently worn by the Queen and Princess Margaret in the 1960's were included in the ranges available to

238 (opposite)   Slim-fitting hostess dress in washable cotton by Horrockses, Spring, 1972. Handkerchief sleeves edged in fine lace

the public. Famous actresses were devotees. One group of shops bought £200,000 worth a year. It could not go on for ever, and the Cotton Board ran into organisational difficulties for a time. But it established cotton as a fashion fabric, which it has been ever since. The Cotton Board's methods of promotion became the general pattern followed by many newer fashion interests.

I.C.I., which dominates the nylon market for hosiery and underwear in Britain, also found it important to offer an advisory service as the range of its fabrics increased. Terylene in 1951-1952 and Crimplene ten years later both advanced in the fashion field and proved widely acceptable. A technical service that would follow them through from polymer to purchaser was developed. Special attention was given to fashion trends and close co-operation was set up with the fashion trade at all levels, from Paris leaders to new designers.

Du Pont's man-made fibres played a considerable part in British fashion from the late nineteen-fifties, when Orlon and Dacron came to the fore for outerwear and Lycra and Antron began to be used extensively in foundationwear and swimwear. By the 'seventies Qiana was successfully established. Du Pont's British promotional activities have developed on a large-scale since then. Their aim was to support their fibres through from spinners and throwsters to the consumer and in the fashion sector this meant that they followed their fibres through to the fabric and garment manufacturers and thence to the retail shop and the customer.

They offered a variety of design prototypes to clothing manufacturers and twice a year presented a knitwear collection of this kind, designed by the Countess de Vautibault, to manufacturers throughout the country. The designs were all available to them. There was also close collaboration with colleges of fashion, whose design students were guided in the use of the various Du Pont fabrics, including new fabric constructions coming on the market.

Du Pont were among the first to present fashion spectaculars to fabric and garment manufacturers and members of the retail fashion trade. Every year from 1961 until the end of the decade they showed outstanding collections of fashions made from their fabrics.

11   Changes from the 1970's: revolt, unexpected influences and Punk

I

In the early 'seventies two-track fashion was proceeding apace, but it was against all probability that it would continue on that course. Not even in fashion can our one world be thus divided up and the two motivating forces could not go on ignoring each other. Interaction was inevitable. What, then, would happen next?

The giants, on the one hand, were potentially capable of introducing and maintaining, within a comparatively short time

239 (left)   Classic co-ordinates by Alexon in double knit jersey: sweater, cardigan and trousers. 1972

240 (right)   A classic three-piece in Dacron polyester, by Act III. 1972

and without any acute internal revolution, a computerised, mechanised, engineered and technologically-geared species of fashion manufacture. A wealth of devices existed which could be put into large-scale use for this purpose. There was nothing to stop the general introduction of computerised sizing and grading; spirit duplicating; electronic photo-copying and spray techniques for laying and cutting; sewing machines with photo-electric eyes which could follow the most intricate curves of a pattern. Sewing might be superseded in a foreseeable time by welding processes. Clothes could be produced by built-in programming and every kind of garment could flow off the production lines as smoothly and on as vast a scale as packaged foods or motor cars. The machinery would be costly to install, but if a large enough market were won over it would pay off.

Clothing, yes, but fashion, no. The trouble, as John Fairchild pointed out in 1965 after working in fashion for several years in New York and Paris for *Women's Wear Daily*, is that 'high fashion cannot be mechanised and new ideas are not born out of mass production thinking'. Fashion means new ideas all the time, and how would potential mechanisers know what to feed into their computers in order to ensure that a complete range of fashion was the end product? Their position was made more complicated because the traditional long-accepted leadership of Paris couture had been declining since the 'sixties. The respectful deference which good quality ready-to-wear fashion had been wont to pay to the leadership of the French capital was breaking down. No alternative leadership had arisen and public attitudes and taste were against acceptance of dictated standards.

Moreover, while fashion manufacture moved forward technically, the trend-setters who made up the other side of fashion were also winning an increasing share of the market and were becoming increasingly individualistic. Some of them were not only turning their backs on mass production but were even going back to pre-machine days, to doing their own weaving and hand-printing their own fabrics. In the early 'seventies *Harper's Bazaar* became excited at discovering an aspiring ex-college of art student who took months to make a dress she had designed. Every seam was hand-rolled. The material was dotted all over with tiny sewn-on clusters of artificial fruit and leaves. Every berry was hand-made, every leaf was put together from pieces of gauze and every motif was stitched on by hand. At the same time boutiques were becoming more and more way-out. There was no end to doing your own thing.

242 Hand-printed knitted Terylene linen for two outfits. Bra top and sarong skirt on left and on right a long-sleeved dress for beach or city street. By Frank Usher 1971

241 Spotted silk jumpsuits topped by exotically printed sleeveless coats, for new-style evening wear. By Lanvin 1970

*243 Increasingly individualistic:
Mary Quant's 1970 bloomers suit*

Alongside the great factories small production units continued to flourish to meet this need. Sir Dudley Stamp and S.H.
Beaver in *The British Isles* said of the clothing trade in 1971 that
'the little dressmakers and tailors' establishments which were so
important in the past still persist in towns of almost every size up
and down the country; indeed in 1948 over 40% of all the 12,000
firms in the industry employed less than ten persons each'. No
comparable later figure, they state, exists, but they note that the
Census of Production, 1963 recorded that in the manufacture of
women's and girls' tailored outerwear 678 out of a total of 1135
firms employed under 25 people. Leonard Halliday, in the mid-
sixties, stated that of between 9000 and 10,000 establishments
engaged in making women's clothing in Britain some 4000
employed less than ten people. Of the remaining 5000 more than
half had less than 50 workers and only 75, or less than $1\frac{1}{2}$% of the
whole, had more than 500 on their pay rolls. In America the
position was much the same. In the 1960's only 2.1% of firms
there were on record as having more than 250 employees and
72.2% had less than 50.

The future course of fashion, however, is not likely to be
dictated solely either by further developments in mechanisation
or in a greater return to old-time craftsmanship. The factors
which will determine it are sociological rather than technological. They are new to our time; vast and momentous and very
much part of an upheaval in society which is greater than any
previous revolutions though, mercifully, less bloody than most
of them.

In regard to fashion, the background of the change was that
fashion throughout its history had always been a status symbol.
Its existence depended on a class-conscious society dominated by
an accepted hierarchy, below which a strong body of the
population had the power to rise towards that hierarchy and was
intent on doing so. That way progress lay. Only western society,
based on and developing under a system of capitalism, has
possessed this kind of class mobility and, accordingly, only
western society has developed and fostered what we call fashion.
For centuries the ruling classes, the hierarchy of birth and
wealth, set the pace in a display of personal adornment, even
resorting at times to sumptuary laws which forbade the wearing
of certain kinds of rich apparel by those below a certain station.
From the early nineteenth century the male had, indeed, opted
out of this and taken on a new guise as a pillar of industry and
commerce, suitably attired in muted formality. But ostentatious
female fashion, as a sign of the success and importance of the

individual and the family, remained part of the accepted social pattern until World War II, although it was being undermined by then.

The status symbol aspect of fashion was, however, consistently coloured by another factor. This was women's concern to attract men; what James Laver has described as the 'seduction principle' was closely bound up with the 'status principle'. Fashion's changes were not purely arbitrary. Women still derived their position mainly from their relationships with men, so fashion aimed to attract men and in its development the 'seduction principle' was closely bound up with the hierarchic or status one. But with the change in the status of women and in the social stratification both influences declined.

The rise and expansion of the middle classes from Victorian times coincided with a spread of fashion because of the increased opportunities which were created for the movement from one class to another or to a higher place within a class. The leisured (or idle) woman, resplendent in a kind of elaborate dressing which proclaimed that it took up much time and money to sustain, was one of society's chief symbols of social and material success. Keeping up with her or following close behind her was a measure of achievement for the rest of women. That meant that the fashion leader had to be constantly changing her image in order to preserve her lead and her exclusiveness. 'Living up to your position' and 'dressing according to your position' were phrases much heard up to World War II, but they meant imitating those immediately above. In terms of feminine thinking fashion meant aspiring to a world where one was perpetually striving to keep ahead of the crowd. Fashion had, however, to carry the crowd with it – you could not lead unless there were followers and the followers, similarly, had to find leaders.

This pattern of fashion assumed that the leadership of the Establishment was accepted by the rest of the community. Such acceptance remained as a convention even when, with the rise of the middle classes and women's entry into public life, personal attitudes were changing – as witness the Edwardian 'New Woman'. The 'youth explosion' of the later 'fifties and the 'sixties is usually credited with having dealt the death-blow to this concept, but this is only partly true. A vast social and economic upheaval was in full swing. Youth was expressing only a small part of this revolution when, possessed of new-found freedom and independence and with more money than ever before to back up its self-assertion, it made a break with the

244   Individuality in fashion: a hand printed evening dress in lilac georgette with its own transparent wings. By Frank Usher. 1972

established fashion leaders and blew the social status concept of fashion sky-high. Fashion became a proclamation of individuality. It became functional. It became fun. It became everything at once. It had nothing to do with status or class any more. There was a new orientation, a new social grouping. What people wore no longer symbolised their social or material alignments in the old vertical pattern. This applied before long to all ages, though the young were the first to proclaim it in the most obvious form.

The first phase of this quite monumental change brought a period of confusion in fashion trends, but soon there were signs that the brouhaha and the phase of what almost amounted to anti-fashion passed their peak and were dying of their own surfeit. The young generation which started it all was, moreover, not so young, not so fiercely head-in-the-wind in its fashion attitudes. But it remains assertive and highly personal in its demands for its own needs.

This is not to say that fashion was going out of fashion or ceasing to exist in a new evaluation of life which was unlike anything that had happened before. What was happening was that fashion was becoming part of the general design for living.

245 (left)   Functional fashion: a midi trench coat by Rosewin in Qiana in double breasted cover-up style, worn with practical boots. 1972

246 (right)   Fun fashion: party dress in 'Western' style, blue and white print, with many flounced skirt and puff sleeves also edged with flounces. 1972

247 *Fashion with a personal look in Autumn 1972 by Jaeger*

More and more it expressed the personal taste of the wearer, indicated the kind of person she was and where she belonged in a new orientation of the social order which was proceeding everywhere. It is a natural corollary that fashion was once again becoming the concern of men as well as women. Whatever the course this re-grouping took, it seemed certain that it would not lead back to the bygone acceptance of arbitrary social and class values of the keeping-up-with-the-Joneses kind. It had already become impossible to imagine the drop of a hem or the shape of a neckline or sleeve, the raising or lowering of a waist causing the excitement that used to greet such innovations at the Paris collections. Your hem stops where you want it. You follow this or that fashion if you like it, by pass it if you don't. 'A striking feature of consumer attitudes towards clothes', says *Your Future in Clothing*, the industry's blue-print of things to come, published in 1970, 'is the development of a "Personal style".

248   Design for living. Sporty pants suit and short tailored skirt co-exist in 1972

249   Mary Quant in 1972 in varied moods: youthful smock, spotted crepe de Chine suit with a 'thirties air, cotton suit with flared skirt and evening suit in white crepe de Chine with wrap-over top and flowing trousers

This "personal style" transcends the changes of various fashions and appears to change very slowly, sometimes in fact appearing to last virtually throughout an individual's adult life.'

Fashion as a result came from all kinds of sources. It is already strange to reflect that only a few years ago authoritative writers could say things like 'All new fashion is born in Paris'. Couture there had dwindled and been siphoned off into the ready-to-wear to such an extent that it was going back a hundred years and again concentrating on the private customer, the *rara avis* who has time and money to spare for that kind of dressing, but who is no more a general leader. Paris fashion is only incidental news. The *Evening Standard* voiced the new viewpoint when it announced in April, 1972 that 'we won't be spending any more time reporting the funeral obsequies of a moribund institution', because, it continued, 'the old couture emporiums have got nothing left to offer the ordinary woman'. London couture had followed the same course as Paris. The two main survivors, Hardy Amies and Norman Hartnell, the Royal dressmakers, were both deeply involved in other fashion activities. When Michael closed his house in 1970 he spotlighted another secondary cause of the decline of couture: 'I am finding it increasingly difficult to get the tailoring staff that is essential to a haute couture house. Art schools are turning out designers, not tailors. But you can't have an army of generals and no privates.'

Mary Quant who, more than any other single individual, had instigated the breakaway from conventional fashion standards from the mid-1960's and created revolutionary clothes to meet the needs of the clamorous young, succeeded triumphantly in her aim. But she did not want to stop there and as she herself grew further out of that particular generation she moved into a quite different area of activity in the early 1970's. It was that of general 'design for living' thinking, because she designed almost everything that came into the category of personal needs, though with a bias towards the woman's side. Her products included tights, hats, shoes, foundationwear and cosmetics – but also linen and beds, carpets, table-ware, writing paper, wallpaper and furnishings. In fashion she produced only small collections, for selected shops, intended not for any fixed age group but for a certain kind of taste. She did not manufacture any of these items; instead she licensed her designs to appropriate manufacturers well-established in each area, undertaking for her part only a certain amount of marketing and promotion at home and overseas. This approach flourished – and continues. It was a procedure that was to be widely followed.

The centuries-long fashion lead set by the establishment and its chosen couturiers had been on the wane for some years before the 1970's, but its decline was accelerated from the start of that decade by another factor, the precise timing of which was largely coincidental, though it was bound to happen and fairly soon. In a few years many of the leading long-established personalities in the traditional couture world died at comparatively short intervals from each other: Chanel in 1971, Balenciaga in 1972 (though he had retired and closed his house

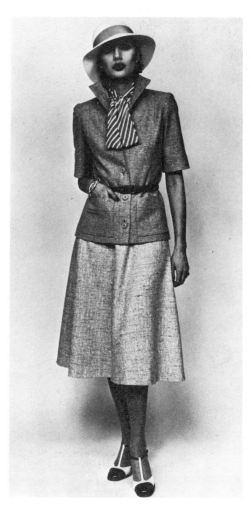

250   The Chanel suit, as fashionable as ever in 1964, is still in favour in the 'seventies at all levels of fashion, including mass manufacturers and multiples

251   The 'thirties look, with longer flared skirt, slouch hat and co-respondent shoes in a grey flannel jacket and grey and white tweed skirt by Dior, spring-summer 1974

252 *Reminiscent of the 'thirties is Balmain's spring-summer 1974 evening dress in black organza with embroidered corsage and frilled top*

253 *Return of the coat-dress: by Ungaro for spring/summer 1984 in lightweight pure wool gabardine, with contrasting tightly folded waist sash*

some years earlier), Schiaparelli in 1973, France's Vionnet and Britain's Victor Stiebel in 1975. America's leader in the wholesale fashion world, Norman Norell, died in 1972.

Last of the great names in traditional fashion was Pierre Balmain, who died on 29 June 1982 at the age of 68 while still very much in harness, after a brief illness. He dressed queens and princesses of West and East, stars of stage and screen, famous and elegant women in all spheres, among them Queen Fabiola of Belgium, the Duchess of Windsor, Katharine Hepburn, Sophia Loren, Vivien Leigh and Bridget Bardot. The 'jolie madame' was his image, a symbol of high-fashion elegance and the hallmark of his whole career. He established his own house in 1946, after serving in the war and having previously worked with Captain Molyneux. The last of the traditionalists, he was succeeded by the Danish Eric Morgensen, who had been his assistant, and maintained the name and the business, but the day when his kind of fashion was dominant had gone, probably forever.

In the face of these losses there were, of course, the new arrivals, many of whom were to make their names and in some cases operate on a scale that surpassed, in commercial terms and world coverage, that of previous top designers. But it was to be a different kind of success, signifying a new era in couture and fashion in general.

Those who had gone had crowned what was probably the last great epoch of authoritative fashion and had worn their crowns for a lifetime. Now even though their houses continued to flourish, there were to be many changes and adjustments. Paris couture was, in the early 1970's, going back to the place it had held at the opening of the century, when it catered for a group of the privileged, for the private customer, the woman with the leisure for complicated fittings and elaborate dressing.

The new generation, headed by Courrèges, Ungaro, Cardin and above all, Yves St Laurent, operated in new ways. By the 1970's even in Paris the *prêt à porter* wholesale trade was increasingly ahead of couture and couture was operating in different ways, keeping pace with changed times. Women, for instance, no longer went to Paris for laborious fittings and consultations. Instead, the fashions came to them, usually through boutiques run by the couturiers.

Yves St Laurent, born in Algiers in 1936, was trained under Dior and for a time was expected to be his successor. But he opened his own house in 1962, after leaving Dior, and followed with his first boutique in 1966, the first of the Rive Gauche chain, which was to amount to 160, all over the world. It was his métier. He did not design couture clothes in the old tradition, did not believe in the seasonal collection or in the 'line' dictated each season from the top and followed sedulously at all levels.

He designed jeans, introduced a blazer jacket in 1962 which was worn over a printed dress. It was still in favour in the 1980's and the revival of the woman's suit, one of the main features of fashion from the later 1970's, owed much to it. He sought his inspiration everywhere – even from peasant dress, an important trend – and once said that he designed for the flea-market.

254 *Lean, clean lines for matching coat and skirt by Sonia Rykiel in checked wool with wide shoulders, from Paris ready-to-wear collections, 1984*

255   *The casual look in fashion. Long trench coat in wool poplin with soft safari jacket and trousers, Guy Paulin 1984*

In 1971 St Laurent announced that he would abandon couture completely, but was persuaded to present seasonal collections of this kind as part of his many activities. He continued to do so. He remained, however, insistently anti-status. He attracted the go-ahead, the young, the adventurous – and moneyed. He designed for both men and women; in addition to his clothes he had 50 other products carrying his name as trademark. But, despite all his breaks with tradition, he was the first living designer to have a collection of his clothes presented with great éclat by the Metropolitan Museum of New York – this occurred in 1983, to celebrate his completion of 20 years in the fashion world. They were all, perhaps disappointingly, couture models.

Chanel's house remained in business during the 1970's, but the big shot in the arm that looked like putting new life and vigour into it did not happen until 1983, when Karl Lagerfeld was appointed chief designer. He had been with Chloé in Paris for 20 years, winning success with his bold designs, assertive and colourful, for the manufacturing trade. In 1983 he did a 'Farewell and Hail' act by presenting his last Chloé collection in the spring and his first Chanel one that autumn.

It was a surprising move; Lagerfeld's style was flamboyant, dramatic and in many other ways violently contrasted to Chanel's understatement and 'poor look'. His arrival brought changes but a distinction which was further revealed when, in 1984, he also opened his own house under his own name, showing with the Paris *prêt à porter* collections and selling in London exclusively through Lady Rendlesham in Bond Street.

Lagerfeld's work was in line with the new mood of revolt against the status quo in society. This was further expressed in the 1970's by a distinctive movement of fashion to find its new trends well away from any adaptation or revival of past lines or looks. Instead there were moves towards the ethnic, to the adoption of eastern trends, of peasant styles from far places, garments unknown to western fashion such as djellabahs, caftans, flowing tunics.

Most unexpected, long-lasting and strong was the influence of Japan. It was in 1971 that *The Times* first wrote about Kenzo Takada, who was to have a strong influence on fashion from the mid-seventies right into the 1980's. He introduced fuller, wider skirts, deep wide kimono sleeves, squared-up shoulders. His knitwear was based on full, loose kimonos. He featured shawls, layered looks, and probably reached his peak about 1978. Kenzo was based in Paris at this time, and in London a similar influence was exercised by his fellow-countryman, Yuki. He was respon-

sible for similar trends, and was particularly successful in his use of soft silk jersey, showing himself a master of skilful cutting and draping, thereby producing fluid but very elegant lines. He sold all over the world, including licensees in his native Japan. Issey Miyake and Hanae Mori are among the influential Japanese designers to emerge in the 80's.

Laura Ashley was linked to the new group of inventors only because she too was in revolt against the status quo of dress, the formal, class-conscious high fashion. As a force and a personality in fashion, Laura Ashley developed in exactly the opposite way from Mary Quant. She moved from textiles and furnishings to fashion and general items of dress with an increasing momentum through the 1970's and 1980's. (She died in a tragic accident in 1985.)

The business now universally known by her name began early in 1953 when her husband Bernard Ashley started printing textiles in a small Pimlico workshop. He designed furnishing fabrics and Laura began with little table mats and napkins. Heals

256   *A Karl Lagerfeld design for Chloé: Lady Silvy Thynne models the dress of the year, 1981*
257   *Softer lines for the suit in 1984. Karl Lagerfeld's is part of a three-piece ensemble in lightweight wool gabardine, with long lapels, knotted waistline and slim skirt*
258   *Dress of the year 1977: a stylish loose-cut design by Kenzo for Jap*

and Liberty became early customers. Ashley next began to produce his own printing machines. Pictorial tea-towels became the first speciality to carry the Laura Ashley name.

The tea-towels led to matching aprons with a country look and to gardening overalls which were so attractive that they began to be worn as dresses. This was in 1961, when the company moved to Carno, in Mid Wales, making more and more overalls and wörking dresses with their own machines and machinists.

Finer and more fashionable dresses were developed in the following years, and by the 1970's Laura Ashley dresses were elegant and had their own special style. To start with traditional country prints were their hallmark, and soon they were being sold in a constantly increasing chain of their own shops and other stores. Success in Europe, Canada, the U.S.A. and Australia followed and in 1974 the company opened in Paris. Dress textiles and furnishing fabrics also expanded. By 1976 a private aircraft linked them with Europe. There were 1500 employees, a multi-million pound annual turnover and continued growth. Furnishings and wallpapers as well as all kinds of fashions for women and children grew, and menswear came also to be included. Shops world-wide totalled 153.

By the mid-eighties there were five factories in Wales, and two in Holland. The prevailing country theme was widened and varied, ranging through all types of dress, but mainly on casual lines. Knitwear, suits, hats and accessories were added. There was a huge E.E.C. involvement and late in 1984 the possibility of the whole enterprise being transferred to Holland, but with assurances of British government aid the expanding operation was sited in Mid and North Wales, with the prospect of still another 500 jobs for local workers. Both fashions and furnishing textiles were involved in this.

In the face of all these influences, dress by the mid-1970's presented a bewildering variety of styles, from which it was difficult to pick out the trends worth recording, and to guess which ones would prove to have been evanescent. But two items were so widely worn that they cannot be overlooked by any survey. Jeans and T-shirts were almost a uniform for all ages and types of people.

Why jeans? Why this garment should have enjoyed a prominence and duration far beyond that of any other modern fashion has never been satisfactorily explained. It is almost absurd to call it a fashion, for it has become more a way of life, universal, classless, irrespective of age or sex. The appeal of jeans

259   Denim as worn in 1974. Canadian group Bachman-Turner Overdrive pose in jeans, tee-shirts, flying jackets

cannot be ascribed to the pop music scene, but probably music and films had rather more to do with promoting them than any other recent influence.

Jeans became fashionable among students in America as early as the 1930's. America became the pace-setter for young men's fashions after World War II and jeans were worn by young men more and more extensively in the 1960's. As the culture of youth became wider in its impact, there were more jeans, but it was not until the early 1970's that jeans began to be adopted throughout society as a whole and by all age groups. Even Yves St Laurent made them.

Jeans were often too tight to be in any possible way working clothes. There was a special panache about their being deliberately faded and worn, frayed or even patched, too long and turned up roughly. They often cost more that way. They were the star turn of the unisex movement. But the most important thing was that they went on and on, a way of life rather than fashion.

They were washable, hardwearing, but that did not explain

260 Denim 1982. British group Dexys Midnight Runners in unisex, post-punk denims

them. Men had been wearing trousers of various styles for about
150 years, and a change from wool, flannel, tweed and other
conventional fabrics was perhaps reasonable. Apart from the
immense flannel Oxford bags of the 1920's there had been no
novelties in legwear worth mentioning. Jeans were at any rate
different.

As the eighties moved on jeans became less dominant, at any
rate among young women, women in the High Streets, and men
about the house at week-ends. But they were by no means 'out'
as fashions can be. Nothing was replacing them, though more
and more new man-made fabrics were being produced. They
remained symbols of a denial of past social traditions in dress, a
proclamation of contemporary values. Yet in 1984, the jeans
firm of Levi Strauss, the biggest clothes manufacturer in the
world, launched out into the making of traditional-style men's
suits in conventional material, such as wool, and in conventional
designs – but in an immense variety of sizes and fittings. The
success of this project has yet to be clearly demonstrated.

3

For some time after it began to attract widespread attention in
the late 1960's the youth explosion in fashion was regarded, at
any rate by conventional (mostly older) devotees of dress
history, as a limited and probably short-lived euphoric phenomenon which would no doubt soon give way to something at least
related to previous fashions and social traditions and to other age
groups in the community.

The frivolities of the mini-skirt and other extreme youthful
assertions of independence did indeed disappear fairly soon
except for a small minority of wearers. But the old ways did not
return. Behind the strange new fashions lay a revolt of a more
potent kind than dress alone had so far expressed. The young by
the early 'seventies were often in revolt against the world as it
was, against mechanization, materialism, industrialism, current
ways of life among their elders. The iconoclastic urge found
expression most loudly literally in the pop and rock music which
blared out in all directions. The heroes of the movement were
pop stars, David Bowie, Mick Jagger, Keith Richard and dozens
more, and pop and other groups became famous and sometimes
violent and disruptive.

As far back as the 'fifties, youth cults became more and more
identified by extremes of dress, culminating in the 'sixties with

various specific costumes adopted by certain groups – mods, rockers, skinheads, flower people, and many more. The main centre of these cults in London became the King's Road, Chelsea, with its boutiques of rivalling eccentricity.

It seeemed to have little to do with dress as a whole, but it was part of the social history of the day. The dress influence evolved mainly from the pop punk phenomenon, which had a positive link with the dress world.

The punk movement was foreshadowed in the mid-seventies by groups such as the New York Dolls, but came to widespread public attention after boutique-owner Malcolm McLaren became manager of the Sex Pistols, in 1976. Featuring the notorious duo of Johnny Rotten and Sid Vicious, and extraordinary outfits of shredded and tattered clothes with safety pins passed through garments, ears and even nostrils, the Pistols personified the punk style to an outraged public. They gained enormous (and free) publicity from a scandalized press and TV as their records climbed the charts. Green or pink hair was soon

261 Culture Club: punk and Japanese influence combine in the mid-eighties

added to the punk image. The word 'punk' originally meant 'rubbish' or 'rotten' but eventually became used, from that time till today, for a general style of particularly outrageous dress.

The first performance of the Sex Pistols is said to have been at St Martin's School of Art, which had a department for training fashion students. E.M.I. signed them up, but got cold feet and cancelled the contract. A chat-show interview with Bill Grundy created an uproar and they were then banned from T.V. and radio, which naturally led to even greater notoriety.

Whatever was said of them, punk rockers came to be regarded as the spearhead of what was called the New Wave. In 1977 punk rock bands began to make the Top Ten of the record charts. The cult was working class, sometimes left-wing oriented.

Then Zandra Rhodes, established as a distinguished *avant garde* dress designer, brought the fashion craze for punk to a climax, whether a triumph or a disaster is arguable, when in the autumn of 1977 she created a Punk Chic collection. It received widespread attention, bringing punk to the notice of the rich and talked-of section of society. The dresses had gold pins and the holes were embroidered with gold. There were embroidered, tattered hems. Zandra herself modelled some of the collection with green hair, which she wore for years to come. But after that punk seemed to run out of steam in 1978, when it sought its audiences on the football terraces. What remained was the word, used generally by people outside the pop movement to describe certain way-out and freakish elements in dress, coupled to rowdy and iconoclastic music.

The pop movement also produced its own top designer, who made a considerable impact on fashion for some years. Ossie Clark, trained at the Manchester School of Art and at the Royal School of Art, was for some years, from the late 1960's to the start of the 1980's, the wonder boy of the 'pop' movement in fashion, raising its image to the couture level. When he graduated in 1965 he went first to a department store in Knightsbridge. Then came a spell with Alice Pollock at a boutique in the inevitable King's Road. From 1969 to 1978 he was designer with Radley. There he created fashions that won immense acclaim and were notable for the skill and grace with which they used soft fabrics for evening wear, and for his bold adventurousness in devising new looks for the young and chic. But it was a fickle market, and Clark fell victim to the recession in 1981, when he was declared bankrupt, fading from the fashion scene for the forseeable future.

Malcolm McLaren followed up his gambit with the Sex

Pistols by taking charge of various other pop groups, from Adam and the Ants to Bow Wow Wow, and also by a much-publicised partnership with Vivienne Westwood, among the most sensational of dress-designers. Hers is the only name from the revolutionary youth movement to have survived into the 1980's and to have attained an international reputation, with headquarters in Milan. Her famous shop she had named World's End in 1980, after a series of other names for the premises at the end of the King's Road.

It is perhaps not wholly irrelevant that when that mature and wide-ranging television personality Alan Whicker chose the speakers for a tri-partite discussion on fashion in *Whicker's World* early in 1984, his selection was Lady Rendlesham, managing director of the London *Rive Gauche* shops of Yves St Laurent; Molly Parkin, novelist and former fashion editor; and Malcolm McLaren. At the close of the talk, asked what final verdict each had to voice on fashion, Lady Rendlesham gave as her fashion basics a knitted woollen jacket and scarf. Miss Parkin thought all heavy expenditure on fashion was immoral. Mr McLaren believed in ranging the world for one's choice, picking up what appealed from every age and place to create one's own completely individual effect.

12 Ready-to-wear: manufacturers give a lead in the 1970's and 1980's

I

An exaggerated degree of attention is frequently given to extremes and vagaries of fashion, because they make news. This is particularly true in the present media-dominated times. The imbalance was increased by the fragmentation of fashion, the breakdown of established and long-accepted social structures and a general lack of clear leadership in dress, from the couture level downwards, in the later 20th century. This was demonstrated early by the youth movement of the sixties and seventies.

Fashion, however, must involve the styles of dress followed by sizeable and cohesive sections of the community if it is to have any lasting credence. Too little attention is paid by the fashion records to what ordinary people wear, to what common features can be seen there, where these fashion trends come from, how and by whom they are produced.

All in all, the clothing industry is one of the oldest in the world and one in which billions of pounds have been invested for home production and overseas trade. Most of this production is maintained for and by ordinary people.

The high quality and wide variety of dress offered by the British ready-to-wear clothing manufacturers have been the main steadying and stabilising factors in the clothing industry since the 1930's – and above all in the women's side of the industry during recent decades. This has been due mainly to the leading group of well established companies, many of whose equally important earlier histories have already been dealt with in these pages.

Usually starting as small tailors last century or as part of the activities of the immigrants who established a great part of the modern women's clothing trade, the best of such firms grew and flourished. Many of them also bought up and rescued from

262   *Romantic short dance dress by Frank Usher for 1982, in taffeta with pleated ruffles and petal frills*

263   Lacy knitted two-piece in acrylic and nylon from the Frank Usher Designer Collection. Wide dolman sleeves, peplum effect and pleated skirt. 1983

collapse small, good companies, undercapitalized and badly organized, often still privately owned, during the chaotic 1960's and early 1970's. In many cases the new owners respected the individuality and recognizable 'signature' of clothes produced by such firms and kept a large degree of their autonomy while running them as part of a group. Separate designers, fabric selection, the maintenance of quality production and the continuance of separate showrooms all benefitted the ready-to-wear side of fashion in its times of change. A practical example of this was the fact that in 1973 a Royal wedding dress, that of Princess Anne, was designed by Janice Wainwright, chief designer of Susan Small. In November 1983, incidentally, Susan Small's prestigious and sustained fashion record collapsed when the company crashed, owing nearly £300,000 to creditors. It had been acquired by Courtauld's, who sold it for £50,000 in 1983 to new owners. After a 30-year life it ended with assets of only £7,000 and was voluntarily wound up.

From the 1970's the ready-to-wear clothing trade went through as many basic changes as couture. Perhaps more, because in addition to adjusting to the changing U.K. economy ready-to-wear needed to compete with the successful manufacturers of the Third World, especially in the Far East. This meant imports of cheap – and not-so-cheap – manufactures and also the use of cheap labour in Third World countries, to make up designs produced in Britain.

The unexpected recession in the late 1970's in the U.K. and in Europe was, however, a more serious problem for the top firms in the manufacturing trade. Combined with the uncertainties of fashion trends, it led to some periods of difficulty for most companies. The established leaders met and countered the challenge in various ways, with changes and adjustments which quickly paid off in renewed success. The rise in clothing imports in recent years had, however, been a matter of concern not only to the U.K. clothing trade but also to the economy as a whole. In 1982 clothing imports amounted to £1500 million.

How the established companies, with sufficient capital, organisation, reputation and enterprise to weather the troubles dealt with their particular problems is best seen by following the later histories of some of those already recorded from their beginnings.

The Selincourt Group, now a public company with 15 subsidiaries, recently added to its record of progress through more than 130 years of business. As at January 31, 1983, its assets were approximately £45 million, its turnover £65 million, both increases on those of the previous years. Its profits were £407,000 for 1983, compared with £375,000 for 1982. Sales outside the U.K. were £20,000,000 per annum. Its employees totalled about 3000. Most of its subsidiaries were mainly engaged in women's fashions, with three leading fashion houses in Frank Usher, Jacqmar, and Tricosa. Their interests in women's fashions, as manufacturers and merchandizers, comprise about two-thirds of their activities. Fifteen per cent of their output has recently been for Marks and Spencer.

In the past 25 years they had also penetrated in depth into specialised areas of the textile industry, including gaining leadership in the field of curtain nets and becoming strongly established in the lace and pile-fabric industries. There had also been considerable re-organization within subsidiaries. The growth potential of certain of their companies was engaging their special concern at a time when the textile industry as a whole was not regarded as likely to enjoy a share of the anticipated general economic upturn. Improvement therefore must come, they felt, 'from our own efforts'. They placed strong emphasis on market research, investment in their own design and product development activities, in efficient production and distribution systems and financial controls and, in the case of their manufacturing companies, on new technology. Employee involvement, maintained by regular communication between management and employees, was also a part of their policy. Close relationships with the bigger chains which took advantage of the large spectrum of products which they offered also featured high on their programme for the future.

At Aquascutum, who started their business over 130 years ago as small tailors in Regent Street (opposite the present premises), the developments which have been proceeding throughout their history began when they discovered a new way of shower-proofing wool cloth in 1853 and became specialists in raincoats for men and later, in 1909, for women also. Thus they took their first step into the women's market, where they have made immense advances in recent years.

For them the difficult years of the early 1980's have been a challenge met by the creation of a new image and a much broader alignment with current fashion trends at the up-market level which has always been their chosen field. They now dress their customers from top to toe and even from childhood (a girls' section opened in 1984), for all seasons and all weathers, with an emphasis on a sporty look and casual elegance. They have developed their overseas trade with such energy and success

264   Slick city-suit for 1984 by Aquascutum, in boldly striped pure new wool. Short jacket has mandarin collar, padded shoulders and puffed sleeves. Fuller, longer skirt

that they now export 65 per cent of their output. External group sales recorded in their 1983 report amounted to £25,024,352.

Their managing director, Mr Frank Larcombe, who succeeded Mr Gerald Abrahams (who remained chairman) in 1983, sees in the present difficult situation of the clothing trade a special diversity of problems for Aquascutum because the parent company is responsible for manufacturing, wholesaling, retailing and exporting high-quality clothes and accessories for both men and women. Despite this, Aquascutum added to their tally of Queen's Awards for Export in 1976 and 1979.

The world recession of the few years since then has considerably affected their overseas interests, says Mr Larcombe. In the European and North American markets it has been impossible to increase turnover, despite special sales drives. But home turnover has risen in that time, due to the continuing broadening of the Aquascutum approach. Their four factories, two for men's wear, at Kettering and Corby, and two for women's, at Bletchley and St Albans, employ together an average of 1356 people. Today 50 per cent of output is menswear, 36 per cent womenswear, the remainder comprising the new range of clothes for children.

People today, says Mr Larcombe, do not spend a bigger proportion of their income on clothes, but they buy more variously. This is due to a great rise in casualwear, which usually comprises less expensive garments, but these are also easier to import, especially from the low-labour-cost countries.

In compensation, the good-quality clothing industry has benefited from the E.E.C., where new facilities for trade are opening up. From 1972 Aquascutum was building up a favourable balance of trade with all the E.E.C. countries. Competition from low-cost countries is, however, causing some erosion in the present economic recession. Australia used to be a good Aquascutum customer, in the 1960's, but a 50 per cent duty on imports has reduced this. Commonwealth countries as a whole have become less important, as has America.

Meanwhile, Japan has become the big new market for Aquascutum, largely opened up by that country's increased affluence. Japan is today very dress-conscious and notably well-dressed, not only for formal occasions but also for leisure and sportswear. Men used to be the main customers but now women too are giving increased attention to fashion from the west. It used to be only Japanese men who travelled abroad, but now it is women too.

Japan, adds Mr Larcombe, is also very brand-conscious, with

265 Casual elegance is Aquascutum's sleek navy blazer, cream skirt and checked waistcoat, all in pure wool. 1984 an emphasis on luxury, especially if the labels are outside the clothes or the material is a 'signature', like the Aquascutum checks. With English the second language, English clothes are in demand. Aquascutum sells its whole range of coats. Men's suits are made under licence, under a recent agreement made with the Mitsubishi Corporation to supervise the manufacture there of certain ranges of merchandise which cannot be exported from the U.K. A new company, Aquascutum of England, has been formed to control these activities; similar arrangements have been made with Spain and the U.S.A., for tariff reasons.

The main recent developments at Aquascutum are the refurbished ladies' department, now featuring a comprehensive range of 'sporty' designs and leisurewear for all occasions, and the addition to their many accessories of a range of men's toiletries. These are proving as successful as the other accessories, which range from shirts and ties to luggage. These they do not manufacture themselves, but buy from specialist companies.

Elegant, adaptable, fashionable but never extreme, Aquascutum make full use of co-ordination of colours and fabrics so as to form a versatile wardrobe for town and country. The emphasis is on the finest Scottish tweeds, cashmeres, worsteds, with silk and cottons for summer. From coats and tailored suits to separates and a formal wool-and-mohair dinner suit the whole gamut of fashion is there.

2

Ellis and Goldstein, now with Mr. B.A. Barnett as group managing director, has achieved a successful and enterprising adjustment to changing conditions by means of a kind of roundabouts-and-swings operation. Its branded merchandise, Eastex and Deréta coats, suits and casualwear, together with Eastex, Elgora and DuMansel dresses and co-ordinates, is sold to independent retailers at home and overseas. Its retailing division operates more than 300 shops within stores, mainly in the U.K., selling both the Group's branded merchandise and also active leisurewear under the name Dash, a new range introduced late in 1982. This was aimed at a younger age group than had previously been their main target. With its emphasis on youth and a more casual look it met with an enthusiastic reception and high sales. The Group thereupon extended it to a still younger market, that of seven-to-fourteen-year-old girls.

During the year ending 1983 these innovations, and also

266   *Puff-sleeved top and full skirt in Deréta's two-piece in black cotton/polyester with multi-coloured overchecks*

increased sales to multiples, especially of knitwear, began to make themselves felt. Though the year's profits declined marginally due to a slight drop in traditional sales, the new moves began to offset that. Profits for the year to January 31, 1983 were £1,026,000 as against the previous year's £1,419,000.

During 1982 Ellis and Goldstein spent £1,027,000 on additions to their fixed assets, most of it on sophisticated plant and machinery for the knitting machines which were occupying more and more space, in accordance with the general trend of fashion towards knitwear, the leader in the favoured casualwear, and in growing demand at all levels of fashion and dress. The company now produces knitwear to the special requirements of multiple and chain store customers. Fixed assets amounted to £4,225,000 in 1983, having increased by £374,000 during that year.

The intention in 1984 was to maintain existing ranges but also look for new customers and markets by offering new ranges in accordance with the continued mobility of fashion's demands. In line with this is a move within the Eastex range, first introduced in 1952 for the five-foot-two woman, the height and proportions of whom, according to market research, were the predominant ones in British women. Eastex is still made for the shorter group, but the company say they have 'adjusted the lengths'.

Their managing director, Mr. B.A. Barnett, discussing the previous ten or twelve years, said in 1984: 'The biggest changes are from the tailored image of the suits to those of a softer but dressier nature, and of course, we have expanded greatly into the field of co-ordinated casualwear which has been so successful.'

A similar change has affected Dereta, in the same group. 'The *Deréta* label,' said the managing director of that subsidiary, Mr. Simon Lebor, 'is related to "executive dressing" in today's image, while *Deréta Sport* is a more casual form of dress for relaxing and leisure, perhaps for watching sport rather than participating'. Garments sold under the *Concept* label are, he continued, 'top end of fashion – dressy, unbusy'.

During the past decade or so Windsmoor also has changed and grown considerably, but the emphasis on quality has been maintained. Windsmoor is still owned and run by the same family which started it – the Greens, famous in the story of fashion manufacturing. But now members of the third and fourth generations have taken over. They still have their factory at Tottenham, and all models and model collections are made there, but there is now also a factory in Hong Kong, opened in

267   *Slacks, shorts and casual tops by Deréta Sport for summer 1984*

1973. Like other manufacturers they have diversified and in addition to Windsmoor they make another range, Planet, started in 1979 and comprising mainly separates, co-ordinates and casualwear, maintaining the company's high quality but aimed at a younger life-style, with emphasis on adaptability and 'middle' prices. For the two ranges the company operates more than 450 concession departments in almost all leading department stores throughout the country.

Tops, blouses, knitwear, jackets, waistcoats, skirts and pants are all included in the Planet range, in all materials according to season, and a summer 1984 innovation was the addition of accessories, including hats, belts and scarves. The theme goes from tailored to sporty and to appealingly pretty and feminine – for all occasions.

Windsmoor, the main collection, also moved from the

269   *Black, taupe and white combined in Windsmoor's swashbuckling summer outfit for 1984: jacket, button-through skirt and jersey*

268   *Bold dark grey and white stripes for Windsmoor, summer 1984. Two-piece, lace trimmed at neck and hem, highlighted by magenta accessories*

earlier, classically tailored tradition to include a great variety of 'looks'. From the more inventive tailoring of today and the familiar beautifully simple but cleverly accented classic lines, it now extends to some adventurous and even exotic co-ordinates in special design collections for a limited number of top stores. Colour contrasts are often unexpected and venturesome, ranging from subdued to very bold indeed.

Paradoxically, what is now the Steinberg Group was set on a course of far-reaching expansion by the general recession in clothing at the start of the 1980's. The momentum thus set up resulted in loss being turned into a profit of about £1,000,000 in the year ended March, 1983. This was based on changes and adjustments which led to the division of the company into two sections, the Contract Manufacturing Group and the Branded Products Group.

270   Co-ordinated separates by Planet. Blouse in navy/pink/green stripes, skirt in navy print. Summer 1984

The former, based at Peterlee, Co. Durham, employs 1550 people in four factories, manufacturing exclusively for Marks and Spencer, which accounts for 25 per cent of the total Company output. The expansion involved in this was made possible by the previous purchase of a successful company, Claremont Garments Limited, which broadened the product image built up by the Contract Group. A substantial pro-gramme of up-to-date technology furthered the project.

The Branded Products Groups was not left behind. Alexon was expanding and flourishing, with over 150 shops-in-shops and hundreds of retail outlets. Horrockses Fashions, acquired in 1964, was also doing well and the first of its shops-in-shops were opened in the summer of 1984. The Chairman could say in the annual report of 1983 that 'Alexon is emerging as a major brand in British women's wear'.

Behind the success lay two main moves by the Group. One was the move from the Aldersgate Street headquarters in 1974 to a purpose-built storage headquarters and distribution complex at Milton Keynes, which also became the general headquarters of the Group. Technology here includes a computer system whereby every garment produced is recorded from its begin-nings to its retailing and final shop sale. The distributing plant can handle half a million garments at any one time. One visitor there wrote: 'They are shipped inexorably off the sort of machinery you see in James Bond films onto lorries belonging to the firm and thence without packing and creasing on to the rails of two hundred shops within stores.'

Before this happens every garment has been ticketed with its style number, colour and size. Girls work up to 2,000 key impressions an hour to get this vital information on to the computer. As each garment is sold the fact comes back to the computer on the tickets from the shops, both on monitor screen and on tapes. This information is linked to the factories, also by computer, so that there is a complete feed-back for planning replacements.

The Times, writing about the Milton Keynes operation in 1977, estimated that it dealt with 500,000 items a year, at the rate of 62,000 a week. To complicate the matter further, Alexon's sizing system means that each garment comes in five figure-types, within each being as many as seven and never less than three sizes. It must be a very very difficult figure that Alexon cannot fit.

The Alexon style is, as ever, towards the tailored look. Yet today it is very much an updated tailored look, in an uncluttered

271 *Relaxed suit in grey flannel with bolero jacket and full skirt by Alexon, with toning blouse, for spring 1984*

English style, ranging from the classic to the casual, from the suit to leisurewear, from the holiday to the informal evening, from knitwear to cover-up coats.

Celebrating the centenary of British production of their famous clothes, Jaeger seems in many ways to have moved far away from the original 'sanitary woollen' system set forth by the learned Doctor. But they claim nevertheless to have definite affinities with him. He was a pioneer in 'natural' clothes that were thought of as workwear, and the leisurewear, which is a main feature of fashion and dress in the 1980's, is based on the same thinking.

Jaeger today are equally intent on using the best materials, achieving an excellence of design and cut, high standards of making-up and finishing. Their successes of the eighties have been 'vintage Jaeger' – ski-ing, handknits, cashmere coats, herringbone tweeds, fine woollen garments – even to the natural yellowy-grey jersey of the original Jaegers.

They recall how they have 'pursued and used fine lines-people – like Jean Muir in her learning days' – and she is now recognised as one of the finest designers in Britain. Of their designs today, Jaeger declare, 'Herr Doktor himself would call them his own'.

As all these designs are now available in the latest colours – bright blues, reds, greens and yellows for leisurewear, sophisticated terracotta, putty and black for busy times, 'to keep hard-working women feeling good'. Jaeger feel they are selling the best of old and new. Woollens are still there of course, but so are pure cottons, textured cotton mixes and wool and silk blends.

3

Considerable services to fashion at many levels have been provided in recent years by various organisations which represent fibre and fabric producers and manufacturers. These bodies mastermind the progress of carrying the textiles used in clothing through from the raw product to the retailer, not only in the interests of technical efficiency but also with attention to the requirements of the final product – its colours, quality, fashion suitability. They display and exhibit fabrics, provide advance fashion news from the world's main centres, link weavers and mills to tailors and other clothes manufacturers, and keep the public knowledgeable about new advances and developments and the trades concerned in a prosperous state.

The first of these to be established was the International Wool

Secretariat, representing the textile fabric with the longest history in Britain. Formed in 1937, it is a world-wide organisation aimed at promoting the demand for and use of wool. With headquarters in London it has permanent offices in 32 countries and operates in 18 more. It is financed by the wool growers of Australia, New Zealand, South Africa and Uruguay, who between them produce 80 per cent of the raw wool entering the world trade. It undertakes advertising and marketing campaigns in media ranging from the press to radio, television and the cinema.

The International Wool Secretariat provides a wide range of services covering all aspects of fashion design and new technology affecting wool. It co-operates with all areas of the wool industry from processors and manufacturers to retailers. Its famous Woolmark, introduced in 1964, sets standards of quality and performance for 100 per cent pure new wool products. More than 25 million Woolmark labels are used every month by over 15,000 licensees in 58 countries. The main International Wool Secretariat technical development centre is at Ilkley, Yorkshire, with additional centres in the U.S.A. and Japan. Machine-washable wool was one of its main innovations, which have also included flame-resistant treatment, shrink-proofing and moth-proofing, crease-resistance and printed effects both for woven and knitted wool fabrics.

Nearly half of all the fibre used by the world for major textile manufacture is cotton. It is grown in 90 countries. World sales in raw cotton total about 7.5 billion dollars yearly and despite today's competition from man-made fibres cotton is increasing in popularity. The International Institute for Cotton, established in 1966, operates at an inter-governmental level and its members, drawn from Western Europe to as far afield as Japan, account for about 60 per cent of raw cotton production and raw cotton exports from non-centrally planned countries. Funds come from a levy on exports of raw cotton with additional contributions in recent years from international organisations and national aid agencies in developed countries.

The Institute carries out a comprehensive programme of co-operation with the industry at every point, and its activities range from technical research to market stimulation. A colour forecast two years ahead of retailing is one of its services to the fashion industry, and it also presents its own advance collection of fashion designs for men and women by well-known designers. Co-operation with the industry at all levels from the spinner to the retailer is its aim and its effectiveness is shown by

272 Coat dress for 1984 by Jaeger keeps a link with the original principles of the name as it is a blend of wool and polyester, but up-to-the-minute in style

273 Cotton styles for winter 1984/85: the family as seen by the International Institute for Cotton

the increasing popularity of cotton. The rise of cotton as a valued fashion fabric for all occasions, all the year round in all countries, has been continually enhanced, the fabrics themselves being developed to an immense degree by technological advances.

Man-made fibres and fabrics have had a chequered history in the past 50 or 60 years, during which they have come to play a greater and greater part in the wardrobe. Technology has also gone through immense changes and development. Materials once well known have disappeared.

I.C.I. fibres dominate the man-made textile industry in Britain and have always been in the forefront of new technology. I.C.I. invented Terylene, launching it into the fashion world in 1951–2, and then some ten years later the popularity of Crimplene revolutionised the mass market. Through the 'seventies various new products were developed to meet fashion requirements. By the end of the decade and into the 'eighties the emphasis was heavily on to those which resembled natural fibres, in touch and appearance. Sportswear as a market also grew in size and influence and impacted directly on the design of casual and street clothing in man-made materials.

The first new-generation fibre to be introduced by I.C.I. was Mitrelle, a polyester which weaves into fabrics very like silk, and it was followed six months later in November 1981 by Terinda for look-alike suedes and fleeces. The next big advance – the most significant for 20 years said the industry – came in 1983 with the launch of Tactel, a family of fibres which opened new horizons for designers and manufacturers by adding a whole range of natural aesthetics to the qualities of strength and easy care traditionally offered by a polymer.

In addition to supplying the fashion business with the yarns and fibres it needs, a key service offered by I.C.I. Fibres has always been prediction of colour and style. This is supported by technical assistance which sees a product through from polymer to garment manufacturer and is an indication of the central rôle the fibre producer plays in the industry.

While the fashion spectaculars of the 'sixties no longer happen, Du Pont continued in the 1980's to have shows for Lycra in specific end uses such as sportswear, bodywear and leotards. In addition they offered the U.K. manufacturing industry design prototypes, together with styling and colour predictions for all types of clothing.

Du Pont withdrew from the European manufacture of Orlon and filament Dacron in the early 1980's, which meant that they were no longer involved with either knitwear or ordinary outerwear fabrics. In place of domestically produced traditional fashion, they concentrated their efforts to meet the trend towards casual, sports and leisurewear and the bodywear which goes with it.

The development of Lycra in deniers as fine as 70, 40 and 20 has made possible an entirely new area of elasticated fabrics and garments – worsted trousers, denim jeans, leotards and tights. This is one of the most important fabric and dress developments of recent years; a special boon and source of attractiveness in casualwear.

Hosiery has become a very important fashion accessory and

274   Lightness and elegance in a Tsarina coat which also provides maximum warmth by means of Dacron polyester used for quilting, worn with quilted trousers. Du Pont

the addition of a small percentage of Lycra gives greatly improved comfort and fit. It is used in control tops for a smooth unbroken line; in the leg portion with nylon to improve fit and performance; with wool and other fibres for hosiery that keeps its shape. As well as leg warmers, various kinds of socks are being worn, short, medium and long, as well as stockings and tights: 'legwear' is another useful new word in the clothes vocabulary.

Finally comes a whole variety of filling products in Dacron for every sort of padded garment, from sportswear items, with down-like softness, lots of warmth and high bulk, to high-style winter wear with warmth through light insulation, with good drape but without bulk.

In the 1970's and 1980's, British clothing manufacture was a successful industry, earning a surplus in trade with the E.E.C. countries. Since the late 1960's productivity had increased faster in the clothing trade than in U.K. manufacturing as a whole.

That was the summary put forward by the clothing section of the Economic Development Council, which was responsible for the exhibition *Better Made in Britain*, held in March 1983 and attended by H.R.H. The Princess of Wales and a considerable number of V.I.P.s from many areas of life. All sides of the clothing industry were represented by 600 exhibitors. The fashion show organised for it by the Clothing Export Council included companies at all levels, from Aquascutum, Jaeger and other prestigious names to volume stores and chains, among them Marks and Spencer, British Home Stores and C & A; there were also British designers like Jasper Conran, Janice Wainwright, Bellville Sassoon, Bruce Oldfield – an impressive illustration of what British clothes could present at home and abroad.

In recent years knitwear has become an increasingly important and successful part of British clothes production. The trend towards more casual dress operates strongly in its favour and it seems beyond all reasonable doubt that such a trend will continue, even increase. It was therefore a very practical move for the Clothing Export Council to amalgamate with the corresponding body representing knitwear, and from January 1, 1984 the British Knitting and Clothing Export Council offered combined services to the industry as a whole. It was estimated that joint exports for 1985 would exceed £900 million, and the target for 1990 was set at £2 billion.

All areas of export sales and marketing are covered in detail by this self-financing, non-profit-making body, and there are about 400 companies as members. Specialized committees deal with

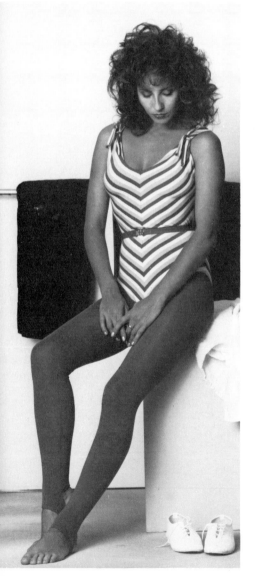

275　Cotton/Lycra elastine brings a new look to leotards for keep-fitters, combining body-shaping, fit and comfort. Worn with matching footless tights. Du Pont

each of about a dozen main categories of personal and household textile manufactures. Particular attention is being given to the Middle and Far East, to Japan and North America. There are other activities, especially in regard to exhibitions, trade fairs and market research projects, and an information service covering all aspects of exporting. A close liaison is maintained with all Government and other organizations concerned with export.

The task is no small one. In 1983 clothing imports into the U.K. rose by 2 per cent compared with 1982. The number of people employed in the clothing industry fell by 6,400 to 201,300 in the year 1983. The import of textile yarns and fabrics also rose by 17 per cent in value.

The 1984 British Fashion Week was evidence of the growing determination of British fashion to make its mark on world markets. For the first time this annual spring drive was highlighted by a celebratory reception held at 10 Downing Street by the Prime Minister – Mrs. Thatcher received 200 guests, British designers and manufacturers and overseas buyers from all over the world, including famous American stores. There were more than 30 British designers present including Zandra Rhodes and Jean Muir, along with representatives of leading manufacturers and retailers. As part of a drive to increase British clothing exports to over £1,000 million in 1984 it went with a swing and an enthusiastic reception was accorded, for example, by representatives of American store groups. Mrs. Thatcher said at the event: 'The whole industry ... is big business. We tend to think of it as not quite so important because it is fashion.' The collections shown by individual manufacturers and designers for the week were the biggest ever seen in London, a sure sign of the determination of the trade to inject new life into European fashion. It seems to be happening.

13 Changes in the shops, 1970's and 1980's

I

To turn from developments and changes among manufacturers to the shops where the actual garments are purchased, is to find corresponding changes in attitudes to dress, new demands and new ways of life among the public. New opportunities and new areas of successful retailing have been opened up and old systems have diminished or gone altogether.

Since the beginning of the 'seventies, a number of traditional and famous names among stores have disappeared. There have been take-overs galore among big groups, which have grown bigger and more centralized. Many stores, however, have survived the changes, opening new and more specialized departments, giving more emphasis to presenting garments in effective displays to enable busy customers to do their own selection. There are many more shops-within-shops, increasing the prestige of the manufacturers. There is, obviously, greatly increased attention given to leisurewear, casuals, co-ordinates. Some departments, on the contrary, have almost disappeared. Evening dress commands less attention. Hats, at any rate until very recently, no longer provided a focus of excited attention at the start of each season.

The most adventurous idea for updating a big store was that put into action at Derry & Toms in 1973, under the aegis of Barbara Hulanicki of Biba boutique fame, who had a part-share in the shop and visualized bringing the coffee-bar and leisure atmosphere of the boutique to it. In the event, people came to relax and enjoy themselves, but they did not buy. The project disintegrated in confusion and rows between the various managers. Hulanicki left and pursued her activities in Brazil for five years. Derry & Toms closed in 1975.

276 Strong contrast in casual co-ordinates from Windsmoor's 1984 Designer Collection, combining blue, black and white, jacket, blouse, skirt and sweater

On the shopping scene generally, the boutiques that burgeoned so profusely some twenty years ago continue to flourish, less boisterously, less given to coffee-bars and excitement, but still appealing mainly to the young and venturesome who were their original inspiration. They have not greatly extended their orbit to keep pace with customers growing more mature. These turn to new outlets.

In the 'eighties it was this group – the women aged 25–40 plus – who were engaging the attention of many clothes retailers, and a number of new arrivals are breaking new ground on the shopping scene. The chosen location is no longer the trendy 'King's Road' kind of area, but the familiar High Streets of towns and suburbs everywhere.

The outlook for the High Street chains has been greatly enhanced by the opening-up of new up-market outlets; an example is the group Solo, which used to sell within stores but early in 1984 opened the first of its own chain of shops in High Streets, aiming at reaching a total of 41 shops during the spring, in different parts of the country.

It was a vote of confidence in the High Street and also a good augury for the future, when, in 1982, Sir Terence Conran acquired a large interest in the 211 Richard Shops, paying £30 million for a 48 per cent share. This enterprise had had a successful record, but at that time was ready to benefit by being updated and showing a more sympathetic flair for 25-to-45-year-old women High Street customers who had lived through and outgrown the boutique market. They were busy women, with many interests, young families. They had also often returned to their careers and had to be well turned-out but had a strong preference for shopping locally, seeing the stock quickly and conveniently. This the big Richard Shops – renamed simply 'Richard' – could provide, but some of them needed clearer space, less clutter.

Conran had established a reputation for revolutionizing British design for ordinary people in his Habitat furniture shops, the first of which was opened in 1964. He was an innovator, but always a practical one, and so was an ideal entrant into the fashion field at the age of 51. What Conran had already done for furniture, making it functional but with a new look at a keen price, was an apt summary of what dress needed in the 'eighties, for the majority of women. Co-ordination had been a basic part of his thinking in dealing with household furnishings, carpets and accessories, so it was natural to apply it to dress. In the previous year at Mothercare, which he acquired, and in the chain

Next, launched by Hepworths, of which he was chairman, Conran had already had some experience of the clothing business.

From its long-established basis in the large-scale production of men's suits at economy prices but with individual fitting, offered in every High Street, Burtons have in recent years captured much new High Street territory and have built up a new image in both men's and women's markets. Their success in the early 1980's increased steadily year by year in both sectors. In women's wear their Dorothy Perkins, Evans and Peter Robinson chains increased turnover by a substantial percentage and in the year 1982–3 their emphasis was increasingly on the 20-to-40 age groups. That continued to be their policy and at the end of 1983 Burtons were operating from 955 womenswear outlets. The next target was 1,425 stores, of which 250 would be devoted to the new womenswear over-30 look. Their policy was towards further expansion and development, particularly in this area.

Chain stores in general showed some of the most notable changes and new thinking in their selling policies in the 1980's. Specialized ranges for distinct groups and types increased, with sporty, formal and casual styles being shown separately. Colours too engaged close attention, with co-ordination between different items. British Home Stores introduced a new colour labelling system to assist the matching of clothes and accessories. Tesco concentrated on beach and sportswear.

Marks & Spencer, while retaining their main emphasis on classic lines in dress, diversified to an increased degree. In 1984 they made a feature of special colourways for cottons, plus designs that ranged from safari suits and kimono tops to cropped pants and low-backed summer dresses. Their spring ranges included a small group of *avant-garde* cotton separates designed by students of the Royal College of Art and aimed at the 17-to-25 year olds, offered at selected branches.

Mrs. Thatcher's morning spent going the rounds of Marks & Spencer's, including their dress departments, naturally created something of a stir in April 1983, when she spent more than ninety minutes in their 'pilot' shop at Marble Arch, London; subsequently a selection of men's suits went to 10 Downing Street, for husbandly attention. The chairman of the group, Lord Rayner, appointed in succession to Lord Sieff and the first man outside the family to hold this key position, had been a special advisor on cost savings and Civil Service efficiency in Mrs. Thatcher's first government.

277 Colour theme in summer separates by Planet. Skirt in white/blue/grey print, with blouse in grey, strawberry, purple and yellow, 1984

278 *Big enveloping winter coat in double-face grey and electric blue wool broadcloth, worn with grey flannel dress. By Guy Paulin, Paris ready-to-wear 1984*

A long and eventful span of fashion history was recalled for many people when Sir Norman Hartnell died in 1979, just before his 78th birthday.

Hartnell was famous for his formal dresses, and for the embroideries designed by him and carried out in his own workrooms, where at one time he employed a staff of 85 on this work. He created the clothes for innumerable royal occasions, all over the world. In addition he produced large and outstanding couture collections, worked as designer with wholesale manu-facturers and created a considerable range of accessories, including perfumes, cosmetics and hosiery.

From 1951 Hardy Amies shared the honour of dressing the Queen, showing a particular skill in tailoring, but also excelling in clothes for great occasions. In the early 1970's Ian Thomas, who had formerly worked for Hartnell, but had now set up his own house, joined the team of royal dressmakers. The trio maintained an impeccable harmony of style and a flawless consistency of co-operation, and had equally successful associ-ations with milliners and other makers of royal accessories. The tradition was maintained since 1979 by the remaining two designers.

Hardy Amies, who celebrated 50 years in couture on February 1st, 1984 and was 75 in that year, has had one of the most diversified and continuously successful careers in the world of dressmaking and clothing in general. He has produced regular seasonal couture and boutique collections throughout his career in fashion, achieving great distinction in both. But licensees also produce his clothes round the world, including America, Australia, New Zealand and Japan. He has been closely identified with the large scale market for men's suits, shirts and other items of wear. He told his full story in his second book of reminiscences, *Still Here*, published to celebrate his 50 years, and bearing witness to the blend of creative talent, business acumen and personality which have made his career in fashion probably wider and more varied than that of anyone else. Inventive and enterprising, he has always been a stabilizing influence in a period of change.

Jean Muir has continued on her course with something of the quality of Chanel, going her own way, maintaining her own characteristics regardless of fashion's upheavals. The main change in the early 'eighties was some lower-priced clothes, woollen dresses plain and plaid, shifts, separates, available in shops for from about £100 per garment. She also moved towards seeing a basic wardrobe – jacket, with skirt or trousers – as important.

Bill Gibb, in a career of considerable variety and change, ranged through a series of outlets, from the personal to department stores, from boutiques to newspaper and magazine fashion features. He has always been an individualist, always faithful to his own tenets, which centre on the enterprising and ingenious use of textures and weaves and patterns in fabrics and knitting. Boldly inventive to the point of wildness at times, he combined, matched and mixed materials and colours. The mood was romantic and way-out, the effects usually larger than life and unmistakably his own.

3

The 1970's were a period of fragmentation in dress, however they are approached, and it is difficult even in retrospect to pick out all the most significant trends in them. A very widely worn item of fashion at all levels during those years was the long evening skirt, which became almost a uniform for all but the most formal occasions; it could be in black, and most frequently was, in silk or velvet (the latter sometimes accompanied by a tailored jacket to make a suit, which survived fashion's changes and continued to be worn). The skirt could also be in tartan wool, based on the traditional kilt, or in any kind of patterned fabric. With such a skirt went a blouse, tailored or frilly and Edwardian, or a knitted top, casual or sophisticated, or a pullover for cold weather.

279   Jean Muir continues to go her own way in the 80's: Bath exhibition, 1981, at the Fashion Research Centre

The long evening skirt went out of favour, because it became too monotonous to remain interesting. The shorter daytime or evening skirt, with a blouse or other top, remained in vogue and with a cardigan added was the most generally worn of all daytime outfits all the year round. It was probably the return of the shorter skirt which led to the revival of the suit for women's wear. This became as popular from the late 'seventies as it had been long ago when the New Woman of the 1900's took to it – and from then it had been worn fairly continuously until the 1950's.

In the 1980's, the casuals, the layered looks, the endless variety of mix and match found a contrast in the suit with its hint of formality and a new variety in that it was not always as strictly tailored as of yore, and was often looser, with wide shoulders, a

280   Slim chemise dress with matching hat by Jaeger in elegant printed cotton for 1984

more relaxed line. It was rarely bespoke, as in the old days, but it was available in a greater number of fittings and, as with men's suits, it became usual to be able to buy skirt and jacket in different fittings – to have your choice of plain or flared or pleated skirt, your own particular size of waist or jacket. This variety extended from the costly to the moderately priced, but was specially featured by large scale retailers such as Marks & Spencer. Plain and checked materials could also be allied.

The suit was particularly acceptable to the age-group of about 25 to over 40 which in the 1980's received the priority of attention which in the 1960's had been lavished on the very young. It was women in their middle years who dressed with the most discrimination, who were increasingly continuing or returning to their careers as children grew up. Homes were increasingly mechanized, family life was more casual and flexible. Such women often had more money than the very young as times became more difficult and jobs scarcer.

To the clothing trade the more mature market was profoundly welcome and a period of more stability in fashion and dress in general seemed to be setting in. In 1984 well-made, unfussy, carefully finished clothes made a return to favour in the stores and in the increasingly popular High Streets, where this kind of woman found her most favoured market for shopping.

The main trend of fashion and dress in general in recent years has been the increasing importance of casual wear in everywoman's wardrobe. A survey undertaken in 1983 by Textile Market Studies included an analysis of how this had happened in the years between 1970 and 1982. The conclusion was that the overall amount spent on clothing and footwear by the individual did not change perceptibly in real terms.

At 1982 prices the clothing market was estimated to be £11.5 billion. The average British resident spent £165 a year on clothes and just under £50 on footwear. Spending on women's items was highest at £250 a head per annum, that is £5.6 billion, 49 per cent of the total. The ratio of outerwear to underwear was nearly 70:30 within the clothing total. The largest single component of the market was the £3.4 billion spent on women's outerwear, that is 38 per cent of the total, with 26 per cent or £2.3 billion spent on men's outerwear. Children's wear takes up 12 per cent.

Between 1970 and 1982 in the women's outerwear market, casualwear, from being about a quarter of the total, rose progressively to account for three times as much in sales volume as formal wear. There seems no likelihood of that trend being

281 *Shirt-waister in colourful stripes by Jaeger, 1984*

reversed or even reduced, but it is noticeable that in the 1980's there has been an emergence in women's dress of something like the men's distinction between formal and casual dress. After a period when a woman could appear at any but very formal parties wearing anything from a full-scale evening gown to jeans and T-shirt or sweater, there came a return of the woman's tailored suit. It was widely welcomed by women of all ages and all types as 'correct' for almost any occasion, business or social, as it had been up to the 1950's.

Since fashion must perforce have contradictions, it ran true to this form in the early 1980's. Just when the lead was going to the not-so-young woman, the chief fashion leader for women everywhere came to be the young Princess of Wales. But she moved right away from the 'young' fashions of recent decades, opted mainly for long lines, soft textures, classic two-pieces, long coats – and hats which turned the head of every woman and put hats back into the fashion scene with an effectiveness which startled a languishing millinery trade into unhoped-for activity. Other royal ladies had been wearing hats on formal occasions for most of their lives, but no one noticed. Now no one failed to notice. If that could happen in the hatless 1980's, it cannot be said that fashion is dead. What will happen next is unpredictable, since mechanisation and technological invention are likely to continue to influence the production of dress, but the status and social connections of fashions of the past have little place in today's and tomorrow's worlds.

Bibliography

Adburgham, Alison, *A Punch History of Modes and Manners*, Hutchinson, 1961

Adburgham, Alison, *Shops and Shopping, 1810–1914*, George Allen & Unwin

Amies, Hardy, *Just So Far*, Collins, 1954

Arlen, Michael, *The Green Hat*, Collins, 1924

Ballard, Bettina, *In My Fashion*, Secker & Warburg, 1960

Balmain, Pierre, *My Years and Seasons*, Cassell, 1964

Battiscombe, Georgina, *Queen Alexandra*, Constable, 1969

Beaton, Cecil, *The Glass of Fashion*, Weidenfeld & Nicholson, 1954

Bernard, B., *Fashion in the Sixties*, Academy Editions, 1978

Bertin, Celia, Trans. M. Deans, *Paris à la Mode*, Gollancz, 1953

Bell, Quentin, *Bloomsbury*, Weidenfeld & Nicholson, 1968

Bell, Quentin, *On Human Finery*, Hogarth Press, revised ed. 1976

Bradfield, Nancy, *Historical Costume of England, 1066–1968*, G. Harrap, 1970

Brittain, Vera, *Lady into Woman*, Andrew Dakers, 1953

Carter, E., *Twentieth Century Fashion. A scrapbook 1900 to Today*, Eyre Methuen, 1975

Carter, E., *The Changing World of Fashion*, Weidenfeld and Nicolson, 1977

Carter, E., *Magic Names of Fashion*, Weidenfeld and Nicolson, 1980

Chase, Edna Woolman and Ilka, *Always in Vogue*, Gollancz, 1951

Cohn, N., *Today there are no Gentlemen*, Weidenfeld, 1971

Cooper, Diana, *The Rainbow Comes and Goes*, Rupert Hart-Davis, 1958

Creed, Charles, *Maid to Measure*, Jarrolds, 1961

Cunnington, C. W., *Englishwomen's Clothing in the Present Century*, Faber & Faber, 1951

Davis, Dorothy, *The Second Industrial Revolution*, Routledge & Kegan Paul, 1966

Dior by Dior, Trans. A. Fraser, Weidenfeld & Nicolson, 1957; Penguin Books, 1958

Disher, M. L., *American Factory Production of Women's Clothing*, Devereux Publications, 1947

Dobbs, S. P., *The Clothing Workers of Great Britain*, G. Routledge, 1928

Dorner, J., *Fashion in the Twenties and Thirties*, Ian Allan Ltd., 1973

Dorner, J., *Fashion in the Forties and Fifties*, Ian Allan Ltd., 1975

Duff Gordon, Lady (Lucile), *Discretions and Indiscretions*, Jarrolds, 1932

Fairchild, John, *The Fashionable Savages*, Doubleday & Co. Inc., 1965

Fashion 1900–1939, Exhibition Catalogue, Scottish Arts Council & V & A, 1975

Forbes-Robertson, Diana, *Maxine*, Hamish Hamilton, 1964

Garland, Madge, *Fashion*, Penguin Books, 1962

Garland, Madge, *The Changing Form of Fashion*, J. M. Dent, 1970

Garland, Madge, *The Indecisive Years*, Macdonald, 1968

Glynn, Prudence, *In Fashion*, Allen & Unwin, 1978

Greer, Howard, *Designing Male*, Robert Hale, 1952

Halliday, Leonard, *The Makers of our Clothes*, Zenith Books, 1966

Hartnell, Norman, *Silver and Gold*, Evans Bros., 1955

Howell, G., *In Vogue*, Condé Nast Publications, 1975

Huggett, Renée, *Shops*, B. T. Batsford, 1969

Jarrow, Jeannette A. and Jondelle, Beatrice, *Inside the Fashion Business*, John Wiley & Sons Inc., 1965

Jefferys, James B., *Retail Trading in Britain, 1850–1950*, Cambridge University Press, 1964

Journal of the Costume Society, 1967–1985

Kennett, F., *A Collector's Book of Twentieth Century Fashion*, 1983

Keppel, Sonia, *Edwardian Daughter*, Hamish Hamilton, 1958

Lambert, Richard B., *The Universal Provider, A Study of William Whiteley and the Rise of the London Department Store*, G. G. Harrap, 1938

Laver, James, *Costume*, Cassell, 1963

Laver, James, *Costume and Fashion*, (new ed.) Thames and Hudson, 1982

Laver, James, *Taste and Fashion*, Harrap, 1937

Laver, James, *Women's Dress in the Jazz Age*, Hamish Hamilton, 1964

McDowell, C., *McDowell's Directory of Twentieth Century Fashion*, Muller, 1984

de Marly, Diana, *The History of Haute Couture 1850–1950*, Batsford, 1980

Mayer, Mrs. Carl and Black, Clementina, *Makers of our Clothes*, Duckworth, 1909

Maugham, W. Somerset, *Bondage*, Heinemann, 1915; Re-issued as *Of Human Bondage*, 1934

Poiret, Paul, *My First Fifty Years*, Gollancz, 1934

Pound, Reginald, *Selfridge*, Heinemann, 1960

Priestley, J. B., *The Edwardians*, Heinemann, 1970

Pritchard, Mrs. Eric, *The Cult of Chiffon*, Grant Richards, 1902

Quant, Mary, *Quant by Quant*, Cassell, 1966

Raverat, Gwen, *Period Piece*, Faber and Faber, 1952

Rees, Goronwy, *St. Michael. A History of Marks and Spencer*, Weidenfeld & Nicolson, 1969

Saunders, Edith, *The Age of Worth*, Longmans Green, 1954

Schiaparelli, *Shocking Life*, J. M. Dent, 1954

Settle, Alison, *A Family of Shops*, Marshall & Snelgrove

Settle, Alison, *English Fashion*, Collins, 1959

Settle, Alison, *Fashion and Trade*, Journal of the Royal Society of Arts, 1970

Spanier, Ginette, *It isn't all Mink*, Collins, 1959

Spanier, Ginette, *And now it's Sables*, Robert Hale, 1970

Stewart, Margaret and Hunter, Leslie, *The Needle is Threaded*, Heinemann/Newman Neame, 1964

The Present Position of the Apparel and Fashion Industry, A Report, AFIA 1950

The Times

The World in Vogue, 1893–1963, Condé Nast Publications, 1963

Tweedsmuir, Susan, *The Edwardian Lady*, Duckworth, 1966

Waugh, Norah, *The Cut of Women's Clothes, 1600–1930*, Faber & Faber, 1968

Westminster, Loelia Duchess of, *Grace and Favour*, Weidenfeld & Nicolson, 1961

White, Cynthia, *Women's Magazines, 1693–1966*, Michael Joseph, 1970

Wilcox, R. Turner, *Five Centuries of American Fashion*, A. & C. Black, 1963

Wilkinson, Marjorie, *Clothes*, B. T. Batsford, 1970

Wray, Margaret, M.A., Ph.D., *The Women's Outerwear Indus-
try*, G. Duckworth, 1957
Yarwood, Doreen, *Encyclopaedia of World Costume*, B. T.
Batsford, 1978
Yarwood, Doreen, *English Costume*, B. T. Batsford, Fifth
Edition, 1979
York, P., *Style Wars*, Sidgwick, 1980
Your Future in Clothing, Clothing E.D.C., H.M.S.O., 1970
Yoxall, Harry, *A Fashion of Life*, Heinemann, 1966

Index